A BAND OF
MISFITS

Tales *of the* **2010 San Francisco Giants**

ANDREW BAGGARLY

TRIUMPH
B O O K S

This book is available in quantity at special discounts for your group or organization. For further information, contact:

Triumph Books LLC
814 North Franklin Street
Chicago, Illinois 60610
www.triumphbooks.com

Printed in U.S.A.
ISBN: 978-1-62937-098-9
Design by Patricia Frey
Editorial production by Prologue Publishing Services, LLC
Photos courtesy of AP Images

"It's strange to say, but the weirder you are, it seems like the more you win."
—*Aubrey Huff*

Contents

Introduction

There was a powerful odor traveling through the Giants' clubhouse, and it wasn't the smell of victory.

The Giants had just been embarrassed by the powerful Philadelphia Phillies in Game 2 of the National League Championship Series, trounced 6–1 in a contest that wasn't as close as the score indicated. For the first time, the Giants looked and played like the subordinate team everyone believed them to be. Their defense broke down in several key areas. Phillies right-hander Roy Oswalt carved up their lineup by throwing no-nonsense fastballs over and over. Leadoff man Andres Torres struck out four times. Their own pitchers seemed afraid to throw strikes to the Phillies' fearsome lineup, as if tossing glasses of water at a raging brush fire.

After the game, though, something else was blazing.

The pungent, skunky aroma was unmistakable.

"Ohhhh," said one of the coaches. "That's really not good."

I was the only reporter still in the visiting clubhouse at Citizens Bank Park. Most of the players had showered, dressed, and were heading to the team bus. Above my head, I could see wisps of smoke.

"It's coming from the dugout," a PR official told me. "Some Phillies fans might have snuck past security."

I pointed to the huge fan in the tunnel. It was blowing out, not in.

"Well then, it must've been the grounds crew," he said. "They know grass, right?"

Right. Sure.

I never found out for certain who was lighting the world on fire that night in Philadelphia. So I couldn't write a word about it for the newspaper or in a blog post—not so much as a Tweet. But suffice it to say the 2010 San Francisco Giants were a little different than your average group of major league baseball players.

From Aubrey Huff and his immodestly skimpy Rally Thong to Tim Lincecum's penchant for dropping F-bombs on live television, Brian Wilson's curiously strong black beard, and Buster Posey's too-good-to-be-true rookie season, the Giants featured more zany characters than a whole team of sitcom writers could conjure.

To them, they added spare parts like Cody Ross and Pat Burrell, who were unwanted by their former teams. And this band of misfits, against all odds, fit so perfectly together.

They believed in each other, even if no one else did. They played with confidence and attitude. And when they were set back by a tough loss, they didn't panic or give in to thoughts of fear or inadequacy. They simply put it aside and rolled with it.

Manager Bruce Bochy lovingly referred to his collection of kooks, crackpots, and castoffs as his "Dirty Dozen." And with his grinders and golden arms, Bochy's team willed its way to an NL West–clinching victory on the last day of the regular season. There was a magic within their ranks as they dispatched the Atlanta Braves, upended the heavily favored Phillies, and, yes, overwhelmed the Texas Rangers to win the first World Series in the Giants' 53-year existence in San Francisco.

The biggest crowd in the city's history jammed the streets for the victory parade. The speeches were made, the crowd dispersed in a gleeful haze, and the players scattered to their off-season homes.

And long after the celebration had ended, I sat in the press box at AT&T Park, finishing one last blog post—a final mile marker in an unbelievable, 9½-month journey. The stadium was pitch dark. The parade had ended eight hours earlier. Even the gift shop had locked its doors, finally accommodating a line that snaked all the way across the Lefty O'Doul Bridge.

Yet I could still hear the celebratory blasts of car horns, the constant buzzing of passersby, occasional chants of "Let's Go, Giants," and one determined dude, as punctual as a cuckoo clock, yelling the same phrase at the top of his lungs every five minutes:

"F— YEEEEEAH!!!!"

There wouldn't be another baseball event at the ballpark until FanFest in February. The light standards were off. Nothing to see here. But for the fans milling about, it didn't seem to matter.

Maybe they couldn't tell you why they were hanging around. They only knew they didn't want to leave.

They were high on life—among other things—and that was to be expected. San Francisco had gone without a World Series championship despite so many Hall of Fame–studded rosters. Even Willie Mays and Barry Bonds, perhaps the two greatest all-around National Leaguers to ever put on a uniform, hadn't been enough.

No matter what form it took or who achieved it, the first World Series title in San Francisco was sure to result in a joyous, momentous, over-whelming celebration.

So on the night of November 1 in Arlington, Texas, when Posey caught the final pitch from Wilson that made the Giants champions, it was a moment that stirred the soul of an entire region. The Giants arrived home at 3:00 the following morning and were surprised that hundreds of people were there, waiting in the dark, for no other reason than to cheer and say thank you.

The players hadn't seen anything yet.

They understood what they had accomplished that night in Texas. But until their parade cars turned from Montgomery onto Market Street, they hadn't realized what it all meant.

The players and coaches were blown away as they went along the parade route. They saw moving seas of orange-clad fans, holding signs that conveyed thousands of messages of grace and gratitude. People flew from all over the country on short notice to be there. BART trains packed in fans and families from the East Bay like sardines, each car already full before they reached the stops in Oakland.

San Francisco is no stranger to social movements. This is a city that unites for a common cause. And it is a city that knows how to party. These Giants brought out the best of both.

But there was something extra with this team. They *were* San Francisco. This was a team that lived out loud, played hard, and partied harder. Lincecum would look right at home with a flower child headband. And Wilson had the most famous beard since Jerry Garcia.

It wasn't just baseball fans who got caught up in this team. It was the entire city, from the Sunset to the Marina to the Castro to the financial district, all finding a character who spoke to them or a player with whom they could identify.

Even if your thing was half-naked men wearing leather S&M masks. (We'll get to that, I promise.)

These were the people's champions. They were accessible and lovable, raucous and rowdy, a little bit kinky and a little bit freaky. They were punk rock, classic country, and a whole lot of soul.

This was San Francisco's team, and their clubhouse dynamic fit the city. They accepted outcasts. They tolerated a diversity of opinions and beliefs. They played hard for themselves and for each other.

And in the end, they nailed it.

No year stands alone, though. For these Giants players, coaches, and executives, the 2010 season was a place and time in which their fates intersected and their individual stories reached an epic arc.

As I look back on this group of World Series winners, so many things stand out. Sure, they stood in fourth place at the All-Star break and overhauled their Opening Day lineup during the season. But more than anything, I'm struck by the number of compelling characters who populated their roster.

As a beat reporter, I'm not supposed to root for wins or losses. But there's no harm in hoping for good stories to write. And the Giants provided no shortage of them.

There was Huff, the charming rogue, whose famous unmentionables were first mentioned in my Extra Baggs blog. (No, I never envisioned that one of my biggest journalistic scoops would involve a 33-year-old Texan and his butt floss.)

There was Torres, the career minor leaguer, who refused to give up on himself and inspired his teammates time after time. There was Juan Uribe and his joyful spirit that needed no translation. There was Wilson's uniquely odd personality and even odder television interviews, Burrell's second chance, and Ross's whirlwind of a postseason. There was a brilliant rotation, from Lincecum's carefree brilliance to Matt Cain's zero-tolerance mound presence to Jonathan Sanchez's boldness to rookie Madison Bumgarner's unflinching gaze. And in the end, there was perhaps the most unlikely MVP a World Series has ever seen—a beat up veteran shortstop with a torn tendon in his arm who almost didn't make the postseason roster.

The night before Edgar Renteria hit his three-run home run and Lincecum pitched the Giants to their World Series title, I sat with a glass of scotch in my hotel room in Arlington and considered a rather sobering thought: of all the great writers and reporters who covered the

Giants over the years, people like Bob Stevens and Nick Peters who are in the Hall of Fame, none of them got the chance to cover a World Series winner in San Francisco. They had recorded so many seasons over so many summers, following teams from the day pitchers and catchers reported to the inevitable day they were eliminated.

And here I was, nine clean innings away from writing a game story that had never been written in 53 seasons of major league baseball in San Francisco. It was an awesomely humbling thought.

This was my seventh year on the Giants beat, and it had been a long, strange trip. My very first morning on the job, I arrived in Scottsdale in the spring of 2004 and got a breathless call from my editor at the *Oakland Tribune*: the *San Francisco Chronicle* had just reported that Barry Bonds and five other players had received steroids from a lab in Burlingame called BALCO, and could I get Bonds to comment on it?

Wonderful.

Bonds, BALCO, and controversial home run records would dominate every story line about the Giants for the next four seasons. There wasn't a single division title or playoff run to distract from it. The team was miserable, bordering on hopeless.

I don't believe in jinxes, but I was well aware that I'd never covered a playoff team. And some of my near-misses were downright spooky. I was on the Anaheim Angels beat in 2000–2001, then switched to cover the Dodgers. The Angels, of course, won the World Series in 2002. After two years on the Dodgers beat, I packed up and headed to Northern California. In my first year on the Giants, I was there to see a team clinch the NL West. But it wasn't the Giants. It was the Dodgers, and Steve Finley hit the grand slam off Wayne Franklin that gave them the division title.

Did jinxes exist after all? Well, it turns out they don't.

Who could have predicted that two years after celebrating on that night in Texas, the Giants would be rushing the field on another foreign mound in another American League city, awash in another World Series celebration?

The 2012 team had a nearly identical pitching staff, but a whole new cast in the lineup—and its own story to tell. That team will be remembered for its six elimination victories to squeak past the Cincinnati Reds and St. Louis Cardinals—two playoff rounds that included Hunter Pence's "I want one more day with you" sermons, the high school football rallies in the dugout, Buster Posey's grand slam off old foe Mat Latos, Sergio Romo's fearless battle with the Reds' Jay Bruce as a season teetered on all 12 pitches, Barry Zito's most graceful moment as a Giant to force the Cardinals back to San Francisco, a triple-hit double from Pence that defied physics, and Marco Scutaro, his arms outstretched, welcoming a cleansing rain as the Giants clinched the pennant in a Biblical downpour.

Then, apparently bored with playing from behind, they went out and swept the shocked Detroit Tigers. For the second time in 24 months, a bearded closer threw a bold third strike—it was Romo this time—and the nation was left to wonder just who these guys were and how, once again, they were the last team standing.

The 2012 team had its own compelling characters, perhaps none moreso than Ryan Vogelsong, the 35-year-old who spent six years overseas or in the minor leagues, only to return to the Giants a decade after they traded him to the Pittsburgh Pirates. Vogelsong narrowed his eyes and set the tone for the Giants when they had to go to Cincinnati and sweep a Reds team that hadn't lost three consecutive at home all season. Vogelsong started Game 3 and somehow kept pace with Homer Bailey, even though the Reds' hard-throwing right-hander yielded just one hit and struck out 10 in seven innings.

Zito was left off the postseason roster in 2010. Two years later, he pitched in the World Series for the first time—Game 1—and he won it. He was backed by three historic home runs from Pablo Sandoval, who lost his job down the stretch in 2010 but stood in company with Babe Ruth, Reggie Jackson, and Albert Pujols after that stunning opener.

And there was redemption for Tim Lincecum, so dominant as a two-time Cy Young winner and so suddenly bewildered and betrayed by a dimming fastball. He had the worst ERA of any National League starting pitcher in 2012 but set aside his ego when asked to pitch out of the bullpen. He became a weapon in that role in five postseason relief appearances, allowing just three hits and one run while striking out 17 in 13 innings. Once, before entering a game, he made just three warm-up tosses.

There was another parade, of course, and another wheat field of humanity on the steps of City Hall—and then, to everyone's surprise, the even-year phenomenon held true again in 2014.

No World Series champion has ever been welcomed home with a yawn. But although the Giants defied expectations in all three of their World Series seasons, there will always be something unique about the 2010 club. The draught tastes sweetest when it breaks a 50-year thirst.

All of San Francisco drank deeply in the Autumn of 2010 while toasting the greatest band of misfits baseball has ever seen. And it's my great privilege and pleasure to share all of their stories with you.

This book wouldn't be possible without the support of Bud Geracie, executive sports editor at the *San Jose Mercury News*, a mentor and good friend who understands that a 162-game season isn't just a grind for the players. My gratitude also to Mark Conley, Darryl Matsuda, Randy Sumimoto, Richard Parrish, Laurence Miedema, Darren Sabedra, and everyone else on our undaunted sports copy staff. They begin each day with a blank section and they absolutely nail it. Thanks to Jon Becker, who brought me to the Bay Area more than seven years ago, and to colleagues Dan Brown, Carl Steward, and Alex Pavlovic, who enthusiastically feed the beast and keep the beat so well tended during my absences. A special mention to Bay Area News Group columnists Tim Kawakami, Mark Purdy, Gary Peterson, Monte Poole, and Cam Inman for being such outstanding team players during the playoff run, and also to the Giants PR department, including Staci Slaughter, Jim Moorehead, Matt Chisholm, Eric Smith, and Erwin Higueros, for all their hard work. I'd also like to acknowledge the many others in the industry who have helped me over the years, including the late, great Terry Johnson, Paul Oberjuerge, Mike Davis, and Josh Suchon. I'm especially grateful to my family, beginning with my parents, Brad and Harriet, for their love and encouragement. Most especially, my love and gratitude goes out to my MVP, Aliya, who has made countless sacrifices and endured so many long absences while I followed this band of misfits around the country. You show me the meaning of teamwork every day.

A final thank-you to all Giants fans who followed the team through my game stories, notebooks, features, Tweets, and posts on the Extra Baggs blog, which has migrated from the Merc to my new home at Comcast SportsNet Bay Area. So many of you have gone out of your way to share your kind thoughts with me. Thank you, and I hope as you turn these pages, you enjoy one more ride through this incredible, magical, mystical, and totally memorable 2010 season.

Foreword

by Duane Kuiper
Giants broadcaster and former big-league infielder

Back in 1975, my first full season in the big leagues, I had a hopeful feeling as I arrived for spring training with the Cleveland Indians.

This could be the year, I thought.

We finished a game under .500, in fourth place. But the next year, I had that same feeling. We finished in fourth place again. The year after that, I truly believed we were destined for a different outcome. And we were. We finished fifth.

Now, understand, the feeling doesn't go away. Baseball begins in the spring, which everyone knows is the season of hope. You always arrive in spring training with that little jolt of excitement in your chest—the hope and belief that this year could be *the* year.

But the more time you spend in this game, you start to know when you're fooling yourself. So I'd nod my head whenever a Giants fan would come up to me before the 2010 season and say, "This is the year! This is the year they're going to do it!"

Yeah, sure. I played for the Cleveland Indians for 10 seasons, pal.

But now that I reflect back on it, I wonder: what did those fans know that I didn't know? Or did they say the same thing every year? Did they really believe it, or were they fooling themselves?

As for me…well, this team was somewhere in the middle. Maybe if they could score a little bit, yeah, you could see them making a run. You knew the pitching was good enough. But as it turned out, this was the most unique bunch of guys that I've ever encountered, and I'm not just talking about talent.

Since you were a kid, you've had coaches and parents explain to you what a team is. "T is for talent, E is for effort, A is for attitude," and on and on. Well, Giants fans didn't need anybody to tell them what a team was all about. They got to watch one. This was the truest form of a team that I've seen in a long time. They had a different hero every night. It could be Darren Ford, who didn't even have an at-bat, for crying out loud, but won a game as a pinch runner. That was the essence of this team—a bunch of misfits that other teams didn't necessarily want or care for, with the exception of that wonderful pitching staff, and they played as a group.

They showed everyone in the Bay Area what the true definition of "team" was, and it was fun to watch. It really was.

I saved a copy of the *Philadelphia Inquirer* when we arrived for the NLCS. You know how each paper does the position-by-position rankings to see who has the edge? They didn't give the Giants an edge at any position. Not one. So they didn't really have a chance, right?

But they did. Because they had their starting pitchers, they had their bullpen, and they had their closer. Those guys gave them a chance in every game they played this year. That was the one difference between this team and all the great Giants teams in the past.

It might have seemed like getting past the Phillies was even tougher than winning the World Series. But you have to remember that the Giants weren't just taking on the Texas Rangers. They were taking on the 1962 Yankees, they were taking on the '89 Oakland A's, they were taking on the 2002 Angels. They'd gotten so close in the past. Everyone had expectations for what it would be like when they finally did it.

But after they did, it exceeded anything you ever thought it could be. It was like, "Man! This is great! This is unbelievable!" And as it turned out, the World Series victory wasn't the dessert. It was the main course, and the parade was the dessert.

We saw grandpas and grandsons, daughters and granddaughters. We saw the joy on so many faces. You could see the generations who had their hearts with the San Francisco Giants ever since they came to town. And they were all expressing themselves like they thought they'd never have this chance.

It was, without a doubt, the single largest group of happy people that I've ever seen.

When we took the left from Montgomery Street, we were warned ahead of time that we would not believe it. Well, I said, "I've been the Grand Marshal with my friend Mike Krukow at the Half Moon Bay Pumpkin Festival. I know what loud is."

But when we rounded that corner, we swallowed hard. Because it was breathtaking.

We saw more "torture" signs during the parade, and I appreciated the people who understood that we were talking about baseball torture. It's something we've all had to live with. And when Brian Wilson struck out Nelson Cruz, the torture truly was over.

But it's funny how all the people were saying, "This is killing me! This is too much!" Now those same people come up to me and say, "We miss it! Life is boring! I need some more torture!"

As the weeks and months have passed since November 1, I've taken time to reflect on everything. And I keep thinking about Hank Greenwald and all the years he announced Giants games and never had the chance to make that final call. I think about Lon Simmons, and how close he came. I thought of all the people who came before us and held that microphone and thought as much of the Giants as we do.

And I thought of Herb Score, who announced all those years in Cleveland. In his last season, he had told his audience that he would retire, and his final broadcast turned out to be Game 7 of the 1997 World Series. His team had the lead in the ninth inning, and Jose Mesa blew the save, and the Florida Marlins won. That is how he ended his broadcasting career, having to describe a defeat that broke hearts in Cleveland all over again.

And I thought of that, and how privileged I was to be in position to make the call that would make every Giants fan, all around the world, the happiest that any Giants fan had ever been. I think about it all the time. People often tell us gut-wrenching stories about how they wish their dad or their grandmother or brother had a chance to listen to that final game. We don't discard those stories. Those are very special to us.

Really, when you think about it, every season is its own storybook. As bad as some of those Cleveland Indians teams were, each of those seasons was like a book. It's the chapters upon chapters of what happened to those individual players, where they came from, and what happened during their summer together before they went on separate paths.

The 2010 Giants were a storybook, too. The only difference is that theirs had a happy ending—the happiest of all.

This is a book about teamwork and toughness. It's about belief and perseverance. But more than anything, it's a book about relief. That's the one word I'd use to describe this World Series championship season.

I mean, do you know how hard it's been to be a Giants fan since they came to San Francisco? Of course, you do! McCovey's line drive and earthquakes and Scott Spiezio...

Well, there's a new story. The torture is over. Now feel the relief and enjoy.

Chapter 1

Adios, El Caballo

The Giants were descending from 35,000 feet, and word began to travel.

One player saw the news on his PDA. Another was surfing the Web on his laptop. The Fox Sports report had been linked on MLBtraderumors.com, which passes for wildfire in this information era.

Bengie Molina had been traded.

Teammates began to approach the proud veteran catcher, stretched out in his own row, listening to music on black, oversized headphones.

"Are you okay? I'm so sorry, man."

"Good luck. It's been an honor playing with you."

"Wow, what a shock."

The headphones came off, and Molina met the news with stunned silence. The Giants were on the verge of announcing a deal with the Texas Rangers. They were getting a right-handed middle reliever, Chris Ray, along with a minor leaguer—a seemingly small return for a former Gold Glove catcher who had been the heart of his team, a two-time winner of the Willie Mac Award as the most inspirational Giant, and a steady guide during both of Tim Lincecum's Cy Young–winning seasons.

Molina would be leaving a flawed, fourth-place team for a surprising Texas club that was leading the AL West. But he was not happy. He was confused, angry, and, most of all, hurt to receive the news from

1

teammates as their charter flight from San Francisco—where the archrival Dodgers had just swept them—descended into Denver.

Molina had a hunch he might be traded at some point. He knew it was a matter of time before the Giants would clear his position for bright young catcher Buster Posey. But it was June 30. The non-waiver trade deadline was a month away.

"They're getting rid of me now?" he thought. "After all I've done?"

This was not the first time the Giants had stung his pride. Two years earlier, on the day the club drafted Posey with the fifth overall pick, general manager Brian Sabean made a reference to Molina's "clock winding down." The longtime GM was referring to the expiration of Molina's contract after the 2009 season, but his language was inelegant. Molina took it as a comment that his skills were eroding.

After the 2009 season, when a reporter asked Sabean about re-signing Molina to a one-year contract, the GM said, "That ship has sailed."

Molina didn't get the two-year contract he wanted—that he felt he deserved—from the New York Mets or any other team. So it came as a surprise to everyone, the Giants included, when he took slightly less money to return for one more year.

On his first day in spring camp, Molina pulled up his black socks in front of his locker and smiled.

"I guess that ship sailed back," he said wistfully.

The catcher is supposed to be the toughest soul on the diamond—constantly pelted by foul tips, mentally tested by the thousands of decisions he must make every game, and prone to full-frontal collisions by runners flying down the third-base line.

Molina handled all those burdens with quiet grace. But inside, he felt wounded. He was sensitive to every passing remark, glum over any perceived slight. He never trusted the baseball establishment, never forgot that scouts passed him over twice in the draft while at Arizona Western

College. He returned home to Puerto Rico, and after playing a few games for a local semipro team, he quit the sport he loved with one symbolic act.

He kicked off his cleats, knotted the laces together, whipped them over his head like an Argentinean bolo, and flung them to the humid trade winds. The shoes stuck in the power lines, as tangled up as his emotions.

What next? Bengie didn't know. His father, Benjamin Sr., came home every day before dusk to play catch with his sons. He never waved a tired hand or begged off grabbing his worn mitt, even though he started his 12-hour shift at 4:00 AM. Maybe there would be a job for Bengie at the Westinghouse factory, too.

There was something else Bengie didn't know: a scout from the Angels, Ray Poitevint, had happened to see him swing the bat during that last semipro game. Poitevint came to Vega Alta to work out Bengie's little brother, Jose, a catcher with a strong throwing arm. From across the street, he spied Bengie line a single to right field. He liked the swing. Then he saw Molina run to first base.

To call Bengie a below-average runner would be charitable. Even when he was younger and carrying around fewer pounds, scouts almost needed a sundial to clock him in the 60-yard dash. It's the reason he never received a shot at a pro contract.

But Poitevint had seen enough players overcome marginal tools. The old scout once signed a Hall of Famer, Eddie Murray, but he was much prouder of another signee, Enos Cabell, who made it to the big leagues through force of will and fashioned a respectable career.

"Scouts are trained to look for flaws, and when they see one, they'll just pass and go to the next guy," Poitevint said. "We're always looking for perfection."

Another scout would have turned away. But Poitevint kept an open mind and walked across the street to see another at-bat. It so happened that Bengie hit another line drive to right field. And as fate would have it, Poitevint took a seat next to Gladys Molina, matriarch of the family and an unflagging supporter of her three boys.

"Please," she implored, "you have to see my Bengie."

The next morning Poitevint asked Jose if his older brother could join them for a workout. Jose immediately rushed back to the family house, crashed through the door, and nudged his big brother awake.

"Quick! Grab your hat. Get your bats. A scout wants to see you," Jose said. "Put on your shoes!"

Bengie was wide awake now. He jolted out of bed.

"My shoes!"

Years later, Bengie couldn't remember if he wore sneakers to the workout or borrowed his brother's cleats. He was sure of one thing, though: he didn't try to shimmy up into those power lines.

He put on a tremendous round of batting practice for Poitevint, spraying line drives as his father pitched to him. Then Poitevint asked him to crouch down, receive the ball at home plate, and make a few throws to second base. Bengie hadn't caught before. He pitched, played a little outfield and even some shortstop in junior college. Jose was the catcher in the family. But Bengie was willing to do anything, and the Molina brothers had the same strong arm and quick release.

Poitevint signed Bengie on the spot. He received the grand sum of $500.

"I would have signed for nothing," Bengie would say, much later. "I would have signed for nothing."

Now holding a professional contract, Bengie almost killed himself to get into the best shape of his life. He ran hills with a truck tire around his waist and had deep cuts from where the steel belting poked through the rubber. He chopped wood for hours. His family called him "El Caballo Loco"—the Crazy Horse.

Big-hearted catcher Bengie Molina was shocked to learn of his midseason
trade from the fourth-place Giants to the first-place Rangers.

When he arrived in the Angels minor league camp, a coach told him there wouldn't be time for extra hitting. He was an organizational player—a non-prospect. He was here to catch in the bullpen. And when he went to Cedar Rapids, Iowa—another planet to a kid from the Caribbean—he was a backup who played in 48 games.

Bengie knew he needed to improve his catching skills, so he accepted an invitation to play winter ball for Mayaguez. But it came with a catch: he would have to catch all the bullpens they wanted.

He once caught seven bullpens before a game, then three more during it. If he was lucky, he'd get an at-bat and maybe a few innings behind the plate. El Caballo was being whipped.

That wasn't the worst part. Mayaguez was on the east coast of the island, a two-hour drive at top speed in clear weather. Bengie couldn't go at top speed. He didn't drive his father's old Chevy Nova through the commute so much as he coaxed it through. The entire chassis shook if he went faster than 55 mph. The tires were bald, slick, and the wrong size. When he made a right turn, they scraped the frame and made a terrible screeching noise. Driving in the rain was the worst. The wipers didn't work, so he had to roll down the window and crank them by hand.

All while the car slid across the wet road.

One time he had his baby daughter in the back seat and was so scared that he began to cry.

"I didn't know if I could keep doing this," he said.

But in those moments, he would think of his father, his back aching after those 12-hour shifts but always returning home early enough to take his sons to the practice field. With the light fading, they would hit and run and throw together. Baseball wasn't just Bengie's career. It was his father's, too.

Over the years Bengie made believers in the Angels minor league system. He caught the eye of Mike Scioscia, who skippered the Dodgers'

Triple A affiliate before the Angels hired him to manage in 2000. One of Scioscia's first and boldest moves was to hand the big-league catching job to an unproven non-prospect. Bengie rewarded Scioscia's trust, and in his third season, he was the starting catcher on a World Series winner. The Angels, with their collection of tough outs, wrested the title from Barry Bonds' Giants in seven games.

Poitevint would have another Enos Cabell to think about and smile during lonelier moments on the road.

Not only did Benjamin Molina Sr. see all three of his sons reach the major leagues, but he would boast something that no other father has ever boasted in the history of baseball. He saw all three sons—Bengie, Jose, and his youngest, Yadier—win World Series rings.

In October of 2008 Benjamin Sr. was returning to the baseball field across the street from his house—the field he had built, that he mowed and groomed and maintained for the community—carrying more baseballs for an afternoon game. He grabbed his chest and collapsed. He was 58.

The sudden loss affected Bengie deeply. He carried a photo collage of his father in his locker, home and away during the 2009 season, his third with the Giants. His mood darkened. And he knew free agency was coming up after the season. All the old thoughts flooded back, and he felt wounded again.

But the ship turned back around, and Molina was happy to return to a city that his daughters and wife, Jamie, loved. He exchanged text messages with Posey, the young catcher that he admired and supported. He pledged that spring to be a good teammate, always, and accept whatever happened. He finally found peace with his father's passing, and after a cold winter as a free agent in which nobody showed him the respect he felt he deserved, he entered 2010 assuming it would be the last season of his career. There was a peace in that, too.

He would be able to spend all his time with Jamie and the girls. After a while, he might even look for a job in baseball. But not as a scout.

"Because I'd sign all the guys who are 5'8"," he said, "and have a heart the size of a building."

Then came that ink-black night in Denver. The Giants' jet touched down with a jarring thud.

Molina took a few minutes to collect his thoughts, and a text message from Jamie confirmed the news. He had been traded.

What was he supposed to do now? Check into the Giants' hotel or catch a flight to Anaheim, where the Rangers were playing?

Giants Manager Bruce Bochy told him to stay with the team and be prepared in case he had to report to Coors Field the next afternoon. No trade had been finalized. It turned out that Major League Baseball had to approve the financials of the deal because the Rangers ownership was emerging from bankruptcy. The Giants would be sending roughly $2 million to Texas to offset the salary difference between Molina and Ray. When Molina heard that, it only stung him further. They were *paying* the Rangers to take him.

Molina exchanged hugs with teammates on the tarmac, then boarded the players' bus. He did not go quietly. He had something he needed to say.

He rose and walked to the front of the bus, stood in the center aisle and poured out his heart. He thanked his teammates and said he would miss them. He reminded them that they had his cell phone number and to call or send him a message whenever they wanted, not only during their baseball career, but in whatever life held for them beyond that. He said he would always be their friend.

And he said something else.

"You have what it takes to win this thing, and I'm going to be watching as much as I can."

The players began to applaud, then rose and gave him a standing ovation.

But the Giants were a fourth-place team, just three games over .500. They had a five-game losing streak. Their Opening Day lineup of old, injury-prone players already had broken down in a couple of key areas.

In a few days they would play the longest game in Coors Field history—a torturous statement if one ever existed in baseball—and lose.

Molina was going to a first-place team in Texas. The Giants were going nowhere.

Chapter 2

Hail to the Buster

Demp Posey heard another commotion from inside the house. This time he didn't even bother to investigate. He kept right on flipping his special-recipe jalapeño cheeseburgers on the barbecue, the smoke rising into the Georgia night.

"Would you believe it?" he thought to himself, shaking his head. "He's done it again."

It was May 29 and his eldest son, Buster, had been called up by the San Francisco Giants that morning. In his season debut the much-hyped prospect hit an RBI single. Then he hit another. And another.

"Naw, he cannot have another hit already," Demp Posey thought as he heard another round of muffled hoops and hollers from his wife and in-laws, glued to the TV. "This has got to stop."

There was no stopping Gerald Dempsey "Buster" Posey III. Not in high school, where he was a strong-armed pitcher, pure-hitting short-stop, and the talk of tiny Leesburg, Georgia, population 2,900. Not at Florida State, where he volunteered to catch his sophomore year even though he didn't know how to buckle up a shin guard. And not in the minor leagues, where he matriculated faster than Doogie Howser.

Posey awakened the morning of May 29 in Salt Lake City, where the Triple A Fresno Grizzlies were finishing up a road series. He owned a

.349 average in the Pacific Coast League, an unreal .442 on-base percentage, and 21 of his 60 hits had gone for extra bases.

It was time.

The Giants were coming off an embarrassing sweep at the hands of the crosstown A's in Oakland the previous weekend, scoring a total of one run in three losses, but they had rallied to take three of four after that. The situation wasn't good—the Giants were treading water, just three games over .500—but it had stabilized a bit. The weight of the world wouldn't be on Posey's shoulders.

He caught a flight at dawn to San Francisco and batted sixth in the lineup that night. And to a series of standing ovations in a 12–1 rout of the Arizona Diamondbacks, he lined a run-scoring single in the first inning. He shot another RBI single up the middle in the fifth. And he grounded a single through the left side with the bases loaded in the seventh.

Then the stoic 23-year-old with the Eagle Scout's demeanor stood on first base and finally cracked a smile.

"It was great. It was fun. It's humbling," he said. "I have to slow myself down because it can get you going a little bit."

In spite of his memorable season debut, Giants officials took plenty of criticism over the timing of the promotion. To many, Posey clearly was the best hitter in Sabean's organization—including the major leagues—and it was borderline criminal to keep him in the minors while the Giants' meager offense struggled in April and May.

Others railed at Sabean for calling up Posey too soon. Another three weeks or so in the minor leagues and he wouldn't have accrued enough service time to be eligible for arbitration until 2013. Now he was likely to qualify a year earlier. The team had just experienced the downside of making a similar move with ace pitcher Tim Lincecum, who had been called up in May 2007 and made a multimillion dent in the Giants' 2010 payroll as a result.

"Let me dispel all that, all right?" said Sabean, when asked about the service-time issue on May 9. "When we think Posey's ready, just like when we thought Lincecum was ready—and this starts from ownership—he'll be in the big leagues.

"We can't be on a strict clock. Shoot, we're trying to get back to winning ways and get to the playoffs, and everybody understands it."

Sabean insisted he kept Posey at Triple A because the front office wasn't convinced the rookie could excel behind the plate in the big leagues. Yet when Posey came up, he played mostly first base. So on the surface, Sabean's rationale didn't make much sense.

Fact is, the front office was scared to death over when to introduce this sweet-swinging kid with the intelligent approach and consistently crisp contact—petrified because they simply couldn't afford for him to fail.

A Giants homegrown position player, drafted and developed by the organization, hadn't made an All-Star team in a San Francisco uniform since Matt Williams—and it had been two decades since he broke into the big leagues. It was an embarrassing drought, even if it had a basic explanation.

All through the latter stages of the Barry Bonds era, the Giants gave away draft picks like surplus firewood. They knew Bonds remained a force of nature, even as he approached his forties, and they couldn't afford to let their window of opportunity pass by relying on long-term strategies. Because of the debt service they paid on their privately financed ballpark, they couldn't just splurge on their choice of free agents. They had to cut someplace. So they took money from the draft budget and diverted it to the major league payroll, allowing them to sign quick-fix veteran role players.

In the most famous instance, prior to the 2004 season, they agreed to terms with marginal outfielder Michael Tucker a day before the deadline for the Kansas City Royals to offer him arbitration—a necessary step to receive draft-pick compensation, but a move nobody expected the Royals to make. The Giants made it an easy call for Kansas City. They *wanted* to give away the pick, so they timed their strike accordingly.

Even with their go-cheap strategy in the draft, the Giants farm system continued to produce pitchers, both to use as trade bait and to fill out their rotation. Such was the talent of Dick Tidrow, Sabean's top lieutenant. A former Yankees and Cubs reliever, Tidrow kept his intimidating handlebar mustache from his playing days. He also retained his nickname, "Dirt," which was an appropriate description for his no-nonsense personality. Legendary Yankees clubhouse man Pete Sheehy bestowed Tidrow with that name because of the pitcher's over-exuberance in a pregame diversion that relievers called "flip." The game was played like hacky sack but with your fielding glove, and if you dropped the ball, you excused yourself from the circle until only the winner remained. Tidrow was so competitive that he'd often dive on the track, dusting up his uniform and creating more laundry for Sheehy.

Dirt's name stayed with him as a scout, and as Sabean's closest advisor. Despite his daily uniform of white dress shirt and black slacks, Tidrow looked more like a gunslinger than a front-office executive. Minor league pitchers called him "the Ninja" because he'd drop in to see an affiliate and silently watch the action from dozens of angles. He'd be somewhere behind the plate, then suddenly someone would spot him in center field. The next thing anyone knew, he was on the third-base side to get a better look at a right-hander. Then through almost magical stealth, he'd be right behind the pitcher in the bullpen, tapping him on the shoulder with a thought about how his hands break or how he wasn't selling his change-up.

Tidrow had an eye for the ideal pitcher's body. He liked size, strong legs, and loose, easy arm action. A promising high school kid might need to overhaul his mechanics, but that's okay. The Giants had smart people to

Catcher Buster Posey tags out Dodgers right fielder Andre Ethier. Posey's rise to the majors was swift—from the 2008 draft to replacing Bengie Molina behind the plate in July 2010.

help with that, he thought. One day, when a game at Ohio State rained out, Tidrow drove to see a left-hander from little Ohio Dominican University whom the Giants' local scout had written up. Tidrow liked how the lefty appeared to throw easy but had a fastball that just exploded on hitters. The lefty couldn't stay on line to the plate and didn't have a consistent breaking pitch, but the arm worked. Then Tidrow got out of town and covered his tracks. It was Jonathan Sanchez—a little gem as a 27th-round pick.

But there also were times when the Giants' thriftiness in the draft kept Tidrow from getting the pitcher he wanted. In 1998 he liked a big high school left-hander out of nearby Vallejo with the regal name of Carsten Charles Sabathia. No, Tidrow was told. He didn't have the money needed to buy out Sabathia's football offers from Cal and Hawaii. So the Giants took another local player who wasn't projected to go in the first round, outfielder Tony Torcato, because they knew he'd sign quickly.

Sabathia owns a Cy Young Award and a World Series ring. Torcato had 53 plate appearances in four big-league seasons. When Sabathia was pitching for the New York Yankees in the playoffs, Torcato was playing for a team in Grosseto, Italy.

The Giants had five of the first 41 picks in that 1998 draft—a huge chance to restock the system. They took five players who signed for bonuses below their expected slot value. Torcato ranked as the success story. He was the only one to reach the major leagues.

Even on the rare occasion the Giants were able to draft a decent hitting prospect, they failed to reap results. Todd Linden won a batting title in the Pacific Coast League but was a wreck at the plate and a strikeout machine in the majors. Lance Niekro fared no better. The Giants weren't getting the same inventory of high-ceiling hitters as other teams, but their problems went beyond that. Whether it was faulty predraft evaluations or a flawed player development system, there was a disconnect somewhere. The Giants simply weren't growing hitters.

The fallow farm led to famine in 2005. Bonds, the greatest offensive force the game has ever seen, missed nearly the entire season because of a surgically repaired knee that became infected and required two more procedures. And the Giants were exposed.

A year earlier Bonds had destroyed the major league records for walks (232) and intentional walks (120) in a season—cartoonish totals that almost certainly won't be approached again. Despite playing on a marginally talented roster with holes in the rotation and a burned-out bullpen, Bonds was such an on-base engine in the middle of the Giants' lineup that they won 91 games in 2004 and remained alive in two playoff races until the season's final weekend.

The Giants were about to learn the true scope of the Bonds effect, though. They were 75–87 in 2005 and finished just one win better in '06. Most baseball fans around the nation, convinced they were seeing a pumped up, steroid-fueled sham, sat on their hands when Bonds broke Hank Aaron's all-time home run record in 2007. The team finished 71–91, as if anyone cared. Every night in that strange season the only result on the scoreboard that mattered was whether Bonds went deep. It made for a fractured, tense clubhouse best summarized by Matt Morris, a free agent arrival from St. Louis.

"I don't even know what the goal is anymore," said Morris after a loss at Wrigley Field. "Is it to win games?"

Morris was banished to Pittsburgh in a trade shortly thereafter, and although Bonds raised his arms in triumph when he became the first human to hit 756 home runs in the major leagues, the season did not end the way he wanted. He whined for another contract and felt spurned when Giants owner Peter Magowan finally showed enough backbone to say no. The Giants were just 72–90 in 2008, their fourth consecutive losing season. It was the worst run of baseball in San Francisco since 1974 through 1977, the bleakest days in the history of blustery Candlestick Park, when the Giants blew through four managers in four campaigns.

The Bonds era was over. A vacuum was ready to take its place.

Sabean, despite a comfortable existence since he took over in 1996, was under the gun and unpopular with the radio callers and message boarders, many of whom were discovering the advanced statistical methods for evaluating players that worked so well across the bay with the small-revenue Oakland A's. Giants fans felt no special attachment to Bruce Bochy, either. He wasn't seen as an inspiring choice to replace Felipe Alou and manage the club through the Bonds hullabaloo in '07, and it seemed suspicious that the NL West–rival San Diego Padres encouraged him to leave with a year still remaining on his contract.

Magowan retained Sabean after the '07 season, quietly acknowledging that many of the GM's mistakes were made because he was following orders. But the ownership group demanded changes. Tidrow, despite his acumen with pitchers, needed some boundaries. It was time for new faces in baseball operations. Jack Hiatt, the longtime farm director and former big-league catcher, turned over his duties. "It's time for some younger blood," said Hiatt, who was 65. The club promoted field coordinator Fred "Chicken" Stanley. He was 60.

Most significantly, the Giants hired a bright and upbeat scout named John Barr away from the Los Angeles Dodgers. Barr was energetic and talkative, the kind of guy who could meet 100 people at a cocktail party and call them each by name the next time he saw them. He'd return your call promptly while apologizing for the delay, and he always asked about your family. He had worked for the New York Mets and Baltimore Orioles, among other teams, and couldn't enter a scout's section at any ballpark in the country without a flurry of handshakes. He brought a new, personable dynamic to a somewhat hostile front-office cabal that often felt like a meeting of capos from *The Sopranos.*

And John Barr knew a major league hitter when he saw one.

The Giants gave Barr a long-winded "special assistant" title rather than calling him their scouting director. But those were his duties. Find bats.

As a cross-checker with the Dodgers, Barr had unearthed a number of successful hitting prospects in the lower rounds of the draft, including catcher Russell Martin and center fielder Matt Kemp. Now he had to find those kinds of players for the Giants. And he'd have a decent budget allotted to sign them.

There were even bigger changes taking place atop the Giants' organizational pyramid. Magowan had led the effort to save the Giants from moving to St. Petersburg, Florida, in 1993, and he ensured the health of the franchise by pushing through the construction of the Giants' gorgeous ballpark on the waterfront. But the Mitchell Report, baseball's official record of the steroids scandal, portrayed him as an enabler who allowed Bonds' personal trainer, a convicted steroids dealer, to have free run of the clubhouse. Perhaps even more damaging to Magowan among his fellow investors was the disastrous decision to give former A's left-hander Barry Zito a ridiculous $126 million contract.

Saying he wanted to spend more time with his family, Magowan stepped down in May 2008. He turned over managing partner duties to Bill Neukom, one of the club's principal investors. Like Magowan, who had followed the Giants from their days in New York, Neukom was a lifelong fan of the team. He grew up in San Mateo, and one of his father's earliest gifts was 10 shares in the National Exhibition Corporation—the name that Giants owner Horace Stoneham gave to his investment group upon bringing the team west in 1958.

Many years later, Neukom had the wherewithal to purchase a much larger stake. He had graduated from Stanford Law and was working in a Seattle firm when one of the chief partners asked him to help his kid incorporate a fledgling business. The partner was Bill Gates Sr., his teenage son's business became Microsoft, and Neukom got in on the absolute ground floor. He made a fortune during the boom times of the software goliath and became a legend in the arena of intellectual property rights while serving as Microsoft's chief legal counsel for almost a quarter century.

Neukom approached his new appointment with the Giants in the same fashion in which he ran Microsoft's legal department. He wanted to create a meritocracy that rewarded talent and results. He set to work on a mission statement and outlined a *Giants Way* publication that would be distributed to everyone from the lowest minor leaguer to the ace of the big-league staff. And Neukom, more than anyone, understood the value of cultivating talent from within. For the first time in decades, the farm system would be a top priority.

Barr would have the fifth overall pick in the '08 draft, the highest the Giants had selected since they took pitcher Jason Grilli fourth overall in 1997. Prior to that, they hadn't had a top-five pick since 1986—when they took a square-jawed infielder out of UNLV by the name of Matt Williams.

Barr knew all about Buster Posey. He personally scouted him as a high school pitcher in Lee County, Georgia, down in the rural, southern part of the state an hour's drive from Albany. Then again, everyone else knew about Posey, too. As a high school junior, he was 10–1 with a 1.53 ERA, he hit .544, and he struck out just nine times. All year. He won the Gatorade and Louisville Slugger Georgia Player of the Year awards.

As a senior, he led Lee County to the 2005 state Class 4A championship series, where he was 6-for-8 with a home run and four RBIs in three games, while also pitching five innings of one-run ball.

But a rangy 16-year-old sophomore from Henry County High School, an hour outside of Atlanta, was just as fearsome at the plate in that series. He was 6-for-10 with a home run and eight RBIs, including a tying, three-run double in the third and deciding game.

His name was Jason Heyward, soon to be the biggest rookie to hit the Atlanta Braves since Andruw Jones. Heyward's team won that deciding game and the state title; Posey stood in the on-deck circle when a double-play grounder ended it.

The Angels took a flier on Posey out of high school with their 50th-round draft pick, offering him the equivalent of a third-round bonus to sign. But everyone knew the level-headed achiever, who graduated fourth out of 302 students in his Lee County senior class, would honor his commitment to play at Florida State.

That was Buster. The son of a food distribution manager and a special-education teacher, he had all the psychological markings of an oldest child in a family with three younger siblings. He practiced and prepared, silently soaked in his surroundings and worked to master the fundamentals of whatever he chose to do.

His father was the original Buster. His grandmother had called him by that name as a boy until the third grade, when it fell out of use. Soon he went by Demp—short for his middle name, Dempsey, and the same moniker his dad always went by.

But he always liked his boyhood nickname. So when he and his wife, Traci, had their first child, Gerald Dempsey Posey III, they decided against the too-common Southern tradition to call him Tripp or Trey. And he wasn't going to be called Demp. That would be too confusing. So…he was Buster from birth.

"And that's who he is," Demp Posey said. "He's just good ol' Buster."

Demp Posey liked baseball well enough, but he didn't grow up playing it. He was raised on a farm 10 miles from the nearest town, and back then he didn't have time for spring or summer recreation. There were peanut and cotton crops, cattle and pigs that needed attention. He played basketball because it was a winter sport, and he was a local standout.

Demp had the same basketball coach from second grade through high school, a tough but fair man named Cliff Ranew, who drilled his players in the fundamentals. So that's the way Demp taught his own kids when they became old enough to play sports.

Buster tried soccer and football. He played on the basketball team until his sophomore year. He didn't need sports to stay out of trouble—he never ran afoul of authority—although Demp remembered a time when Buster and his brother, Jack, put a few dents in the walls when they chipped golf balls in the house.

But baseball always seemed to take over, and Buster had room to grow. The Poseys built a batting cage on their 50-acre property, which became a social center for the neighborhood kids. Buster wasn't out there to horse around. He liked to practice his swing, but he also repeated drills on the boring stuff, too.

"From an early age, he saw the benefits in working hard on the basics," Demp Posey said. "He's done that with baseball, with academics, and with his personal life. We're proud of who he is today."

He hit .346 as the Seminoles' freshman shortstop, starting all 65 games while winning freshman All-America honors. He made the Dean's List in his first semester, too. But he wasn't a wonder to behold at full gallop, and with Florida State graduating its catcher, pitching coach Jamey Shouppe approached longtime head coach Mike Martin with an intriguing thought. They knew Posey had the arm strength and the intelligence to be a catcher. After one meeting with Buster, they knew they'd have his enthusiasm, too.

Posey would crouch in the catcher's position as he watched TV to strengthen his legs and loosen up his hips. He took countless balls in the dirt from a pitching machine, making his hands pillow soft to smother anything in front of him.

He was the Golden Spikes winner as a junior, honored as the top amateur baseball player in the country. He led Florida State to the 2008 College World Series, also serving as their closer, and memorably played all nine positions in one game. It was a promotional stunt that didn't become Buster, but there was a purpose behind it. Martin wanted to show off the kid's athleticism to the flocks of scouts. That's what a good college coach does when one of his players has a chance to go pro. But there was something more at work with Buster. Martin just had so much gosh darn admiration for the kid.

Buster became as popular as a college athlete can be in Tallahassee without putting on shoulder pads. Old-timers and students alike at Dick

Howser Stadium serenaded him with a song, "Hail to the Buster," sung to the tune of "Hail to the Bus Driver."

"He *sin*-gles, he *doub*-les, he *trip*-les, he *ho*-mers!"

He led the nation in batting average (.467), on-base percentage (.567), and slugging percentage (.864). Behind the plate, he threw out 41.5 percent of attempted base stealers while picking off six others. On the mound, he converted all six of his save opportunities.

As the 2008 draft approached, Martin told reporters that Posey would be Derek Jeter at the plate and Jason Varitek behind it. He was a lock to be taken in the first 10 picks. But even though a multimillion-dollar bonus awaited him, Posey continued to attend classes, study late into the night, and make progress toward his finance degree.

Interviewed for an ESPN.com story, Posey was asked what else he likes to do besides play baseball.

"School?" he said, expressionless. "There's nothing else to do, is there?"

He maintained a cumulative 3.8 grade-point average and was named the Academic All-American of the Year, an award that encompassed all Division I athletes.

"That made us prouder than anything else," Demp Posey said.

Buster married his high school sweetheart, Kristen. He received the key to the city of Leesburg, which has an annual "Buster Posey Day" on the calendar. (They are now looking to move it from February to late autumn.) He was ready to pour his considerable focus and intellect into the next challenge. He would become a full-time student of the game as a professional baseball player.

Now he just needed a team.

"He was in our consideration for this selection," said Barr, "since the day I accepted this position."

The Giants checked and cross-checked on Posey. As a final measure, Sabean sent out Hiatt, his former farm director who knew more about catching than anyone in the organization, to watch the kid receive a game. Hiatt came back with his stamp of approval, saying he liked the way Posey moved his feet and gunned his throws. The rough edges could be smoothed out. It was all the GM needed to hear.

"I'd trust Jack with my life," Sabean said.

Barr and his scouting team rated another college hitter, Vanderbilt infielder Pedro Alvarez, right up there with Posey atop their draft board. But they also had intelligence that Pittsburgh would take Alvarez with the second overall pick. They also knew the Kansas City Royals liked Eric Hosmer, a high school slugger, with the No. 3 pick, and the Baltimore Orioles, who had taken college catcher Matt Wieters with their top choice a year earlier, were committed to taking a pitcher fourth overall.

That left one wild-card—the Tampa Bay Rays, who chose first. When Barr heard the Rays had backed off Posey in favor of high school short-stop Tim Beckham, it was all he could do to keep from dancing around the war room. Fifteen minutes after making the pick, Barr tried to compose himself as he met with reporters.

"He's a team player," Barr said calmly. "And that's what we're trying to develop here—a solid, winning club for years to come."

The Giants barely qualified as a winning club when Posey stepped off that flight from Salt Lake in late May. Their Opening Day lineup featured six of eight position players in their thirties, all of whom were acquired via free agency or trade. Three of them were coming off surgeries, and two of those, Mark DeRosa and Edgar Renteria, already were leaking oil. The third, Freddy Sanchez, had just made his season debut 10 days earlier—a far longer absence than anyone anticipated following a shoul-der procedure in late December that the team had kept hidden from the media until the eve of spring training. Pablo Sandoval, their rotund, 23-year-old switch-hitter who hit .330 while finishing a runner-up for the NL batting title a year earlier, wasn't barreling up pitches the same way and had just hit his first home run in more than a month. Aaron Rowand, an imperfect fit atop the order, had gotten off to a fast start before a pitch from the Dodgers' Vicente Padilla hit him in the cheek, breaking facial bones in three places. Upon his return, he had gone back to lunging at sliders and grounding softly to third base—sights that had become too common as he crashed and burned in the second half in each of the two previous seasons. Molina had gone cold, too, hitting .130 in his last two weeks, and because he was slower than ever, he was like a cork in a bottle on the rare occasions he got on base.

But Molina also continued to handle a young and talented rotation, in addition to a live-armed bullpen. The pitchers were familiar with Molina and trusted him. And Sabean made a powerful statement during the winter meetings a few months earlier, saying he had gone around the table with his staff and "nobody thinks Buster Posey is ready to catch 100-plus games in the big leagues."

It's true, Posey hadn't called games at Florida State; the pitch sequences were ordered from the dugout. He'd have to learn the nuances in Fresno from Grizzlies manager Steve Decker, a former major league catcher who was lauded for his smarts and ability to break down opponents.

"Setting up hitters, controlling their posture, minimizing pitches, knowing who's available in the bullpen—these are all things he needs to know to be an effective major league catcher," Decker said in spring training. "When there's a two-run lead in the ninth, you've gotta be aggressive with the fastball to the leadoff hitter. I could bring up scenario after scenario. You've got to have a reason behind everything you're doing.

"Inevitably, the pitcher has the chance to shake his head. Okay, well, do you let him do that? Or do you call timeout and go talk to him? All the nuances of game calling, the tempo of the game, controlling the emotions of someone like a Brian Wilson out there or whoever it may be…these are all new experiences for a rookie catcher. When you come out to the mound, what do you say to relax a pitcher? Or to get him going? These are all things you learn from experience. He'll be on a crash course to learn all of this."

Some teams handed jobs to rookies. The Giants did not. Bochy's reputation was to play veterans, even if they struggled, and sometimes until upper management released them. Sabean's track record was to trust players with a track record. If a young player like Daniel Ortmeier or John Bowker didn't produce in 150 at-bats, Sabean wasn't going to watch and waste more playing time on them.

It's not like Bochy and Sabean often were proven wrong. Of all the youngsters they jettisoned, only speedy Rajai Davis became a productive player on another team. Of all the young players Bochy benched during his 12 seasons as manager in San Diego, only Xavier Nady went on to post decent numbers elsewhere—for a season or two, anyway.

When Posey made his major league debut in September 2009, ostensibly promoted to give the Giants catching depth while Molina nursed a pulled muscle in his leg, Bochy heard constant braying from fans while he left the kid on the bench. In a month, Bochy only gave Posey 17 at-bats, and the rookie hit .118. Conspiracy theorists wondered if Bochy, a backup catcher during all of his nine big-league seasons, held some malice toward a budding superstar like Posey.

The truth was this: Bochy and Sabean knew the Giants' success would be tied to its high-strikeout pitching staff. So starting the year with a rookie catcher would've taken stones. You don't toss the keys to a Lamborghini to a 15-year-old kid who's just gotten his learner's permit.

So the Giants considered themselves fortunate to re-sign Molina for one more year, and when Posey's bat forced his way to the majors, they introduced him as a first baseman—a position he hadn't played until midway through spring training.

The timing for Posey's 2010 debut was choreographed, right down to the Diamondbacks' starting pitcher that first night. Posey had faced Billy Buckner twice in April at Triple A. He was 4-for-6 with a homer and a double against him.

The Giants sought to take the pressure off Posey however they could. They couldn't afford to miss on him, and not just because his $6 million bonus more than doubled their previous franchise high. He had an entire scouting and player development system—the heartbeat of a franchise—tied to his success.

Good thing for them that Posey had no intention of failing at anything, be it a calculus exam, a new position, or a Saturday night game under major league lights.

Posey followed up his three-hit debut by getting three more hits the next day, to cheers and gasps of disbelief from home fans. The Giants hadn't seen anything like this since a young and brash Will Clark hit a home run on the first pitch of his major league life, off Nolan Ryan, no less, and scowled as he pointed to the stands. A year later, "Will the Thrill" led the Giants to the 1987 NL West title, ending a 15-year playoff drought.

Now Giants fans had a new thrill, a young hitter with a more muted sense of confidence but just as much ability. The thrills didn't stop after two games, either. Posey had multiple hits in seven of his first 12 games, hitting .444 overall. And the best was yet to come.

"Ted Williams was a guy who would hit it out of the catcher's glove," Tim Lincecum said. "That almost looks like what Buster's doing. He's pretty f—ing talented. I don't know what else to say. You don't see this often. I'm just glad he's on my team."

On the day Posey was promoted, Bochy explained it by saying the club had a temporary window while Renteria and DeRosa healed up.

"In a few weeks we'll see where we're at," the manager said.

In a few weeks it was clear to everyone: Buster Posey wasn't going back to Fresno.

"I just expect myself to work hard every day, and when the games come around, try and contribute and help this team get wins, hopefully," Posey said prior to his season debut. "There's a lot of good hitters on this team. I don't feel I have to do extraordinary things to help the team get wins."

That was good ol' Buster, too. Be seen and not heard. Know your place. And if you're boring enough, maybe the reporters will stop coming over to your locker.

Posey knew he had a responsibility to talk to the media. He just wanted to get it all over in one session. One day, after he dealt with a third wave of questions, he had a rare burst of frustration.

"You're killing me!" he said, using two hands to grab a reporter's jacket. Then he softened. "Aw, you know I'm just kidding."

"Just so you know," the newspaperman told Posey, "you ain't seen nothing yet. If this team goes where it wants to go, it's gonna get a lot worse."

The season started to go a little better for the Giants. They exacted revenge on their Bay Area rivals, sweeping three games from the A's at AT&T Park in mid-June. Posey, still mostly playing at first base, had graduated to starting behind the plate once a week.

Aubrey Huff, a designated hitter from the American League who signed with the Giants over the winter, had moved from first to left field to accommodate Posey. To the surprise of many, Huff hadn't been a defensive disaster at either position. The Giants picked Pat Burrell off the scrap heap after the Tampa Bay Rays released him in mid-May and decided to give him a whirl in left field. Huff switched positions again, this time to right field—a treacherous place to play at AT&T Park. He wasn't an embarrassment there, either.

Bochy kept Posey hitting sixth or seventh, far removed from the pressure spots in the lineup. Even as the kid put together good at-bats and knocked in runs, the manager resisted the urge to put him in a higher-rent spot.

"I like him where he is," Bochy said.

The Giants weren't climbing in the standings, though, because they simply failed to match up against their NL West rivals. They finished June with a 13–14 record after the Dodgers waltzed into San Francisco and swept the three-game series.

The team needed a change, and Posey appeared ready to handle it. The Molina trade was made, along with the long-awaited changing of the shin guards.

More than two years after the Barry Bonds era ended, the Buster Posey era had begun.

Chapter 3

Found Material

Pat Burrell wasn't used to rejection.

His whole life, he was the big man on campus—a legend at Bellarmine Prep in San Jose, the alpha male at the University of Miami, and the first player taken in the 1998 draft. With his square jaw and soft eyes, he didn't need to play baseball to be popular with the ladies. Back in college, his teammates called him "Bait." He would walk into a bar and stand in the middle of the room, attracting all the attention from the coeds. He needed multiple wingmen. His buddies were all too willing to help.

Burrell played the first nine years of his career in Philadelphia, and all the locals knew he loved to chase more than fly balls. He averaged 28 home runs and 92 RBIs as a Phillie, hitting a total of 251 out of the park. But he was supposed to be a Hall of Famer with Mark McGwire's power and Jeff Bagwell's all-fields approach. Burrell was a very good player. For many, though, it wasn't enough.

The fans in Philadelphia would boo their own mother for striking out with the bases loaded, and Burrell wore the verbal abuse like coats of lacquer. The taunts often got personal. When it was rumored that Burrell became so drunk one night that he lost control of his basic functions, fans stitched together a bedsheet, spray-painted "BEDWETTER" on it, and hoisted it when he came to the plate.

Burrell always seemed above it all. He would address the media whenever he played a major role in a game, understanding it was part of his obligation. But he wouldn't deign to make eye contact with reporters, instead scanning the ceiling or looking over the tops of their heads. His replies were a recycling of baseball's greatest cliché hits. He didn't need to be genuine. He didn't need to be insightful. He just needed to make himself available.

Although Burrell came off as aloof and cocky in his interviews, he didn't have a reputation as a bad teammate. To the contrary, players lauded Burrell's leadership and loyalty. He didn't look down on rookies. He never yelled at the traveling secretary if a ticket order was out of place. He didn't treat the clubhouse assistants like sub-humanoids. If you were deemed part of the inner sanctum, there was nothing Burrell wouldn't do for you.

The Phillies were mediocre for most of Burrell's tenure with the team, but homegrown stars like Ryan Howard and Chase Utley were changing the dynamic. A new ballpark, built adjacent to old Veterans Stadium, boosted enthusiasm and increased the season-ticket base. The Phillies were generating revenue to go after prized free agents. They said Citizens Bank Park, with its short left-field line, was custom-constructed for Burrell's pull power.

The Phillies made it to the World Series in 2008, and Burrell began it 0-for-13. He felt overwhelmed on the big stage, struggling to control his heart rate. But after the Tampa Bay Rays scored to tie Game 5, veteran shortstop Jimmy Rollins approached Burrell in a tunnel behind the dugout.

"Pat," said Rollins, sticking a finger in his chest, "it's time you joined the show."

Burrell's last at-bat as a Phillie would be his sweetest of all. He hit a leadoff double in the seventh inning, came out for a pinch runner, and the Phillies took the lead on their way to a clinching victory that night.

When the Phillies held their victory parade down Broad Street, their first in nearly three decades, owner David Montgomery insisted that Burrell ride in the first carriage.

The Phillies didn't re-sign Burrell after the season, though, and so he took the highest offer—a two-year, $16 million contract from the Rays, of all teams, to be their designated hitter.

Burrell was miserable. He wasn't a good left fielder, but he didn't like the inaction of getting just four at-bats a night. He wasn't surrounded by all his old running buddies in Philly. Tampa Bay's manager, Joe Maddon, was regarded as one of the most astute in the game. But Maddon and Burrell weren't pals. Maddon often organized team-wide bonding activities, like wearing ugly plaid blazers on flights. Burrell wasn't much of a joiner. He thought players should motivate and police themselves.

Burrell was a flop in Tampa Bay. He hit .221 with just 14 home runs in 2009. He started the 2010 season with a .202 average and just two homers in 24 games. The Rays were a small-revenue club and couldn't afford to eat contracts. But Burrell knew what was happening before they released him in mid-May. He was happy to be cut loose and not completely shocked by it. Yet rejection was an alien feeling for the big man on campus. He was humbled in a way he'd never been.

A Tampa Bay reporter sent him a text message seeking comment on the move.

"Lose my number," came the reply.

But Burrell had not lost Aubrey Huff's number. The two former college teammates remained tight throughout their major league careers, often talking of a day when they might be able to play together. Burrell wasn't sure what he should do next. Huff was.

Two days after Burrell went back home to Scottsdale, Arizona, the Giants were in town to play the Diamondbacks. Huff and Aaron

Rowand, another former Phillie, met Burrell for lunch. Huff and Rowand pledged to put on their most persistent sales pitch to bring Burrell to the Giants.

Bochy, never one to turn down a free roll of the dice, thought it was worth taking a chance. His Opening Day left fielder, DeRosa, already was concerned he'd need another operation on his surgically repaired wrist. John Bowker, the Opening Day right fielder, had massive holes in his swing and wasn't making adjustments. Burrell hadn't played the outfield in two years, and he had been a deficient defensive player for the better part of his career. But the Giants didn't have any right-handed power on their bench. At minimum, Bochy figured, Pat the Bat might be able to come up in the pinch and pop one.

The surprising San Diego Padres, who had leapt to the top of the NL West standings, were expressing interest, too, but they didn't move with enough swiftness or resolve. Besides, Burrell wanted to join his buddies in San Francisco. The Giants signed him to a minor league contract, figuring it couldn't hurt to give him a few weeks at Triple A Fresno to get his swing right.

It had the potential to be a nice homecoming story. Burrell grew up in the Santa Cruz Mountains, and while he wasn't a diehard Giants fan, he attended plenty of games at Candlestick Park. His parents still lived in the Bay Area. The Giants were his hometown team, more or less.

But Sabean didn't have high hopes that Burrell would be an impact player.

"It's lightning in a bottle," Sabean said with a shrug. "It's up to [Burrell] and what he does when the opportunity presents itself."

It didn't take long for Burrell to show the Giants that he was in shape, that he still had bat speed, and that he was motivated. He was 2-for-5 with a home run and an RBI single in his first game for the Grizzlies. He would play just four more games on the farm.

After nine years in Philadelphia and a disappointing season in Tampa Bay, Pat Burrell returned home to California, joining the Giants on June 4, 2010.

Burrell joined the Giants on June 4 in Pittsburgh, and found a No. 9 jersey hanging in his locker. It was the same number worn by Kevin Frandsen, another Bellarmine Prep alum, who had been traded that spring to the Boston Red Sox.

"It couldn't be better, being home," Burrell said.

Bochy didn't define Burrell's role to reporters, saying it was a hard question to answer. But Burrell started the next day, hit a double in his first at-bat and played all nine innings. It was clear Bochy didn't want to invest more at-bats in Bowker. The manager now had an alternative with more experience and, he decided, just as much upside.

With Burrell in left, Huff in right, and Andres Torres establishing himself in center, the Giants had three outfielders who played their college ball in the Miami area.

Burrell came up with another outfield theme. Noting the club had two DH types in the corner positions, Burrell dubbed it the "Wild Kingdom outfield." Torres was the gazelle. Burrell and Huff were the water buffaloes.

Burrell certainly was turning into a beast at the plate again. He had a knack for coming up with big hits in dramatic moments. In his first home game as a Giant, on June 11, Burrell hit a two-run home run to break the spell of an A's staff that had spun 22 consecutive scoreless innings against them. By the time June had ended, Burrell had five home runs in just 65 at-bats—already more than doubling what he'd done in 1½ months with the Rays—and he had a .405 on-base percentage.

His ability to work deep counts and take pitches filled a desperate need for the Giants, whose offense had finished dead last in the majors in walks, on-base percentage, and pitches per plate appearance the previous year. They finished near the bottom in those categories in 2008, too, and the lack of improvement cost hitting coach Carney Lansford his job. They no longer had Barry Bonds' obscene walk totals to provide coal for the fire.

Burrell didn't panic like so many of the Giants' younger hitters. He didn't extend the zone or offer at pitcher's strikes, which were designed to induce weak contact. He still struck out often, especially when his jackknife reaction to an inside pitch didn't fool the umpire. But he made pitchers execute to get him out. He made them work a little harder.

His aloof brand of confidence rubbed off on his new teammates, many of whom had not experienced a true pennant race. In past years younger players felt judged by the veterans in the room, looked at disapprovingly when they would show emotion or be a little outspoken in the media. But Burrell and Huff started to bring a new dynamic. Lord knows, it wasn't their place to judge anyone's behavior. But when something needed to be said, they approached the offending player more like a friendly big brother than a scolding parent.

Get to the park early, do your work, play the game like a professional, enjoy the moment if you win, and forget about it if you don't. Regretting the past only screws up your ability to focus on the present.

The clubhouse vibe was changing, and so were the faces in the lineup. By the All-Star break, you almost needed dental records to prove this was the same team that took the field on Opening Day. Huff had rotated like a volleyball player from first base to left field to right field. Juan Uribe, the Opening Day second baseman, was at shortstop. Molina had been traded to clear the position for Posey. The outfield—DeRosa, Rowand, and Bowker—was completely overhauled. Torres had become the everyday center fielder, and Burrell appreciated the energetic 32-year-old's ability to help him cover part of his territory.

Contending clubs weren't supposed to be made up of career minor leaguers, castoffs, and goofballs. They were supposed to resemble the Phillies, with everyday horses like Utley and Howard in the middle of their lineup.

But with Posey leading the charge, the Giants vaulted themselves into having a relevant second half. And if there was a Bluto Blutarski in their Animal House, the guy with the hedonistic streak who nonetheless kept the group centered, it was Pat the Bat.

"I just think it's simple, really," Burrell would say later that summer. "When you can get 25 guys to believe in one thing, and that's winning, and put that before everything else, it's really easy for the guys to come together and play."

The Giants weren't anyone's trendy World Series pick at the All-Star break, though. They had an embarrassing 9–20 record within the division. And although Posey's promotion gave them a boost, they still had to prove they could beat their NL West rivals.

Immediately after trading Molina to Texas, the Giants lost the first two in Denver, extending their losing streak to seven games—the team's longest in more than four years. Morale was flagging. They would face Ubaldo Jimenez, the Rockies' untouchable ace, the following day. He was 14–1 with a 1.83 ERA in 16 starts.

Huff offered a uniquely insane suggestion.

"Maybe we need to say 'Screw it,'" he said. "Let it all hang out and have fun. I've seen some crazy things happen in this game when you're down and out. This may be the exact guy we need to get out of it."

Crazy is as crazy does. Backup first baseman Travis Ishikawa hit a grand slam in a seven-run third inning as the Giants battered Jimenez. But even in this humidor-controlled era at Coors Field, he who scores last usually wins.

Barry Zito and the Giants' bullpen blew a six-run lead, and the Rockies pushed ahead in the late innings. The Giants responded when Nate Schierholtz hit a leadoff triple and scored the tying run on Torres' single. Then Torres stole third base, positioning himself to score the go-ahead run on a sacrifice fly.

Huff added a two-run home run, and the Giants broke their seven-game losing streak. Crazy stuff, all right. And afterward, Huff welcomed reporters to his locker.

"We let it hang out, didn't we?" he said, beaming with pride. "It gives this offense confidence. If you can get this guy, you can get anybody."

For many teams, an emphatic victory like this would be the turning point in a season, or at least kick-start a winning streak. But the Giants would learn soon enough: nothing would go as expected for them in 2010.

The day after crushing the best pitcher in the game, the Giants would lose the longest game in Coors Field history.

The mile-high ballpark on Blake Street had been the stage for high-scoring theatrics, interminable games, and knock-down, drag-out night-mares. Even after the introduction of the humidor kept baseballs from drying out and flying like Titleists, it remained a place where the scoreboard could turn into a pinball machine at any moment.

For a time, it appeared the Giants might steal an inspiring victory on July 4. They rallied from a three-run deficit to tie in the eighth inning—a dramatic comeback that included Schierholtz's first career pinch home run followed by an inside-the-park homer from Torres. It was the first time the Giants hit consecutive homers that included an inside-the-parker since Willie Mays (running) and Willie McCovey (trotting) did it June 1, 1966, at Atlanta.

But the Giants failed to push ahead, letting chances go by in extra innings. Huff gasped for air after legging out a leadoff triple in the 13th, but backup catcher Eli Whiteside—who curiously pinch ran for Posey earlier in the game—struck out feebly, and Huff advanced no further.

Brian Wilson and Guillermo Mota, the last men standing in the Giants bullpen, escaped two bases-loaded situations in the 13th and 14th before Dexter Fowler tripled to lead off the 15th. The Giants had failed to score Huff from third base, but the Rockies did not fail when given a similar chance. Todd Helton's sacrifice fly won it.

The talk-show callers and bloggers back home screamed for Bochy's head, upset over the decision to pinch run for Posey—a move that looked especially bad after Whiteside struck out twice and popped out in extra innings, twice stranding runners in scoring position.

The season was half over, and the Giants were 41–40—on pace for an unmemorable 82–80 season. They had lost for the 10th time in 12 games, they were in fourth place, and their deficit was a season-high 7½ games behind the Padres. One more losing series or two, and Sabean would have to think about being a seller at the trade deadline.

The Giants were gassed, dejected, and disconsolate—and they had no time to rest. They jetted to Milwaukee, where they had an afternoon game the next day.

Bochy called a quick meeting before reporters were allowed to enter the clubhouse.

"I told them that's a tough loss, but they battled their hearts out," Bochy said. "That's a long day, and they kept fighting. We're just missing one more hit."

The Giants were about to get dozens of them. They were downtrodden, but they had the good fortune to land in Milwaukee just as the Brewers were playing their worst baseball of the season, too. Ryan Braun, their best hitter, was tangled in knots at the plate, and their infielders were booting balls like they were in the World Cup. The Brewers' pitching staff was a wreck. The Giants rolled them with all the subtlety of an oom-pah band.

In the series opener at Miller Park, Bochy broke up the personal battery of Whiteside and Jonathan Sanchez to start Posey—removing the final impediment for the rookie to become the full-fledged catcher from that day forward. Posey homered and hit a single to start a four-run rally.

Huff, so drained after the previous day's loss, somehow dragged himself into the lineup and hit two doubles and a two-run single. Burrell fought off fatigue, too, battling to see 20 pitches in his first two plate appearances. He hit a single on the 12th pitch of an at-bat in the second inning, then worked an eight-pitch walk in the fourth.

Less than 19 hours after the most horrific loss of the season, the Giants won 6–1. This time, it really was a turning point.

After that victory, the Giants remained 7½ games out. And Burrell passed along a piece of advice to Huff.

"Let's make up one game a week," Burrell said. "Just try to see it that way. Then it doesn't seem so overwhelming, does it?"

The Giants accelerated the pace. They won by another 6–1 score the following day. They followed with 15–2 and 9–3 victories to sweep the series, restore their sanity, and thoroughly confuse their longtime general manager.

"Some days we look like the team that's been nine games over .500, and some days that we haven't played well, we look very much like a .500 team," said Sabean, as his fourth-place team entered the All-Star break. "We've got our work cut out for us because we've got to get over three teams. But I like the relative experience we have. The depth and the attitude has been good throughout, the effort has been good throughout, but we obviously have to play better in the division and win more games against teams above .500. It's simple math."

Could the Giants make the playoffs without a major trade?

"I don't know," Sabean said. "Put it this way: they think they're good enough to get to the playoffs, which is important. It really doesn't make any difference what I think.

"They have to think they have a chance. And I have every reason to believe that's their attitude."

Before and after the break, the month of July belonged to Posey.

In the Milwaukee series he destroyed the Brewers' soft pitching staff, going 9-for-15 with four home runs and nine RBIs. He hit another home run as part of a four-hit game in Washington, where the Giants won two of three to enter the break. He became the first rookie in NL history to compile 19 hits, six home runs, and 13 RBIs over a 10-game span.

Posey carried an eight-game hitting streak into the break, and he picked up right where he left off. He extended the streak all the way to 21 games—the longest by an NL player in 2010 and one short of matching the Giants' record for a rookie, set by Willie McCovey in 1959.

Florida's Anibal Sanchez stopped Posey's streak, and the rest of the Giants lineup, with a one-hitter in a July 29 loss. Thanks in large part to their surging rookie catcher, it was just the Giants' fifth loss in 22 games.

Posey was almost happy the attention would go away.

"Indifferent, I guess," he said, asked for his reaction to the end of the streak. "It would've been something cool to have. At the same time, I know who Willie McCovey is. I didn't know he had the Giants' rookie record for a hitting streak. Know what I mean?"

Posey was an easy choice as NL Player of the Month for July after hitting .417 with a .466 on-base percentage. Of his 43 hits, six were doubles and seven were home runs—the most homers by a Giants rookie in a month since Jack Clark in 1977.

He became a puzzle for advance scouts, who couldn't find obvious holes in his swing or approach. He didn't chase much. He was comfortable hitting with two strikes. He'd spoil good pitches on the corners. And he kept his hands inside the ball so well, it was nearly impossible to jam him inside.

Rockies manager Jim Tracy instructed his pitchers to throw inside with runners on base, knowing Posey could be an inviting double-play target. The pitchers hit their spots, too. But Tracy didn't get the result he wanted.

"That sum'gun kept serving it to right field," Tracy said. "The absolute hardest thing to teach a young hitter is to keep your hands inside the ball. And he's already got it. Special player, man."

The Giants needed to add more pieces than just Posey and Burrell, though.

They were 2½ games out on the morning of July 31, the deadline for teams to make trades before players would have to clear waivers. The rival Padres already had improved their unimpressive lineup, engineering a three-team deal that netted slugging outfielder Ryan Ludwick from St. Louis. The Cardinals needed a starting pitcher, and the Padres sent prospects to the Cleveland Indians, who agreed to give up sinkerball specialist Jake Westbrook.

It was the kind of creative deal that many vocal critics believed Sabean was unequipped to pull off. It required engaging in a volume of conversation with other executives that didn't fit Sabean's more isolationist style.

A month before the trade deadline, ESPN's Buster Olney conducted an informal poll of GMs asking a variety of questions. Seven of 12 respondents mentioned Sabean as the most difficult trading partner, and several expressed frustration that he didn't return phone calls.

Sabean didn't appreciate the inference that the Giants' front office was neglecting to do its work.

"Lets not be naïve," Sabean said. "There are 30 teams. Some you don't have anything in common with. Some are young guys cutting their teeth, chatterboxes throwing things against the wall to see what sticks, or gathering intelligence.

"I'm a cut-to-the-chase guy."

He was an old-school guy, too. Sabean, a former scouting director with the New York Yankees, was the longest tenured GM in the major leagues. He was elevated to his position with the Giants in 1996, and over the years the game had changed in many respects. The steroid scandal embarrassed baseball and took a funhouse mirror to some of the game's greatest offensive records. Teams were evaluating talent in different ways, using different tools. After a while, Sabean's counterparts were more likely to have an Ivy League MBA as a background than as an ex-player or scout. It was fair to wonder how much Sabean had in common with them. Nowadays, deals seldom happened at the bar at 3:00 AM, after a few vodka cranberries.

Younger GMs—the chatterboxes, as Sabean called them—were more likely to share information. There was a feeling in the Giants' front office that some of their counterparts were ganging up on them, gathering intelligence to use against them. So Sabean preferred to operate with walls up.

"We do return phone calls. I return phone calls," Sabean said. "But if I don't, it's for a specific reason."

Many of his critics among the Giants' fan base cared little about the process. They simply wanted results. And they saw the Padres think out of the box to get the kind of hitter that Sabean had failed to acquire for the better part of four seasons.

The Dodgers had been active at the deadline, too, addressing their rotation by acquiring left-hander Ted Lilly and infielder Ryan Theriot from the Chicago Cubs. They also got Scott Podsednik from the Kansas City Royals and traded for Pirates closer Octavio Dotel.

With all of San Francisco screaming for Sabean to get a bat, the GM thought he had an angle on a solid, two-way player. Sabean personally scouted outfielder David DeJesus in Kansas City, and by all accounts, he had the Giants positioned to make a deal.

But with Sabean in attendance on July 22, DeJesus crashed into the wall at Kauffman Stadium while chasing a deep drive. He tore a ligament in his thumb, ending his season and turning Sabean's trip into a total waste of time. The GM was livid.

Another rumored name, the Brewers' Corey Hart, also hurt himself in a collision with an outfield fence. And to get a cleanup presence like Adam Dunn, a rental player who'd be a free agent in a few months, the Washington Nationals were strong-arming the Giants into breaking up their rotation. To Sabean, that was a conversation ender. He wouldn't pay that price. And so he wouldn't get the hitter everyone demanded.

But Sabean knew he had another, less sexy priority: his bullpen suddenly found itself without a left-hander. Jeremy Affeldt, whose 1.73 ERA was the lowest among all NL relievers a year earlier, felt something in his side on his second warm-up pitch July 23 at Arizona. An MRI confirmed a strained oblique muscle that would shelve him for a month.

A few weeks before that, hard-throwing rookie Dan Runzler sustained a freakish injury when he dislocated his knee while swinging a bat in his first major league plate appearance. There was additional insult to go with the injury, too. Runzler was carried off the field with a two-strike count, and pitcher Madison Bumgarner was called upon to finish the at-bat. Bumgarner swung through the next pitch, and Runzler got credit for the at-bat. So as Runzler lay on a table in the trainer's room, wondering how badly he was hurt, he also simultaneously earned his first official strikeout as a big-league hitter.

Sabean knew the Giants couldn't survive without a lefty reliever. They had too many games remaining against the Padres, who had Adrian Gonzalez, and the Dodgers, who had James Loney and Andre Ethier. The Diamondbacks had several potent left-handed hitters, too.

Without the injuries to Affeldt and Runzler, the Giants probably wouldn't have given a second look to Javier Lopez, a sidewinding lefty who had pitched in the NL West before with Colorado and quietly was putting up decent numbers in the Pirates bullpen. So on the day of the deadline, the Giants gave up Bowker, their Opening Day right fielder, along with popular right-hander Joe Martinez to make the deal.

It turned out to be one of those little bits of fate that made an enormous difference. Nobody knew it at the time, but out of all the major league players traded at the deadline, Lopez would become the most important acquisition of them all.

The Giants also got a workhorse right-hander, Ramon Ramirez, who might have been in danger of losing his roster spot in Boston. But the scouting reports were encouraging, and Ramirez threw strikes. Sabean nearly pulled off a third trade, too, but a deal for Seattle Mariners closer David Aardsma fell through.

The reaction from Giants fans was less than enthusiastic.

"Bowtie [owner Bill Neukom] doesn't care about a championship," wrote one commenter on a popular Giants blog. "Giants just handed the division to the Padres. Pathetic."

"FIRE BRIAN SABEAN AND GET A REAL GM IN HERE!!!!! Sabean gets schooled every freakin' trade deadline!!!"

"Today is a great example of why the Giants will not make the playoffs, and if they do, they have no chance in the first round."

"The man lacks creativity and a brain. And he was trying to trade for a THIRD reliever, but not a bat??!! The man has lost it!!"

"[Sabean] simply failed miserably at his job. And it isn't the first time."

"Once again, Sabean will say that making the pitching stronger will negate the need for more offense. Once again, he'll be wrong."

"Don't even insult us with the 'Giants will look to improve the offense through waiver-claims/trades in August' crap."

"HAHAHAHAHAHAHAHAHAHAHAHAHA!!!!!!!!!!!!!!!!!!!!!!!!!!"

The mob seemed ready to pick up pitchforks and storm the castle. There was just one thing that could soothe them on the night of July 31, and Burrell provided it. In front of a sellout crowd, Burrell hit a two-run home run in the eighth inning off Dodgers closer Jonathan Broxton, touching off a jubilant celebration at the Giants' waterfront ballpark and sending them to a 2–1 victory.

For the first time in years, it felt like a playoff atmosphere on the shores of McCovey Cove. Burrell took a curtain call after his line drive barely cleared the left-field fence. It was his first home run since June 29; he had been hitting .179 in his previous 21 games.

The game marked a paradigm shift in one of baseball's most heated rivalries. The Dodgers had become far too comfortable in San Francisco over the previous four seasons, all but putting their feet on the furniture when they visited AT&T Park while posting a 23–13 record there. The Dodgers looked to be in control yet again when they beat the Giants in five of six prior to the All-Star break.

But thanks to Burrell, the "BEAT L.A." chant held meaning once more.

The Giants were on a special run. They finished 20–8 in July, a record that was even more remarkable considering they had lost three of four in Denver to start the month. It was the Giants' first 20-win month in 10 years. They had leapt over the Rockies and Dodgers to take second place, where they stood 1½ games behind the Padres.

The Giants won the next day, too—with Matt Cain finally notching his first victory in 15 career starts against the Dodgers—to sweep their archrivals at home for the first time since 2004. Suddenly, the Giants stood 16 games over .500 for the first time in five seasons.

"There's only been a couple other times the crowd sounded the way it did tonight," Rowand said. "That's home-field advantage, right there, when everybody is hanging on every pitch."

Burrell's out-of-the-blue swing against Broxton did more than soothe fans who were upset over the Giants' perceived inactivity at the trade deadline. It also instilled confidence within the clubhouse.

"We don't need a bat, if you ask me," Huff said that night. "We've got problems getting guys in the lineup as it is. We've had guys hurt in the bullpen, so if we needed to make a move, that was it."

The Giants didn't acquire their slugging white knight on a horse. Yet they still defended their turf against their archrivals. Now they had more work to do.

"We're a good team," Burrell said after his homer beat the Dodgers. "We're playing a good team. And we're fighting to catch another good team."

Sabean's lineup was built more like a bird's nest than a skyscraper, made up of found materials, not steel girders. But it would have to hold.

"It's going to be a rough two months," Sabean said. "These games are taking on a playoff atmosphere, and we're chasing a team that's very tough."

The Giants were relevant again, but the Padres had gotten inside their heads. And one player was determined to do something about that.

Chapter 4

Who's Your Padre?

Sigfredo Sanchez didn't want to accept his son's charity.

He had lost his factory job two years earlier, and his other occupation, as a semipro pitching coach in Puerto Rico, didn't pay many grocery bills. But his son, Jonathan, phoned him in July 2009 and offered him a plane ticket to San Francisco. And at the last second, Sigfredo decided to take it.

Sigfredo Sanchez hadn't seen his son pitch in the big leagues in three years, when he sat in the stands at crumbling Shea Stadium as Jonathan made a relief appearance against the New York Mets. Three years is a long time for a pitcher to establish himself in the big leagues, but Jonathan was anything but established. The Giants couldn't figure out what to do with the erratic but live-armed left-hander, and during his first couple seasons, then-manager Felipe Alou yo-yoed him between the rotation and bullpen. Sanchez's easy delivery made his low-90s fastball appear to jump like a rabbit, and when he had his good slider, it swept away from left-handed hitters. The Giants knew they had something. But was he physically strong enough to handle a full season? Was he willing to do the work between starts? Did he have the mentality to face hitters a third and fourth time and make adjustments, as starting pitchers needed to do?

Sanchez had his doubters, both inside and outside the organization. But he added weight and strength in 2008, and he made the most of his opportunity when he began that season in the rotation. He was 8–5 with a 3.97 ERA through his first 19 starts, and the Giants had won 13 of them. Impressively, the club had the same record through Lincecum's first 19 starts—and Lincecum won the Cy Young Award that year.

But Sanchez faltered down the stretch in '08. He had a 7.47 ERA in his last 10 starts, winning just once. He walked too many hitters, and all the little threads in his game were loose. He didn't show much interest in keeping base runners close, even though he had a natural advantage as a left-hander. He wasn't the best at getting a sacrifice bunt down. There were a lot of secondary ways a pitcher could help himself win a game. Sanchez didn't do any of them.

There was a culture change happening with bloggers, reporters, and many fans, who were beginning to understand that the win-loss record was not the best standard, given its highly dependent nature, to judge a starting pitcher. But with Sanchez, his lack of victories was telling. His stuff competed well enough. Yet he wasn't *competitive* enough.

Not surprisingly, trade rumors became one more distraction Sanchez had to tune out. Other clubs noticed his robust strikeouts per nine innings and meager hits per nine innings—the easiest indicators of pure stuff. They noticed he got as many swings and misses with his fastball as Lincecum or Cain. They wondered if the Giants noticed these things, too, and hoped to steal Sanchez away. But while Sabean desperately needed hitters, he couldn't get what he felt was a fair return. So Sanchez remained a Giant.

The left-hander applied himself after that 2008 season, eager to show he could maintain his stuff over 30-plus starts. And the Giants were counting on it. They had designs on contending in 2009 with their young rotation, but they needed steady contributions from all five pitchers—a group that now included 45-year-old Randy Johnson, perhaps the greatest left-handed pitcher of all time, who signed a one-year contract to return to his Bay Area roots while chasing his 300th career victory.

The year did not begin well for Sanchez. He was 2–8 with a 5.62 ERA in his first 13 starts. He issued 46 walks in 64⅔ innings. He was inefficient, and opposing hitters knew it, taking pitches and making him work deep counts while letting him create his own messes. In those 13 starts, Sanchez completed six innings just twice and had retired a total of two batters in the seventh inning.

Once again, the Giants banished Sanchez to the bullpen. They replaced him with Ryan Sadowski, an organizational arm with tame stuff who nevertheless pitched without fear and threw strikes. Sadowski, who overcame a brain hemorrhage early in his minor league career, threw six shutout innings against the Milwaukee Brewers to win his major league debut. It was a magical story, even if it didn't last long.

Three weeks after Sanchez's banishment, the baseball gods provided an opportunity. Johnson, who achieved his milestone victory a month earlier in front of a rain-soaked smattering of fans at Washington, had injured his shoulder while swinging a bat. Sanchez, the 26-year-old who didn't know how to win, would replace an intimidating left-hander who owned 303 of them.

And Sigfredo Sanchez, who had never set foot inside AT&T Park before July 10, 2009, would see his son start a major league game for the first time.

It was an ordinary Friday night when the Giants hosted the last-place San Diego Padres—the second game of a four-game series that would take both teams into the All-Star break. Lincecum and Cain would represent the Giants on the NL squad in St. Louis, and both had flirted with no-hitters a few times in their young careers. In fact, Lincecum took a bid into the seventh inning the previous night.

Cain had the closest brush with a no-hitter, getting within four outs during an interleague start against the Angels in 2006 before Chone Figgins lined a clean single. Just a 21-year-old that season, Cain also owned a one-hitter against the Oakland A's.

It seemed a matter of time, luck, and opportunity before Cain or Lincecum would become the first Giant to break the franchise's lengthy no-hitter drought that went back to 1976 and John Montefusco. Opponents had no-hit the Giants seven times since "the Count" threw his gem more than three decades earlier.

If Sanchez was a candidate to throw a no-hitter, he was on the Peace and Freedom ticket. Maybe that's why nobody saw what was unfolding as the left-hander calmly threw strikes and kept setting down the Padres in order. Whiteside, who started because Molina's wife had gone into labor, didn't realize what was happening until the sixth inning.

"It kind of dawned on me," Whiteside said. "With a runner on base, I'll look over to the dugout for the signs. And I hadn't looked over once."

Sanchez wasn't merely throwing a no-hitter. He had a perfect game, too. And his efficiency allowed him to venture into the late innings for the first time all year.

In the sixth inning a reporter in the press box called his copy desk to make sure his editors had the game on TV. Perfect games and no-hitters were disasters on deadline. Pages would need to be redesigned, plans scrapped, other stories held. It would cause bedlam in the office.

"Don't worry," the reporter spoke calmly into the phone. "No way he throws it."

Sanchez hadn't thrown a complete game in his major league career, after all.

He was about to make history with his first.

The crowd stayed passive until the seventh inning, when Sanchez struck out the side. The fans came to their feet when he set down Tony Gwynn Jr., who had broken up Lincecum's no-hit bid a night earlier with a single in the seventh.

The path to perfection appeared clear after Sanchez survived a 3–0 count to retire Adrian Gonzalez, the Padres' best hitter, on a lineout in the eighth. But Chase Headley followed with a bouncing ball that deflected off third baseman Juan Uribe's chest. The earnest infielder scrambled to pick up the carom, desperate to save his teammate's precious chance. But his barehand attempt failed, and Uribe flipped the ball back to Sanchez with a crestfallen expression on his face.

Error, third base.

This would be the moment of decision for Sanchez. His concentration now broken, would he allow himself to give in, as he did many times in the past when a blooper or a bad call went against him? Or would be stand a bit taller, wipe the slate, and finish the job?

"This is the game. It can happen," he told himself. "It doesn't matter. Just the win."

Sanchez got that and more. Rowand slammed against the center-field wall while making a catch for the second out in the ninth, and the rest all seemed to be scripted. Sanchez struck out Everth Cabrera on a called breaking ball—his 11th strikeout of the game—and raised both arms.

He smiled with nervous surprise. How do you react to a no-hitter? He didn't know. Neither did anyone else.

"All I want to do is pitch," he said. "Tonight, everything went right."

In the stands, Sigfredo Sanchez jumped for joy and hugged the fans around him. He couldn't believe what he was witnessing—or how close he came to missing it.

"I'm very proud," the elder Sanchez said in Spanish. "I was expecting him to get tired. He didn't."

Sigfredo Sanchez disappeared for a time late that night, and nobody could find him. He had gone wandering the city looking for a newspaper—to prove it all really happened.

In the manager's office, the newest Giants legend smiled at Bochy.

"I hope I'm not going back to the bullpen," he said.

The night was profound for pitching coach Dave Righetti, who saw a lot of himself in Sanchez. Righetti was a live-armed left-hander, too, bounced between closer and starter early in his career with the New York Yankees. Righetti appreciated how difficult it was for a young pitcher to establish himself, especially in a pressurized environment.

And now he felt another kinship to Sanchez. Righetti once no-hit the Boston Red Sox on Independence Day 1983—the first no-hitter by a Yankee since Don Larsen's perfect game in the 1956 World Series. He understood what Sanchez's no-hitter meant to the kid and to the franchise.

Long after the toasts and back slaps that night, the big-hearted pitching coach found a quiet place and let slip a few tears.

"These kinds of things bring teams together," said Righetti, with a prescience he couldn't have understood. "It really bonds them in a way and makes them think something good's going to happen to the ballclub.

"You're trying to get through the game and win, and all the sudden, you're talking about immortality. It's a hell of a thing."

Righetti also had a few practical thoughts in the immediate glow of the final out. When he had thrown his July 4 no-hitter, someone had swiped all his stuff from the dugout. So Righetti sent relief pitcher Merkin Valdez to scoop up Sanchez's belongings.

"He picks up the glove, and the ball rolls out," Righetti said. "I yelled, 'Get that ball! Are you crazy?'"

The ball was going to Cooperstown, and Sanchez was going places, too. Finally, he had a winning template in his mind. He knew how everything was supposed to look and feel on the mound.

Jonathan Sanchez opens a champagne bottle after pitching a no-hitter against the San Diego Padres on July 10, 2009.

He pitched with confidence for the remainder of the season, leading to hopes that he would put everything together in 2010. The Giants were confident, too, and when it came time to align their rotation in the spring, they didn't hesitate to set up Sanchez for the fourth game—the club's home opener, in front of a sellout crowd, with all the pregame pomp and pageantry.

If Sanchez could manage to piece together his first half of '08 and his second half of '09, he'd be 13–9 with a 3.91 ERA, 195⅔ innings, and 223 strikeouts. Not bad for a No. 4 starter.

"Different year," he said, a few days after reporting to Scottsdale. "You watch."

Sanchez had talked confidently in the past, but it usually seemed to be more of a false front from an immature kid. There were times when teammates wondered if Sanchez truly would figure everything out—not only how to pitch and win, but how to act like a professional. Years earlier, after a day game, Sanchez put on a Giants hat after changing into his street clothes—a violation of a clubhouse code. Once you leave the room, you don't advertise who you are.

Teammates chided him on his way out the door. "Yeah, go Giants!" shouted one pitcher. "Hey, Sanchy!" yelled another, holding up a fist. "Way to represent!"

With one game, everything changed. Sanchez didn't have to try so hard to be respected. He had earned it.

"This team wants to win a championship, which means going to the park prepared to win all 162 games. In the past, I'm not sure if he understood that or not," said Molina, a few weeks before the 2010 opener. "When he'd get into tight situations, he'd go with the pitch he wanted. I think he just has to understand we're out there to help him. I told him, 'With your stuff, you should have a great career. Just go out and dominate, and the contracts, the wins—everything else—will take care of itself.'"

Naturally, Sanchez's confidence was highest against the Padres. He would start six games against them in 2010, an unusual frequency even in this era of the unbalanced schedule.

He met them for the first time on April 20, on an atypically drizzly and dour night at Petco Park. He dominated again, holding them to one hit while striking out 10 in seven innings. But the Padres countered with Mat Latos, their brutish looking right-hander with the platinum blond hair and hard fastball. Latos held the Giants to four hits in seven shutout innings, and they wasted several scoring chances in a 1–0 loss.

It was the 29th time the Giants held an opponent to one hit or fewer in a nine-inning game in the franchise's San Francisco era. It was the first time that they lost.

"I can't say I've been in a game like this," grumbled Bochy, who bounced f-bombs off his office walls after reporters filed out. "No way we should've lost tonight's game."

Bochy would grumble and swear in that visiting manager's office many more times before the year ended.

The Padres were defying expectations. They were supposed to be relevant to the baseball world only in late July, when star first baseman Adrian Gonzalez, who was getting close to free agency, would be the crown jewel at the trade deadline. Instead, they had established themselves as the NL West's pace car. They no longer had ace right-hander Jake Peavy, but one of the young pitchers they received from the Chicago White Sox in that deal—left-hander Clayton Richard—was churning out one quality start after another. Jon Garland, a bargain free agent who was coming off a mediocre year with the Diamondbacks and Dodgers, found pitching for the Giants to his liking, too. Latos, barely more than a rookie, threw a heavy ball and had learned to control his emotions on the mound.

The Padres' biggest weapon was their bullpen. Their top three relievers, Luke Gregerson, Mike Adams, and closer Heath Bell, effectively shortened every game—and all three were acquired off waivers or in trades.

The Padres' offense, while light on talent, was doing all the little things that the Giants were failing to do. They were opportunistic on the bases, used productive outs to move runners, and reliably scored them from third base with less than two out.

They dinked and dunked the Giants to death while beating them eight times in the first nine games.

It was payback for all the years the Giants destroyed San Diego behind a fusillade of home runs, with Barry Bonds leading the 21-gun salute. Bonds hit more home runs against the Padres than any other team. From 2001 through 2003, the Giants dominated the season series, winning 14 of 19 each season.

But now the Padres were finding ways to beat the Giants with a single hit.

They created their lone run against Sanchez when Headley lined a leadoff single in the fourth inning, stole his way into scoring position, took third on a foul pop that Huff caught while tumbling into the photographer's well, and scored on Scott Hairston's sacrifice fly.

Headley, despite being an average runner, stole three bases on Sanchez during the game. It was the first three-steal game by a Padre in almost four years. Those loose threads cost Sanchez again, and he failed to get down a sacrifice bunt, too.

Meanwhile, the Giants were almost creatively cruel while failing to score on six hits. Schierholtz hit a leadoff triple in the eighth inning but was stranded. The Giants put runners at the corners with one out in the ninth against Bell, but Uribe's fly ball to right field wasn't deep enough to score Torres, and Bowker struck out to end it.

The almost medieval quality of the loss remained in broadcaster Duane Kuiper's mind. And when he opened the next day's telecast with a quick recap of the one-hit loss, he stared into the camera and spoke from his gut.

"Giants baseball," he said.

Long pause.

"Torture."

Kuiper and popular broadcast partner Mike Krukow had a talent for coming up with catchphrases. "Grab some pine, meat!" was one. "Ownage" was another. Every night, fans would bring "Eliminate Me" signs, imploring for Krukow to scribble them out with his telestrator.

Now Kruk and Kuip had conjured a new slogan. "Torture" wasn't the ideal motto for a baseball team, given recent world events. But even in the politically correct Bay Area, the theme immediately caught on. The Giants continued to play excruciatingly tight ballgames. The wins didn't feel much different from the losses. The fans frayed every raw nerve and chewed every last fingernail.

The Giants were Team Torture.

The phenomenon took off on May 15 with a Saturday afternoon game against the Houston Astros. Wilson inherited a 2–1 lead and was charged with protecting Lincecum's fifth victory of the season. But even though Wilson already was an All-Star closer and had saved 79 games over the previous two seasons, he seldom made it easy. The Astros loaded the bases on an infield single and two walks, bringing light-hitting Kazuo Matsui to the plate with two outs.

The at-bat lasted 15 pitches. Wilson refused to throw anything over the heart of the dish. Matsui kept flicking off foul balls. After a dozen or so, Wilson had to step off the mound and laugh.

"I couldn't help it," he said. "It was just comical. It was like, 'What are they thinking [in the dugout] right now?'"

Matsui finally flied out, the Giants won, and in the handshake line Wilson had the nerve to ask Bochy if he was worried.

"Nah," said Bochy to Wilson, one master of deadpan sarcasm to another. "I like seeing a bases-loaded, two-outs-in-the-ninth [pitch] 10 times."

Up in the booth, Kuiper only knew one way to sign off the telecast.

"Giants beat the Astros by a final of 2–1," he said. "Giants baseball: *torture.*"

Fans embraced the theme only because the Giants found a way to win so many of these excruciatingly close games. They had a chance to win almost every night because their rotation was giving them consistent, quality outings. Even Zito, a slow starter his entire career, was 6–1 with a 2.15 ERA after eight assignments. And while the bullpen had some shaky moments in the eighth inning, Wilson always seemed to protect the house in the ninth.

But they always lacked that one hit or one pitch against the upstart Padres.

Latos emerged as an archetypal villain. The hulking pitcher wasn't drafted until the 11th round in 2006, mostly because he had a checkered reputation. But the Padres' area scout in Florida, who happened to be Bruce Bochy's brother, Joe, insisted the kid was worth the risk.

When the Padres visited AT&T Park for the first time in mid-May, Latos did not make nice with Giants fans while shagging fly balls during batting practice. According to eyewitnesses, Latos decided to have a little fun with fans in the left-field bleachers who screamed at him to throw them a baseball. As he headed off the field, he flung a ball over the bleachers and out of the ballpark. Unbeknownst to him, that's where the players' parking lot was located, and the baseball smashed the sunroof of Giants announcer Dave Flemming's new Honda Civic.

Latos disputed the sequence of events, saying the ball must've taken a crazy bounce off a railing. But he pledged to pay the repair bill. The Giants sent it to him.

Latos was doing even more damage to Sanchez's psyche. The Padres' 22-year-old ace won his second 1–0 decision over Sanchez on May 13, finishing mere millimeters away from throwing a perfect game. The

Giants got their only base runner in the sixth inning when Whiteside—
who had become Sanchez's personal catcher—reached on an infield
single. The chopper up the middle went off the heel of Latos' glove;
Headley fielded the deflection, and his throw nearly beat Whiteside,
anyway. Latos didn't allow another base runner. He was dominating the
Giants. It wasn't a good time for Bochy to place a friendly call to his
brother, Joe. Latos was dominating the Giants.

"We've got some guys who are cold right now," the manager said.
"They're not comfortable at the plate. You can see it."

Latos and Sanchez met for the third time five days later in San Diego,
a game in which neither starter would earn a decision and the Giants
would win in the late innings. It was their only victory in eight games
against the Padres before the All-Star break.

The Padres were in the Giants' heads.

"I swear to God, their guys are in the right position every time," Huff
said. "It's like they know what's coming. You've gotta credit their scouts,
I guess, or something."

Sanchez was 0–2 against the Padres in three starts, but he didn't let that
dampen his confidence. This was the team he no-hit last season. This was
a lineup he knew he could dominate. The template was fresh in his mind.

But he still lacked consistency. Heading into August, he hadn't posted
back-to-back quality starts since April 14 and 20. One game, he'd be historically good—such as an August 3 start at Coors Field in which he
struck out seven consecutive hitters to tie Juan Marichal's 46-year-old
franchise record. The next time out, with the Giants needing a quality
effort to earn a hard-fought split at Atlanta, Sanchez couldn't make it
past the fourth inning.

Given his rough start at Turner Field, it was all the more surprising
when Sanchez gathered three reporters near his locker in the visiting
clubhouse. He knew his next start would come against the Padres, whom

the Giants hadn't played in three months. And he wanted to send them a message.

"We are going to make the playoffs," said Sanchez, his chin raised. "San Diego has been winning series all year.... But we're going to play San Diego now, and we're going to beat them three times. If we get to first place, we're not going to look back."

The three reporters at his locker were stunned. Where was this coming from? They reminded him that the Padres beat the Giants in seven of eight games prior to the All-Star break.

"That was a long time ago," Sanchez said. "Doesn't matter. We've got a better team now."

Asked again, for clarification, if he was guaranteeing the Giants would make the playoffs, Sanchez said, "Yeah, we will."

Naturally, all three reporters ran with the story. It blazed across the Bay Area. When Bochy and Sanchez's teammates were asked for reaction the next day, they distanced themselves from the comments. Sanchez didn't have enough service time or stature within the clubhouse to be a team spokesman. It wasn't Bochy's style to blow up bulletin boards, either. Giants coaches met with the left-hander and censured him.

"That's between you all and Jonathan," Bochy told a crowd of reporters in the dugout. "I know some of the guys were giving him a hard time about it."

Outspoken reliever Sergio Romo wasn't among them.

"I'll be honest, he's not the only one in this clubhouse who thinks that's possible," Romo said. "He just happens to be more vocal about it."

The Padres scoffed at the prediction.

"Lotta courage to say that," Padres outfielder Scott Hairston told a San Diego TV station. "I don't think he's too smart of an individual."

Said Bell: "All right, cool. We're going to get swept. Well, I swept my garage this morning."

On the night of August 13, the Padres took great pleasure in smashing Sanchez's crystal ball.

They put up a fight in every at-bat, drove up his pitch count, and forced him from the game in the sixth inning on their way to a 3–2 victory. Huff snapped off his batting gloves in anger after he hit a 420-foot out in the eighth. It was a metaphor for a team that had come up short against the Padres all season.

"You live and die with your park," Huff said. "We died on that one."

Even the Giants' 1970s-inspired orange jerseys—their uniform choice on "Orange Friday" nights at the ballpark—failed to work. The garish jerseys had been undefeated after nine of clubhouse manager Mike Murphy's wash cycles. But they couldn't help the Giants avoid their ninth loss in 10 games to San Diego.

The Padres ended up winning two of three to extend their lead to 3½ games in the NL West. They weren't supposed to be in first place, but they weren't going away. Again and again, they were finding a way to come out on top.

Sanchez's prediction didn't come true. Not yet, at least.

"I believe in my team, you know?" said Sanchez, who didn't duck reporters after the game. "I've got confidence. Nothing against them, but I know we keep fighting out there.

"If we keep playing like this, better and better, I think we're going to make it."

Chapter 5

Putting It Bluntly

It was the day before Halloween, and Tim Lincecum was about to get tricked.

The Seattle native was driving home up Interstate 5 in his Mercedes and had just crossed the Columbia River into Washington, when a patrolman clocked him doing 74 mph in a 60 mph zone.

When Lincecum rolled down the window...

It wasn't quite the scene in *Fast Times at Ridgemont High* when Jeff Spicoli emerged from the van in a cloud of smoke. But the officer smelled marijuana, and Lincecum complied with a request to turn over any illegal substances, producing 3.3 grams of pot along with a pipe. The officer did not deem Lincecum intoxicated, so he cited him and allowed him to continue. But the Cy Young Award winner had a court date, and he knew it was a matter of time before the incident became a public embarrassment.

Earlier that year, Olympic swimmer Michael Phelps paid a steep price when a photo swept across the Internet that showed him inhaling from a water pipe. USA Swimming banned him from competition for three months, major advertising sponsors dropped him, and moralists excoriated his behavior.

For Lincecum, this was no random snapshot from a party. He was caught red-handed, and although prosecutors recommended a lesser charge, the judge assigned to his case in Clark County, Washington, wasn't going to let him off without making an example of him. Even worse, Lincecum was eligible for salary arbitration that winter, and if he and the Giants couldn't agree on a contract, both sides would argue their case to an arbiter in a sealed chamber. If club officials brought up the pot bust, it could turn ugly fast.

Neukom, a buttoned-down, bow-tie-wearing corporate lawyer, made a surprise appearance in the courtroom on the day Lincecum appeared, as if to convey the serious matter of the charges. Lincecum said all the right things, too, when he was finally available to the media.

"I made a mistake, and I regret my actions," he said on a conference call to announce his second consecutive Cy Young Award. "I certainly have learned a valuable lesson in all of this, and I expect to do better in the future."

Lincecum knew he would be open to any manner of insults and jokes on the road in 2010. He would be called a budding superstar in more ways than one.

But a funny thing happened. Lincecum's Q rating actually went *up* in San Francisco. T-shirts with a marijuana leaf and "Let Tim Smoke" became a common sight around AT&T Park. All of a sudden, Lincecum was more than the first two-time Cy Young winner in Giants history. He was a folk hero for a city that once inhaled free love and remained more permissive than the rest of the country.

If Lincecum got razzed on the road during the regular season, it was more tongue-in-cheek than mean-spirited. When he pitched at Atlanta in August, the Turner Field organist played "Puff the Magic Dragon" as he walked to the plate. Lincecum didn't realize it at the time, but his teammates did. And everyone had a good laugh over it.

Besides, it's not as if the arrest came as a shock. Lincecum's black hair got longer every year, he ate breakfast cereal at all hours, he loved video games, and everyone knew he enjoyed a good party. At the news conference to announce his first Cy Young Award, he showed up in a white T-shirt and a black skater-style beanie.

He was at once a slacker and an achiever. And he always made it look so, so easy on the mound.

Lincecum didn't intimidate hitters in the traditional sense. Power pitchers like Roger Clemens whipped themselves into an NFL linebacker's frenzy. Randy Johnson held up his glove while glaring over its laces. Pedro Martinez pitched as if the hitter were contemplating a carjacking attempt, with a "don't even think about it" look on his face. Pedro would remind you again and again that the smaller, more tenacious dog usually wins the fight.

Lincecum didn't pitch angry or aggressive. He certainly didn't cast a long shadow. He stood maybe 5′11″ in his cleats, weighed barely 170 pounds, and shaved as often as your typical high school sophomore. But he was deceptively strong and incredibly flexible—a gymnast in a baseball uniform. He used every bit of that flexibility in his unique delivery—a creation of his father, Chris, an inventory clerk at Boeing who pitched in junior college and had a lifelong fascination with the kinetics of throwing a baseball. Chris Lincecum taught Tim to use every fiber, work every hinge, use every bit of force and momentum that his undersized body could generate.

Most kids have a growth chart somewhere in their childhood home—scratches of pencil along a garage or basement wall—to mark their progress. The Lincecums had an entire video library. Chris would film every practice session, game, or scrimmage, and together they would pick through Tim's throwing motion like NASA scientists. Tim's first lesson came when he was four years old. There is video of him throwing a baseball in Little League, using the same exact delivery; he's 10 years old, his left leg in the air, his glove hand raised above his head, and his back turned slightly toward the plate, looking like he's about to deliver a crane kick straight out of *The Karate Kid*. Then he glides forward with an impossibly long stride and follows through, his hips hinging over his planted, arrow-straight left leg, showing all the flexibility of Houdini squirming out of his chains. His right leg gracefully trails in the air behind him.

Cleats or ballet slippers. Either would work.

It was eccentric. It was poetic. And Chris Lincecum had no modesty whatsoever when a reporter would approach him about it.

"He loads like Warren Spahn or Bob Feller, has an extension and a dangle and the looseness of Satchel Paige with the finish and follow-through of Bob Gibson," Chris Lincecum explained shortly after his son reached the major leagues. "It's pieces of all of them, and it's good for anybody because it's very efficient."

In truth, it wasn't good for just anybody. It required incredible athleticism, balance, coordination, and flexibility to throw that way without falling off the mound. Lincecum was able to repeat it pitch after pitch while still able to control where the ball was going. His head tilted so much in his windup that he relied on his left eye to stay focused on the target. That wouldn't work for most right-handers, who are right-eye-dominant. But Lincecum batted lefty. His left eye was stronger, anyway.

No, this was not the cookie-cutter way to throw. Lincecum simply was gifted enough to pull it off.

It's not surprising that scouts didn't know what to make of him, even while he rocketed baseballs past hitters at every level. Baseball's culture is one of conformity. The season is a 162-game proof kiln. Flaws lead to cracks, which lead to breakdowns. Scouts are trained to identify flaws, raise red flags, and look for dependable projections.

They didn't know what to do with tiny Tim Lincecum or his eccentric father. Many figured he could blow out his arm on any given pitch. But Chris Lincecum knew better. Timmy's power came from his legs, his hips, his seven-foot stride, and his explosive leap off the rubber. His arm was just along for the ride.

"I get so sick and tired hearing them talk about how he's going to break down," Chris Lincecum said. "I've heard that for years. I'm going to tell you right now: he's not going to break down on the field. All he needs to do is keep core muscles in shape and all his hinges.

"I mean, I hit 88 mph at 52 years old, and his mechanics are much more efficient than mine ever were."

It can be mentally draining to prove people wrong all the time, but Lincecum just kept shutting people up. He won the Golden Spikes Award at Washington, the same honor that Buster Posey would capture two years later. Lincecum was two-time Pac-10 Pitcher of the Year. He led the nation with 199 strikeouts in 125⅓ innings.

Yet nine players were drafted in front of him in 2006. Six of those were pitchers. And two of them ended up needing major arm surgery within two years of signing their pro contract. Most galling? One of the clubs that selected a pitcher ahead of Lincecum was the Seattle Mariners, his hometown team. They took a bigger, more prototypical power-pitcher from the Pac-10, Cal right-hander Brandon Morrow. The Mariners tried to use Morrow in the rotation and out of the bullpen, with mixed results. He struck people out, but he walked almost as many. Exasperated, the Mariners traded him a few years later to the Toronto Blue Jays for a middle reliever.

Lincecum recalled attending a banquet in Seattle to honor local players of the year. He was one of the honorees. Bill Bavasi, then the Mariners' general manager, got up to speak and tossed a platitude in Lincecum's direction. What a great talent this kid is. Something like that.

"If that's true," Lincecum remembered thinking, "Why the f— didn't you draft me?"

Lincecum looked nothing like Dick Tidrow's definition of an ideal pitcher, either. But the Giants' guru made one of his Ninja runs up to Seattle to watch the kid throw against Arizona State. He saw how easy Lincecum warmed up in the bullpen, throwing 93 mph. He was amazed as he watched Lincecum play long toss the day after a 130-pitch start, throwing 200 feet on a line.

Sabean called Tidrow. Should he arrange to get a look, too?

"No way in hell," Tidrow replied. "I don't want anybody to know we're on this kid."

Lincecum was there for the taking with the 10th overall pick, and he could've jumped straight to the major leagues. In a brief pro debut at the end of 2006, and five starts at Triple A Fresno to begin the '07 season, he was 6–0 with a 1.01 ERA in a combined 13 starts. He struck out 104 in 62⅔ innings. At Fresno, he gave up just 12 hits in 31 innings.

He didn't belong on the farm. He didn't stay there. Lincecum was in the big leagues by early May 2007.

More impressive than Lincecum's athleticism or his curious delivery was his ability to make adjustments. He got roughed up in his big-league debut against the Philadelphia Phillies, who relaxed when they saw his big, easily recognizable curveball. The Phillies had a lineup full of professional hitters who worked to get ahead in the count, then pounced on overthrown fastballs that hovered at the belt.

Lincecum knew his curveball was close to unhittable in college. But in that moment, he understood that big-league hitters wouldn't chase it. So he continued to experiment with a change-up that he began throwing in the minor leagues. The pitch used a modified split-finger grip—think of Mr. Spock's "Live Long and Prosper" hand gesture—and it had lethal tumble and fade. Lincecum threw it with the same incredible, blurry arm speed as his fastball, making it impossible for a hitter to pick up. With the change-up, it was like he had a personal cloaking device on the mound.

By the end of his rookie season, Lincecum owned more than just the best change-up in the league. It might have been the best single pitch in the majors, and he had learned it within a span of a few bullpen sessions.

Lincecum dominated in each of the next two seasons, racking up consecutive Cy Young Awards despite never leading the league in victories. All his other metrics—ERA, strikeouts, FIP, WHIP, WAR, you name it—ranked him as the most valuable pitcher in the league. Voting members of the Baseball Writers Association of America weren't just picking the 20-game winners anymore. They saw another Dwight Gooden in their midst, and they gave him the prize. He was only the second Giant to win the award, and the first since Mike McCormick in 1967.

It's an outrage to think that Juan Marichal, the high-kicking Dominican Dandy, one of the greatest pitchers of the 1960s, received just one Cy Young vote over his Hall of Fame career. It was a third-place vote in 1971. (The ballots had just expanded from one to three a year earlier.) Other than Marichal and fellow Hall of Famer Gaylord Perry, the Giants didn't have many star pitchers in their five-decade history in San Francisco. They were known as the heavy-hitting franchise of Mays and McCovey, Cepeda and Bonds. Now their fans were learning to cheer strikeouts and Cy Youngs, all unleashed by an unassuming kid who looked like them, talked like them, played video games like them, and partied like them.

Lincecum was a god in San Francisco.

He could've been one of the Beatles. He needed a half-dozen police officers to walk from one autograph station to another at the team's FanFest. He dropped the puck at a San Jose Sharks game, and the crowd couldn't have roared louder if he were hoisting Lord Stanley's Cup.

Lincecum had no trouble adjusting on the mound, but managing his celebrity status was harder. It didn't come natural for him to "big league" people. He had a hard time saying no, and suddenly, thousands of people wanted him to say yes. He was on the front of the 2K9 video game box, had his own ESPN *SportsCenter* commercial and appeared on the cover of *Sports Illustrated*. His teammates called him "the Franchise." The magazine dubbed him "the Freak."

Whatever you called him, Lincecum was making a name for himself. And the pot bust didn't affect his popularity one bit.

For all his talent and accomplishments, though, questions would pop up from time to time about Lincecum's ambition and focus—such as the time in his rookie season when he committed the grave sin of missing a team flight.

The Giants had a 10:30 AM wheels-up time to Cincinnati. Lincecum, who had been in the big leagues only three months, thought the team was meeting at the ballpark at 10:30. He slept in, then got to the clubhouse and knew something was wrong. There were just a few guys doing rehab work.

"Dude," one of them said. "They've been looking for you."

Lincecum called Giants travel coordinator Michael Scardino, who booked him a nonstop flight. The rookie arrived a few hours after the team. No game was scheduled for that day, so no real harm was done—except for the $800 fare that came out of Lincecum's pocket.

But it caused a stir in the Giants clubhouse. As the bus rolled away without Lincecum, Zito took charge.

"I said, 'By a show of hands, how many of you guys have missed a flight in your career?'" Zito said. "And it was just, you know, crickets. So Timmy had to do a little self-preservation on that one."

Barry Bonds, of all people, called a team meeting the following day and got in the rookie's face.

"Are you kidding me, Timmy?" said Bonds, in front of the whole team. "This is ridiculous."

Then he practically pinned a copy of the itinerary to Lincecum's chest.

"Dude, I don't want this thing to leave your fricking sight the entire trip," Bonds said.

When the road trip continued to St. Louis, Lincecum was ordered to carry all the veterans' luggage up to their rooms. He was given one brass cart to do the job. The team walked into the lobby after midnight. Lincecum wasn't finished until close to 3:00 AM.

Lincecum fumed. But as infielder Rich Aurilia said much later, "He hasn't missed another flight, has he?"

The story became public a year after it happened, so it didn't cause much public reaction. But Bochy still tried to downplay it.

"He felt terrible about it," Bochy said. "But you know, just about everyone in the game had a time when they missed a bus or plane. I did once."

Bochy might have been helping Lincecum save face. In this post-9/11 world of scrutinized passenger manifests, it's ultra-rare for a player to go AWOL without securing permission from the manager. Scardino had seen it happen just one other time in his 14 seasons with the team.

Lincecum never forgot his mistake, and his teammates admired the way he handled it. Lincecum wasn't the type to put up walls. He signed autographs every day, sometimes for a half hour or longer. His heart remained in the right place.

"He's grown while he's maintained who he is," Zito said. "He has such a good spirit, a good heart, and this contagious energy. He makes everyone relax a little bit because he just has fun."

Lincecum was coming off his first Cy Young season, when Randy Johnson joined the Giants. It wasn't a surprise when reporters asked the Big Unit, a five-time Cy Young winner, for his thoughts on his much smaller rotation mate. Johnson, a native of nearby Livermore, gave many expansive interviews that season—a yearlong *This is Your Life* with

Two-time Cy Young Award winner Tim Lincecum, with his unorthodox athleticism and free-thinking attitude, has become wildly popular among fans in San Francisco.

reporters, really—and he often said that his fifth Cy Young season was his best. He said he kept on racking up awards because he never stopped working, never became satisfied with what he'd done. The Big Unit didn't know Lincecum well, but he hoped he could impart some career wisdom on the little right-hander.

Lincecum was polite when asked if Johnson provided any lessons for him.

"Well, sure," he said. "I mean, he's had a great career."

But after repeating as Cy Young in '09, there were rumblings that Lincecum had slacked off. He'd become the slightest bit complacent with his success, assuming he'd keep on piling up strikeouts and zeroes. If the hitters made an adjustment to him, he'd just invent something else on the fly. It always worked out for him in the past.

He'd heard doubters his whole life. By now, any criticism had become ambient noise, a buzz that he just tuned out.

For all he'd accomplished, there remained a few shortcomings in Lincecum's game. He didn't pitch well in hot-weather environments like Atlanta or St. Louis, often laboring as his long hair turned stringy with sweat and then running out of gas in the later innings.

He hadn't pitched well in big games, either. Handed the Opening Day assignment for the first time in 2009, Lincecum got lit up by the Milwaukee Brewers. Down the stretch that season, as the Giants remained on the outskirts of contention, Lincecum mixed in a few bad starts. The team had a 7–7 record in his last 14 outings as they faded from the playoff picture.

Lincecum also started the All-Star Game that year at Busch Stadium and admitted he was nervous while the AL scored twice off him in the first inning. At least it had gone better than his All-Star experience the previous year in New York, when he didn't even make it to Yankee Stadium for the game. Lincecum was taken out of his hotel room on a stretcher and received intravenous fluids at a local hospital after experiencing dizziness. The Giants called it flulike symptoms. A suspicious New York media assumed Lincecum had just partied too hard.

It was true, though, that a nasty respiratory illness had gone through the Giants clubhouse in the week prior to that All-Star break, and Lincecum already was exhausted after pitching in hot conditions at Wrigley Field over the weekend. Yes, he said, he had a couple of drinks the night before the game at Yankee Stadium. But he honestly had the flu.

After the pot arrest, though, the door was open for skeptics to look back and wonder.

There was another nagging doubt buzzing around Lincecum as he reported to camp in the spring of 2010. His average fastball velocity had decreased from 94 mph in '08 to 92.4 mph in '09. He didn't top out at 97 mph like he did as a rookie. He had thrown a ton of pitches during his two Cy Young seasons, and the workload might have caught up to him.

Molina acknowledged that Lincecum won a few games in 2009 "because of his name. He wasn't always feeling the best. He wasn't throwing as hard, and his breaking ball wasn't as good. He was beating them because the hitters knew who they were facing.

"Obviously, I'm not trying to put Timmy down. Everybody knows how nasty he is. Even if he doesn't have his good stuff, he knows how to pitch a good game."

Lincecum shrugged. No big deal.

"I'm aware my velocity wasn't where it was," he said. "I don't feel like it's anything to be scared about. I'll just learn how to pitch better."

The questions persisted—the same ones he heard when he enrolled at Washington or the day the Giants drafted him or the times he got stopped trying to enter a big-league ballpark because security assumed he couldn't possibly be a player. And after a rough start in spring training, he got uncharacteristically testy.

"Yeah, I know," he said, to a small group of national reporters. "I'm small and I'm going to break down. Same in high school. Same in college. It used to motivate me. Now it's, 'Get over it. Watch the game.'"

Yet Lincecum knew he had to adjust again. He pledged to throw a ton of sliders and curveballs that spring. He worked on a sinking, two-seam fastball that he could use to get ground balls. He'd figure it out.

He had a 6.94 ERA in just four starts during the spring, a couple times skipping Cactus League games and staying back to pitch in intrasquad games at the club's minor league complex. He didn't look like a pitcher going after his third consecutive Cy Young Award. He wasn't favored to do so, either. The Phillies had acquired durable right-hander Roy Halladay from the American League's Toronto Blue Jays in a megadeal over the winter, and he was expected to dominate the National League.

Bochy answered honestly when asked if he expected Lincecum to repeat his success from the previous two years.

"You know, that's an extremely high standard he has set," Bochy said. "With the bar as high as he's set it, it would be asking a lot. Don't get me wrong, Timmy is capable. He showed it by winning another Cy Young. But it's going to take the other four starters coming through for us, too.

"It's not just Timmy. We can't put it all on him."

For all his troubles in his big-game assignments, Lincecum didn't act tense before his starts. Unlike most starting pitchers, he didn't sequester himself in the hours before taking the mound. He'd chat up the beat reporters during batting practice, crack jokes, anything to keep from thinking too much. "I get bored easily," he'd say.

On Opening Night in Houston, Lincecum spent the early part of his day T-shirt shopping at a mall. He picked up shirts for a bunch of his teammates, including one for Aubrey Huff. He knew Huff was a huge fan of the cartoon series *The Transformers* as a kid—so much so that Huff had huge Autobot and Decepticon logos tattooed on each shoulder blade.

"Aubrey, catch," Lincecum said, throwing him a shirt.

"Thanks," said Huff, who reached in his locker and held up an identical one.

He'd gone shopping at the same store.

Lincecum also bought a shirt for Pablo Sandoval, who hadn't achieved the results the Giants wanted in his off-season weight-loss camp. The shirt said, "I have the body of a god...unfortunately, it's Buddha." Sandoval laughed, immediately modeled the shirt for teammates, and wore it under his batting practice top.

After the anthem and the introductions, Lincecum took the mound with the same carefree spirit. And for all his struggles during the spring, he did what he'd always done.

He shut people up.

He mixed his pitches and didn't walk a batter over seven shutout innings, holding the Astros to four singles while striking out seven. The team with the skinny ace, unimpressive lineup, and chubby third baseman played a near flawless game to beat the Astros and Roy Oswalt 5–2. They would've had their first Opening Day shutout since 1994 if Brandon Medders hadn't coughed up two runs in the ninth.

"I felt a little more in control this time," Lincecum said. "I was definitely excited for this game more than anything. This is where it matters. But it wasn't the uncontrollable hyped-upness, where you don't know what's going on."

Huff, playing behind Lincecum for the first time, was ready to trade in his T-shirt. Maybe for one that said "Let Tim Smoke."

"Just seeing some of those swings, it's like...man," Huff said. "He made some good major league hitters look pretty bad.... Watching him tonight, I really got an idea what it's all about."

But Bochy's concerns were valid. It became apparent by mid-May that Lincecum would have no shot to earn his third consecutive Cy Young Award.

Lincecum's previous high for walks in a game was five. He tied it when he faced the Astros at home on May 15. Then he tied it again in his next start at Arizona. And again in the start after that, against Washington. He issued five walks in four consecutive starts, with the Giants losing three of them. Opposing base runners were stealing on him like mad, further getting in his head.

He didn't allow a single home run at AT&T Park in 2009. He would allow eight of them in 2010, and 18 overall.

"We're talking about a couple starts here," said Bochy in May, trying to downplay a meeting with Lincecum in his office that lasted over an hour. "I mean, c'mon.... Let's give this kid a break here. He's pitched outstanding this year."

But for the first time, Lincecum fretted about whether he'd figure a way out.

"It's completely frustrating," he said, after the loss to Washington. "You can see it in my face. It's something I really don't want to show. You start thinking too much and get away from who you are or what you were before."

His start against the Rockies was marginally better. But Ubaldo Jimenez pitched a six-hit shutout. Lincecum used to match up well against opposing aces. Now he was no match for them.

"There's too much negative going on right now," he said, after that loss.

Bochy didn't panic, saying Lincecum was close to finding a solution. And his ace did, bringing down his fastball and getting enough swings off his still-lethal change-up to make the NL All-Star team as one of the players' selections. He was the first Giants pitcher to be selected to three consecutive NL squads since Marichal in the 1960s.

Lincecum was candid when asked for a reaction to the All-Star nod.

"When you don't think you deserve something, and I'm not saying I don't deserve this, I guess it's not as gratifying," Lincecum said. "I don't know. It feels weird. This has been kind of a humbling year for me. I won't say I was full of myself, but it puts things in perspective."

Then came August. The most humbling month of all.

Until then, Lincecum had not lost three consecutive starts in his 74 career decisions. According to the Elias Sports Bureau, only Sal "the Barber" Maglie had a longer streak to begin his career. Maglie didn't lose three consecutive until his 76th decision in 1952.

August provided a rare instance for Lincecum and "the Barber" to appear in the same sentence. Lincecum lost all five of his starts and had a 7.82 ERA during the month, and every well-meaning piece of advice only keyed him up, reminding him that something was very wrong. He started searching for problems that weren't there, even making a significant change to his delivery that involved raising his hands over his head for the first time. He scrapped it after two starts.

His crisis of confidence started to resemble some of the lower points in Zito's tenure as a Giant, when his $126 million contract became an albatross and he pitched not to fail. After the Padres harassed Lincecum into throwing 93 pitches while he recorded just 11 outs in an August 15 loss, his frustration hit an all-time high.

"I've become a big thinker. That's just the way I am," said Lincecum, who had fallen to 7–7 with a 4.28 ERA since May 1. "Your brain never stops working. You start focusing on the wrong things or the negatives, and they start to manifest and build up on each other.

"I can't keep searching. I've just gotta go out and pitch."

This time, he had to find himself without guidance from Molina, his catcher from the day he entered the big leagues. The night Molina was traded, Lincecum went to his batterymate's hotel room to say good-bye.

They ended up talking for a long time.

"We had our heart-to-heart," Lincecum said. "I've seen a lot of changes in four years. You understand that's part of the game, but it doesn't make it easier. It's obviously tough to see a guy like that go, who's been such a big influence on myself and our pitching staff. I was glad I had the opportunity to work with him at the start of my career."

Molina knew Posey would work well with Lincecum in time, but for now, the pitcher would have to take the reins.

"I had to get used to it, too," Molina said. "Timmy will have to be the driver. He'll have to show Buster what he can and cannot do, and by the third or fourth outing, he'll have a better idea of how he pitches."

Lincecum liked Posey and had confidence in the rookie, but he privately worried about the adjustment.

"This game makes you adapt," he said to himself. "Just know that whoever is behind the dish on a given day is there for a reason."

It wasn't just Lincecum who struggled to post quality starts in August. The entire rotation—the base of the Giants' pyramid—was crumbling all at the same time. Amazingly, the team went 14 games without a victory from a starting pitcher, a streak that Jonathan Sanchez finally broke with a near-complete game at Philadelphia on August 19.

Even as far back as the All-Star break, Sabean was concerned with the rotation. He didn't like what he was seeing from his starting pitchers. They led the league in walks and weren't pitching efficiently. It led to long innings and tired legs on the infield and outfield.

"I don't think our pitching has been as advertised," Sabean said. "It hasn't been close. We've got to throw more strikes. We've got to pitch more to contact.... When you're going through a spot when you aren't swinging the bat, you've got to have some people putting up zeroes or have one- or two-run games, and we haven't had that. It's been disappointing."

Sabean had been unpopular with much of the fan base for the better part of three years because he had failed to trade for a big-time hitter. Now the fans chafed at hearing him criticize his own pitchers for not doing more to help their low-scoring team. But the GM had a point: if this team was built around pitching, those arms couldn't be merely okay. If they only received one run or two on a given night, they'd have to make it hold up.

And what about the adjustment to a rookie catcher? Could that be part of the problem?

"You know the answer to that?" Sabean said. "The pitching staff needs to take it upon itself. They've been around the block. They're the ones throwing the baseball. They're the ones that can shake a pitch or throw what they want. They know the advance reports. And we've failed in that area to some extent.

"Maybe that's because Bengie was so good and they trusted him so much and they didn't take it upon themselves. Now they are more and more responsible and they should be."

The Giants still believed they could catch the Padres and win the NL West, but with Lincecum and the rotation in a slump, they weren't matching up well against other playoff-quality teams. They lost two of three in consecutive series in August to the Cardinals, Phillies, and, yes, the Padres. They simply weren't pitching well enough.

Righetti was one of the best in the business precisely because he didn't put pressure on guys when they struggled. He allowed them to find their own way. He and Bochy subtly suggested that Lincecum do a little more work between starts, build up his legs, put in more time in the gym.

But Lincecum had become harder to reach. Everyone knew he didn't believe in icing after starts like everyone else. He didn't have a normal throwing program. He was the kid who could blow off a class, cram the night before the final, and score an A. The advice that applied to everyone else didn't really apply to him. Why should he take it to heart?

But it was time for a rotation intervention.

Zito got blasted by Arizona on August 28, allowing six runs in the first inning. The game before that, Lincecum took his fifth consecutive defeat, essentially losing in the first inning when Arizona's Adam LaRoche splashed his three-run homer into McCovey Cove.

The Giants were six games out of first place, 1½ games out in the wild-card standings, and their starting pitchers had allowed 13 first-inning runs over their last three games—all losses.

Sabean, who normally stayed out of the clubhouse, marched four-fifths of the rotation into Bochy's office. Only Cain, who was starting the next day, was exempt. And Sabean laid into them.

"It was just telling us to wake up," Lincecum said. "We know what we can do and it's not about stats anymore. It's not about individuals. It's just pick up the f—ing guy behind you. Pick up the team. Do it for the team.

"We know what we can do. Just realize it."

The meeting made an impact with everyone in the room. And afterward, Lincecum privately approached Bochy.

He always assumed he had done his part. He was the defending two-time Cy Young winner, after all. But right then, he understood something for the first time: he hadn't accomplished anything important yet.

"I get it now," Lincecum told his manager. "It's about more than just me."

Chapter 6

A Delicate Matter

Aubrey Huff needed some inspiration.

He was playing in a pennant race for the first time after spending a decade on the wrong side of the tracks in the AL East. Now he was where he always hoped to be. But his body ached all over. He kept fouling balls off his shin. His legs and his lungs burned. He had spent the last several years getting soft as a designated hitter. An off-season workout regimen helped him shed a few pounds, and he entered 2010 in the best shape since he first broke into the league. But it had been a while since he subjected his body to five months of pounding as an everyday player. And as August came to an end, the dog days were barking at him.

Huff was the most consistent bat in the Giants lineup all season, getting nearly as hot as Posey in July and providing punch wherever he played on the field or in the lineup. Now he was entering the first real pennant race of his life, and he was in a 2-for-17 slump.

He needed inspiration, and he found it—in his underwear drawer.

"Here it is, boys," said Huff, holding aloft what would become the most sacred skivvies in franchise history.

It was a piece of skimpy men's thong underwear, bright red with a black waistband, with rhinestone-like studs that spelled out "PAPI" across the front. It fit tight. It looked a fright.

It was the Rally Thong.

"Guys, we've got 30 games left," he announced. "Here's 20 wins right here."

Huff was adamant: this was no personal slumpbuster.

"It's the Rally Thong," he said, four days after slapping it on for the first time. "It's not a slump thong. If I was wearing it to break a slump, I would've burned it a long time ago."

The Giants needed some kind of intervention when they awoke on August 31. They had just lost for the fourth time in five games, and the last defeat was a heartbreaker; Wilson suffered a rare blown save on a broken-bat triple by Colorado's Carlos Gonzalez. Right fielder Cody Ross, who had been acquired on a waiver claim a week earlier from the Florida Marlins, got fooled by the sound of Gonzalez's cracking bat and charged in when he should've sprinted back. It was one of those freaky plays that could happen to anyone, but Ross was disconsolate about letting down his new teammates.

It was the latest in a series of letdowns for the Giants. Their rotation was coming off a terrible month in which their starters had just three victories over a 25-game stretch. Their lineup had cooled down, and Posey, for all his brilliance, had heavy legs, a strained forearm, a chronically sore wrist, and he'd taken his share of foul tips, too. Not surprisingly, he started to swing like he was underwater.

A week earlier the Giants had been shut down at St. Louis by rookie Jamie Garcia, who needed just 89 pitches to fire a three-hitter for his first career complete game. The Giants simply weren't measuring up to quality opponents during the month. They were 4–9 in August against the teams that owned four of the five best records in the NL. Among those losses was an August 25 dogfight against the Cincinnati Reds in which the Giants erased a 10-run deficit—the largest comeback in the franchise's 53-year history in San Francisco—and took an 11–10 lead

Aubrey Huff proudly displays the Rally Thong to the masses during the World Series victory parade on November 3, 2010.

on Huff's sacrifice fly in the eighth inning—after Pablo Sandoval's throwing mistake tied the game in the ninth.

It was the kind of devastating loss that might happen to a franchise once in a decade. But the Giants already had that 15-inning disembowelment at Coors Field on July 4. They'd find a way to rebound from this one, too, and Huff turned the other cheek as soon as the game ended.

"You can't be down," he said. "That game was lost. There shouldn't be one person in here hanging their head."

A few days later, Huff let it all hang out.

He came into possession of the thong as a gag, really, when his wife, Baubi, spotted it during a shopping excursion together. She begged him to buy it. Huff wasn't sure why, exactly. He lives in Florida in the off-season, but he's not a "fake bake" kind of guy. Nobody wanted to see his pale white butt cheeks.

But, whatever. Modesty hadn't been a problem for Huff in a good long while.

From the day he reported to spring training with the Giants, Huff made it known that none of his teammates would be spared from his special brand of harassment. He flexed his muscles as he sauntered out to batting practice, yelling to nobody in particular, "Time for the laser show, boys!" When he gave his first interview as a Giant, he wasn't wearing a shirt, and a reporter commented that he looked trimmer.

"Is that the rumor? That I was a fat ass or something?" he said, smiling broadly.

Huff couldn't take his eyes off teammate Nate Schierholtz's washboard abs. One day early in the spring Huff used his cell phone to snap a picture of Schierholtz's six-pack from close range, then sent it to his wife with the message, "Look honey, I've been working out!"

"I didn't want to put myself out there right away, going to a new team," said Huff a week into spring training. "But it's easy here. Usually every team has one or two guys who are, just...eh, you know. But there isn't one guy like that here."

Huff was a certified expert in keeping a clubhouse loose and having fun. It was the only way to stay sane, really, since his previous teams never had any fun between the lines.

He had spent nearly his entire career with the Tampa Bay Devil Rays and the Baltimore Orioles. In nine years, those teams never finished better than fourth place in the AL East. The Yankees and Red Sox might as well have been playing in another solar system.

"Here's the thing," he said. "When you're playing for a losing team, this is your day: hang out and rag on each other and play for yourself. It's sad to say, but in that situation, that's what you do. If the organization didn't spend the money, if they didn't get players, you have to play for yourself. Otherwise, you won't do anything.

"Nobody will remember you. Nobody will want to sign you."

Huff's humor could disarm reporters who took him—or themselves—too seriously. He once caused a minor uproar among Orioles fans and ownership when he appeared on *Bubba the Love Sponge*, a raunchy talk radio show. The folks in Baltimore didn't seem to have a problem with his graphic comments about his personal sex habits or that he appeared in the same studio with a naked porn star covered in body paint. Their issue was when he called Baltimore "a horseshit town."

Huff was making a joke about the city's lack of nightlife, the same lighthearted way he'd rip on a teammate's travel clothes. He couldn't believe it when people got upset over it.

Not everybody would get Huff's sense of humor. He ripped on people. That was his way. One of his favorite clubhouse pastimes was to sneak up on unsuspecting reporters, knock their notebook out of their hands, point at the tangled pages laying on the ground, and yell, "Yard sale! What a jackass! HA HA HA!"

It was totally juvenile behavior. But somehow, he got away with it. His hazing had an endearing quality. It wasn't malicious, nor was it intended to put people down or make them feel worthless. It came across more like a form of acceptance or inclusion.

He was the charming rogue, not unlike the Sawyer character from *Lost*. Sometimes you wondered why you liked the guy, but you did.

Every once in a while Huff would show his tender side, too. All through his first season as a Giant, he quietly wore an orange bracelet on his wrist that was stamped with "Going To Bat 4 Joe." It was a show of support for Joe Turner, a seven-year-old boy from Texas who had been diagnosed with Wilms' tumor, a rare form of kidney cancer. Huff, who grew up in a trailer park on the outskirts of Fort Worth, learned of the boy's fight through mutual friends and sent him a bat and autographed ball, along with a handwritten letter.

"Keep battling, little man!" Huff wrote. "Never give up, and remember, you're in our prayers here in San Francisco!"

When Huff arrived at his locker in spring training, he entered a Giants clubhouse that was friendly and professional enough. But it lacked an edge.

For years Barry Bonds provided that edge, but it came at the expense of team unity. You had Barry, and you had everyone else, and the reminders were everywhere.

Even after the steroids scandal blew up and personal trainers were barred from the clubhouse, the Giants agreed to hire two members of Bonds' entourage under the guise that they'd assist the entire team: Harvey Shields and Greg "Sweets" Oliver. Essentially, they were Bonds' personal sycophants—on the payroll to be his friends.

One day in spring training, late in Bonds' career, Shields sat at a card table in the clubhouse with a reporter and bemoaned the way the media had portrayed him.

"I was assistant to an adjutant general in Korea with thousands of troops under his command, and I had to train all of them," Shields said. "I have certification. I've taken courses in exercise physiology. I..."

Bonds' voice interrupted, echoing from the shower room.

"Haaar-VEEEE!" he yelled out. "Where's that new lotion at?"

Shields sprang up from his chair.

"Be right there, boss!" he shouted.

Other Giants veterans during those years mostly tolerated Bonds, although there was the occasional scuffle. Left-hander Jason Christiansen once objected to Shields' presence and ended up trying—and failing—to put Bonds in a headlock.

It was a rare breach of an unspoken club policy: stay out of Barry's way. It didn't matter if his reality-series cameramen bothered you, if he refused to be available to pinch hit, or if he decided to change out of his uniform before the game ended. He had his side of the street, and you had yours.

There were attempts to build team unity, though, including a memorable karaoke-style singing competition called "Giants Idol" that pinch-hitter Mark Sweeney dreamed up in the spring of 2007. Lincecum, a rookie in camp that year, put on a zoot suit and fedora and sang Sinatra atop the dugout roof at Scottsdale Stadium. Bonds came out in a wig and falsies, dressed up as judge Paula Abdul, and everyone doubled over with laughter.

But the good vibes didn't last. The whole thing felt contrived. Chemistry didn't come that easily for any team, whether Bonds was on it or not.

Even after Bonds left the scene, the Giants remained a difficult place for young position players to establish themselves. Kevin Frandsen, an eager infielder who was San Jose State's all-time hits leader, grew up idolizing the Giants. He didn't hide his excitement at wearing the uniform and being part of the team. Every day was like a fantasy camp for Frandsen, who had pretended to be all of the Giants' greats when he played Wiffle ball under the Santa Cruz boardwalk with his brother, D.J. The Frandsen family was close with Righetti, who lived down the street from them, and "Rags" was D.J.'s favorite player.

Righetti wore No. 19. D.J. was 19 years old when he lost a lifelong battle with cancer. It was Wilms' tumor.

Shortly after Kevin Frandsen became a Giant, Righetti quietly asked clubhouse manager Mike Murphy to give the kid his No. 19. It was a heartwarming story, and everyone rooted for the scrappy player who seemed to be living out the dream of every Giants fan. But Frandsen never seemed to find an ally in Sabean, who preferred his players on the laconic side.

Frandsen found himself going up and down between the majors and Triple A Fresno, then his career really hit a bump when he missed nearly all of 2008 with a ruptured Achilles tendon. He worked his ass off to make it back for one symbolically important at-bat in the season's final game.

A couple of veteran players on the roster had a different interpretation of Frandsen's charge-through-walls attitude. They thought he acted with a sense of entitlement, talked too much, and wasn't minding his place. Never in Frandsen's wildest dreams did he think a day would come when he wasn't having fun as a professional baseball player, especially in a Giants uniform. But he could read the writing on the wall, and when he reported to spring training in 2010, he didn't have any minor league options remaining.

He wasn't going to make the team. So a few weeks before the opener, the Giants traded him to the Boston Red Sox for cash considerations. Sabean called the move "academic," saying the space on the 40-man roster was worth more than the player who occupied it.

Huff was one of the first players to approach Frandsen, who sat in a chair with his ankles still taped.

"You're going to love it there," said Huff. "If you play well for those people, you're a god."

Frandsen appreciated Huff. He was a veteran who reined in young players, but not in a judgmental way. As Frandsen prepared to catch a red-eye to Florida, he took one more look around the room.

"These guys will go places," he said. "I'm telling you right now, this is a special team. And they'll do something incredible because of that guy right there."

Frandsen pointed to Huff's locker.

It was pure happenstance that Huff became a Giant in the first place.

Although he won the Silver Slugger Award as the AL's top DH in 2008 with the Orioles, hitting .304 with 32 home runs and 108 RBIs, he couldn't get his bat going the following year and flopped after the Detroit Tigers picked him up as a platoon player for the stretch run.

He was a free agent, and Christmas had come and gone. Nobody bothered to call.

"Will I ever be an everyday player again?" he wondered.

But the Giants needed a first baseman, and their initial target, Sacramento native Nick Johnson, spurned them to sign with the Yankees for less money. The Giants had made a two-year, $17 million offer to Adam LaRoche, who turned it down. With that deal off the table, LaRoche ended up signing a one-year, $6 million contract with Arizona, where he could put up numbers in a better hitter's park.

So the Giants turned to Huff, offering him one year at $3 million. Maybe it was a panic signing. Maybe it wasn't. But he clearly wasn't their first or second choice.

Huff couldn't sign fast enough.

"Well, I'll never hit 30 [home runs] again in that park," Huff thought. "I guess I'll try to do the little things."

In his first spring training game as a Giant, on the first swing he took, Huff crushed a home run. Then he grabbed his first baseman's mitt— and dropped the first ball thrown to him. He kept telling reporters that he was a decent defensive player, and that he'd prove everybody wrong. But, after a while, the questions became an annoyance.

"When you're a DH, you get labeled by people who've never played the game," he said. "It's hard to shake. People believe what they read, unfortunately, but I'll play every day and prove that I'm not bad over there."

Huff worried about AT&T Park, though. Its 25-foot wall in right field was death to left-handed power hitters. Its right-field alley stretched 421 feet from home plate at its furthest point. The night games weren't as freezing or windy as at old Candlestick Park, but the ball didn't travel in the cold, damp air. And there was a breezeway through the arches below the right-field arcade—an invisible force that held up well-struck drives.

"You've got to take what the park gives you," Huff said in the spring. Including doubles?

"Including triples," he said with a laugh. "I'm 215 pounds now. I should be flying out there."

The baseball gods must've heard Huff and snickered to themselves. Wouldn't you know it? His first home run as a Giant was an inside-the-park mad dash around the bases.

It happened on April 14 against the Pirates. Huff's deep drive hit off the archway in right-center field and took an extreme sideways bounce away from outfielder Garrett Jones. By the time Huff reached third base, the Pirates were still chasing the ball. He kept running, his stride looking like a wounded herd animal, and he raised a fist as he slid across the plate.

"I didn't need that," he said, in mock agony. "I didn't even know where I was at that point.… I blacked out."

Huff hit two more drives to the warning track in the game. In his mind, it was the first three-homer game of his career.

Eventually, Huff was able to conquer the wall and hit a few conventional homers, too. In fact, each of his first six home runs would come at home. Later on, he would become just the 12th left-handed hitter to achieve a two-homer game at AT&T Park. It had been done 25 times in all; Bonds had done it 13 of those times.

Huff remained productive all season. He was a smart hitter, and he certainly wasn't intimidated to stand in the box against an ace after spending so many years facing Andy Pettitte, Roger Clemens, Pedro Martinez, Curt Schilling, and Roy Halladay in the AL East. It was his dumb luck, he joked, that Halladay had been traded to the Phillies that winter, following him to the National League.

In a late July game at Arizona, Huff hit a home run and heard a few "MVP" chants from a vocal section of Giants fans at Chase Field. Huff was stunned. He had never heard that before in his life from home fans in Tampa or Baltimore. Now he was hearing it as a Giant on the road?

The home fans showed their appreciation, too. In a July 30 home victory over the Dodgers, Huff hit a home run and a two-run double that put the team ahead. He also recorded an assist in right field and made a running catch on the warning track after moving to left.

"That was the biggest atmosphere I've played in," he said. "It was a blast. That was the kind of atmosphere I was waiting my whole life for. I've never been on a team playing for something this late in the year."

Reminded that Huff rose to meet that environment, the longtime Oriole and Devil Ray responded without hesitation:

"If I don't go out there and perform," he said, "those nine years of losing mean absolutely nothing."

Huff made no fuss about moving from position to position to allow the Giants to tweak their lineup and introduce players like Posey and Burrell. And his spring training pledge was dead on the money. He proved all those skeptics flat wrong. The broken-down DH that nobody wanted had turned out to be one of the league's most valuable hitters, and a perfectly capable defensive player at three positions.

In an early June game at Pittsburgh, when Posey made an error at first base that led to four unearned runs, Huff was the first player to give the rookie a supportive swat on the behind. Then Huff hit a tiebreaking, two-run home run in the sixth inning as the Giants came back from four runs down to make a winner of Jonathan Sanchez.

Huff called reporters to his locker, but not to gloat about his big hit.

"Get the young guy off the hook," he said. "That's good for Posey, and it's a little payback for Sanchy losing that one-hitter in San Diego [in April]. He deserved that."

Huff loved to rag on Posey, who just seemed too perfect to be true. On his way to the shower, Huff would shout out "Hay-ZOOS!" whenever reporters converged on Posey's locker following another of the kid's four-hit games. Posey would just shake his head and take it.

But more than anyone, Huff reveled in being reunited with Burrell, his former teammate at the University of Miami. All these years, they dreamed of a day when they might play together again in the big leagues. They knew it was folly. After all, the game is a business, and no player, not even the most attractive free agent, has total control over which uniform he wears. It was even more outlandish to dream that they'd be in a pennant race together, making a drive to the World Series.

Now here they were, taking batting practice in the same group every day, playing cards, and ripping on each other. They were so eager to get their day started, they often arrived at the ballpark at 1:00 PM. for night games. They wore matching, custom-made, mustard-yellow blazers on team flights with the University of Miami logo on the front pocket, looking like a couple of bowl representatives.

When Burrell hit a home run late in the year to beat the Dodgers, the camera panned to the jubilant dugout. Huff looked out of place with an irrepressible scowl. You didn't need to be a master lip reader to know he was saying, "Oh man, I'm going to f— him up!"

The Oakland A's had their Bash Brothers. Huff and Burrell became the punch brothers. The way they saw it, no good deed would go unpunished.

"Hit a home run, punch a teammate in the chest," Huff said. "That's a great time right there."

One time Huff happened to be standing next to Mark DeRosa when Burrell went deep. DeRosa was on the 60-day disabled list after undergoing wrist surgery.

"Oh man," Huff thought. "I can't punch a hurt guy."

Huff would put a little extra behind his punches when Burrell was the recipient. The way Huff figured it, he still owed Burrell a thousand bruises.

Impossible though it might seem, Huff was painfully shy as a boy. Tragically, he was just six years old when his father was shot and killed. Aubrey Huff Jr. was working as an electrician and was on call at an apartment complex in Abilene when he walked into the middle of a domestic disturbance between a man and woman he didn't know. The man shot Huff's father, who was trying to make peace.

Huff's mother, Fonda, was determined that her young son and daughter would have every chance to succeed in life. She worked long hours in the Winn-Dixie deli department while taking night classes to earn her teaching certification. Aubrey would come straight home after school to immerse himself in his Nintendo games or cartoon shows. *The Transformers* remained his favorite.

Baseball was his obsession, though, and his mother saved up enough money to build a batting cage in their yard. Aubrey was awkward in high school—tall, gangly, with acne—and wasn't popular with girls. Other kids would tease him because all he wanted to do was go hit in his cage. They told him he was wasting his time, and it was true, he hit just one home run in his junior and senior years combined—even though the wall was just 350 feet to center field.

"I was a 6'4", 180-pound weakling," Huff said. "I had a nice swing, but I couldn't get the ball out."

Huff began weight training in junior college, and the ball began to jump off his bat. He began to fill out and his skin cleared up. He almost couldn't believe when Miami, a powerhouse program, called with a scholarship offer. He arrived on campus full of nervous anticipation and eager to be accepted.

The first person he met was none other than Burrell—the big man on campus.

"That son of a bitch," Huff said. "I hadn't met such an arrogant prick in my life."

Burrell saw an easy mark. He ragged Huff mercilessly, knowing he'd get only feeble protestations, if any reply at all. Huff lived with a few other players in an off-campus apartment, and it was open season on him. He couldn't stand it. Like a lonely kid at summer camp, he called his mom and said he was coming home.

Fonda dropped everything and traveled to Miami. Sitting in Aubrey's room, she encouraged him to give it a few more weeks. Just stick it out. See if things change.

Just then came a knock at the door, and Burrell barged in, stark naked, dripping wet, with a six-pack of beer in his hand.

Huff jumped up, shut the door, and turned to his mother.

"See what I'm dealing with here, Mom?" he said.

Fonda just started laughing. "Actually, Aubrey," she said, "that's pretty darn funny."

And it struck him: "My God, if my mom can laugh at this, why can't I?"

Huff decided to stay at Miami. And he decided the next time Burrell got on his ass, he'd give it right back. It became a skill he learned to master—almost as important as hitting a curveball.

Later on, Huff came to understand why Burrell was so hard on him. He was feeling him out. He wanted to know where everyone stood. He wanted to weed out the weak ones.

"I really believe that's when I learned to be a ballplayer, man," Huff said. "If I didn't go to Miami, if Pat didn't wear me out, I wouldn't have made it to the big leagues. This is a humbling, challenging game. You have to be mentally tough."

Now teammates in the big leagues, Burrell was teaching Huff new lessons. Although they both had nearly a decade of experience in the majors, Huff hadn't played in the caldron of a pennant stretch. Burrell had been to a World Series. He let the boos in Philly roll down his back for years. His eyes teared up when he went back to receive his ring and those same fans gave him a standing ovation. He knew the crowds sounded different in the stretch drive. Every perception would be heightened and every fear-of-failure impulse would be magnified by a factor of 1,000.

After a late-July game at Dodger Stadium, the two former Hurricanes stayed in the players' lounge for more than two hours, and Burrell told Huff what would await them in September and beyond.

"There's nothing you can do about the anxiety level," Burrell told him. "You'll be nervous and anxious. Trust me, it's a whole different deal. But if you play enough close games, you get used to that."

By the end of August, the Giants and their fans had experienced all the late-inning torture they could handle. But for these final 30 games, the players would have to wince at a new sight every day—Huff parading through the clubhouse, wearing nothing but flip-flops and the Rally Thong.

Chapter 7

Forever Yungo

You couldn't blame Andres Torres for daring to dream that the 2010 Giants might be one of those improbable stories, a little team that could, destined for a glory that almost nobody could have predicted.

Why not? Torres, standing 5′8″ in his bare feet, was having one tall tale of a season in his own right.

He was a 32-year-old minor league journeyman. He'd already burned up his supposed prime years bouncing through the farm systems of three organizations. From June of 2005 to April of '09, he didn't receive a single big league at-bat.

Yet here he was, an everyday player in the majors for the first time. And he was a revelation.

The switch-hitting center fielder from Puerto Rico was making an impact for the Giants almost every night with his magnificent defensive skills, explosive base running, and surprising power.

It had become obvious by mid-May that he was a superior option to Aaron Rowand, who had remained in the lineup despite horrific second-half slumps in each of his two previous seasons. Even as the boos grew louder, it was hard for Bochy to yank a true professional like Rowand, a guy with a good track record who tried as hard as he could and cared as much as anyone. Rowand was in just the third season of a highly criticized five-year, $60 million contract, too. That was no small consideration. Bochy would have to deal with this guy for more than just the summer.

But Bochy couldn't ignore what Torres kept bringing to the field. And it wasn't just the extra-base hits and extra-long pursuits of fly balls in the gap that made the manager sit up and take notice.

Torres' feats were so impressive that they seemed to be unreal exaggerations. He swung a Bunyanesque, 35-ounce war club that looked more like a telephone pole than a baseball bat. Only two or three other hitters in the majors swung a bat so heavy. The little guy generated remarkable bat speed with it, too. When the Giants traveled to Washington and faced Stephen Strasburg, the most hyped rookie pitcher in a generation, Torres hit a home run off him.

It was a 99 mph fastball. And Torres pulled it down the line.

"Dynamite comes in small packages, as they say," Bochy said.

Sure, the Giants might have lucked out by finding Huff in the free-agent irregular bin. They caught lightning in a bottle with Burrell. A year earlier they hit paydirt when they signed Uribe to a minor league contract.

But Torres wasn't someone they found on a bare store shelf. He was still back in the stockroom.

Now he was having a season for the ages, and so many of the Giants' tight victories had his markings on them.

When the Giants finally beat the Padres on May 18 at San Diego, avoiding an 0–8 start against them, it was Torres who cranked the tying, two-run home run in the eighth inning off tough setup man Mike Adams.

When they frolicked on the field after rallying for a 6–5 victory over Arizona on May 30, it was Torres who scored the equalizer in the ninth and connected for the winning single in the 10th.

"They punched me. They hit me. I was trying to cover up," Torres said. "It was a lot of fun."

When they allowed a sewn-up victory to unravel June 6 in Pittsburgh, Torres came to the rescue. The Pirates had two outs and the bases empty when Wilson allowed a two-out single to Ronny Cedeno, who was in an 0-for-20 slump, and a tying, two-run home run to light-hitting Delwyn Young. It had to be the most sudden, most unexpected blown save of Wilson's career.

But Torres refused to let it deflate the club. He lined a double in the 10th, advanced on a wild pitch, and scored on Freddy Sanchez's sacrifice fly.

"Wow. I can't tell you enough about Torres," Sanchez gushed after the 6–5 victory. "He's fast, he gets on base, he plays the game right. He does everything."

The very next day in Cincinnati Torres made a leaping catch at the wall of Ramon Hernandez's deep drive to spare Wilson from consecutive blown saves. And the day after that, Torres robbed Hernandez again, diving to catch a sinking line drive to end the seventh inning and help Cain toss his 11th career complete game.

"Ball right at him, that's not an easy play," Bochy said. "He's so quick and so sure-handed out there. I'd put him up there among the best out-fielders in the game. That's how good I think he is."

Wilson, never at a loss for words, had trouble finding adequate ones to describe Torres.

"I can't explain enough how much of an asset this guy is," the closer said.

How many players could turn a ground ball inside the first-base bag into an inside-the-park home run? That's what happened during the Giants' July 4 loss at Coors Field. Torres hit a smash that never got more than 10 feet off the ground, but it skipped over right fielder Ryan Spilborghs, who had tried to make a sliding stop. Third-base coach Tim

Flannery pumped his arm like a windmill in a hurricane. The Giants were down two runs in the late innings, so Flannery had to be absolutely sure Torres would score. He was.

"Well, I was 99.89 percent sure," Flannery said. "The key was that he never stopped running. That's how you give yourself a chance."

It's hard to throw out a runner when his feet aren't touching the ground. Torres wasn't playing baseball so much as floating. Consider this nine-game stretch:

July 20 at Dodger Stadium: Bases-loaded double in the ninth inning turns a one-run deficit into a one-run lead.

July 22 at Chase Field: Jaw-dropping home run carries over the batter's eye in center field, 414 feet away.

July 23 at Chase Field: Tiebreaking, two-run triple in the seventh inning leads to a victory.

July 27 vs. the Florida Marlins: Faces Josh Johnson, the NL's ERA leader. Reaches base four times.

July 28 vs. Florida: Four more hits, including a home run that splashes into McCovey Cove, to help Giants build a 9–2 lead—and when the Giants pitchers gave that lead back, Torres calmly strode to the plate in the 10th inning and hit the bases-loaded single to win it.

By this time, Torres had been slapped on the helmet so viciously and in so many victory celebrations, it was a miracle he wasn't on the disabled list with a neck injury.

Baseball history is filled with against-the-odds stories and late bloomers, but most are pitchers who overcame arm injuries. A few years ago, when Jim Morris went from high school science teacher to 35-year-old rookie pitcher in Tampa Bay, it didn't take Disney long to crank out a heartwarming feature film.

There simply wasn't much precedent for what Torres was doing, however. Maury Wills didn't establish himself until he was 27. Dave Roberts was another speed guy who waited for his chance.

But Torres wasn't some pitcher filling out the bullpen of a losing team. He wasn't a slap-and-dash hitter, either.

In fact, that style of hitting is precisely what held Torres back all those years in the minors with the Tigers, Rangers, White Sox, Twins, Tigers again, and Cubs. He tried to hit like Ichiro Suzuki, already pivoting his hips toward first base as he swung the bat.

Coaches wanted to utilize his best tool—put the ball on the ground and fly to first base. And Torres didn't know enough about hitting to argue.

He was a former track star who came late to baseball. He ran the 100, 200, and 4x100-meter relay in high school, and didn't play much baseball before a scout handed him his business card one day. Torres ended up at Miami-Dade Community College, where he played baseball and ran track, and he qualified for the national junior college championships after running the 100 meters in 10.37 seconds. But when the Tigers drafted him in the fourth round, he skipped the meet. If someone wanted to pay him to play baseball, hey, that sounded good to him. Based on his speed and fly-catching skills, he would reach the majors in 2002.

One hangup: he still didn't know how to hit.

Torres recalled a day in Kansas City when he was taking batting practice and he heard two fellow Puerto Ricans, Carlos Beltran and Luis Alicea, snickering behind the cage. They pulled him aside. Hadn't anybody taught him to load his hands? Did he know any fundamental principles of hitting?

It wasn't long before the Tigers returned Torres to the minor leagues. He hadn't forgotten what Beltran and Alicea told him, but he was afraid to make radical changes at the plate. Scouts liked his speed, and coaches didn't want to see him strike out or pop up. Torres did as he was told. He was a people pleaser, and besides, he was getting too old to be a prospect. If he struck out 200 times while trying to hit a completely different way, he'd be on a direct path to the independent leagues.

But after the 2007 season, Torres remained stuck in Triple A, and he knew something had to change. With the help of Chris O'Leary, a private hitting coach, he began looking at all the video he could find on hitters he admired, beginning with Albert Pujols. He saw the way they generated power by rotating through the pitch. He began to focus better, too, after he was diagnosed with attention deficit hyperactivity disorder (ADHD) and was prescribed medication. During winter ball in Puerto Rico, he started forming the basis of a swing that wasn't designed just to put the ball in play, but to barrel it up.

The Giants had a decent scouting report on him, and they were light on center fielders for their Triple A roster. So they offered him a minor league contract. They couldn't have imagined that two years later, he'd not only roam center field every day in the big leagues, but rank among the NL leaders in extra-base hits.

Advanced metrics graded Torres' 2010 season even higher than the traditional counting stats did. One of these newer stats, called WAR, or wins above replacement, sought to measure a player's overall offensive and defensive value. Torres finished 2010 tied for fifth among all players in the NL in defensive value. According to WAR, he was the second-most valuable center fielder in the majors, behind Texas' Josh Hamilton.

Torres finished the year with 16 home runs and 43 doubles. His career totals entering the year, over scraps of five seasons? Seven and 12.

Andres Torres scores the tiebreaking run over the leg of Pittsburgh Pirates catcher Ryan Doumit during the 10th inning of a game in Pittsburgh on June 6, 2010. The Giants won 6–5.

Numbers aside, his teammates loved watching him play. They loved the way he ran the bases with the form of a track athlete, his little arms pumping at the elbows and his open hands karate-chopping the air.

They loved the cleat marks he'd leave on the center-field wall when he'd leap to make a grab. They loved the way he circled around a fly ball like a human lariat, making sure all his momentum would go toward the infield when he caught it—even when a slow runner was on first base.

"Does it every time," Bochy said. "He thinks everyone is tagging up."

And they loved watching a truly great season happen to a truly nice guy. Torres couldn't brush past anyone—teammate, reporter, trainer, clubhouse kid banging dirt out of cleats—without stopping to say hello. When Torres began any interview, he apologized for his English, which was perfectly fine. And when he ended the interview, he *thanked the reporter* for his or her time.

Torres couldn't be slowed down to chat for long, though. He was always on the move, whether it was another round of hitting in the indoor cage or more core strengthening exercises. He hardly had an ounce of fat on his chiseled body, and he watched his diet carefully. The medication helped his attention deficit issues, but it would've taken elephant tranquilizers to treat his hyperactivity.

He even ate sunflower seeds like a manic squirrel after a double espresso, cracking each seed individually with his front teeth, tossing the shell, and eating the kernel. No exaggeration: he'd average one second per seed, two tops.

"Salt," he said, wrinkling his nose as he kept right on cracking. "Bad for you."

While some teammates called Torres their Energizer Bunny, he already had a nickname from his youth. In Aguada, his hometown, everyone knew him as Yungo. The name didn't have an English translation, he explained. Then again, Torres shared a clubhouse with a rookie catcher named Buster, so maybe no translation was necessary.

You didn't need to explain Yungo or Buster. Watching them was enough.

Torres' most euphoric late-inning moment of the regular season actually came in a loss. It was the August 25 game against the Reds, when the Giants launched their incredible, 10-run comeback, and Torres provided the equalizer. His tying, two-run double in the eighth inning rattled in the right-field corner, and thousands of total strangers at AT&T Park embraced each other in mass delirium. The Reds came back to win, but for that instant, the ballpark hadn't rocked with that level of jubilation in years. You'd swear the Giants had walked off with the World Series right then and there.

But the fans would file out of the ballpark in silence that day. And a week later, on August 31, things were sufficiently dire that Huff was wearing red butt floss underneath his uniform for the first time.

The team had lost four of five.

Torres made sure it didn't become five of six. He launched a tiebreaking home run to lead off the eighth inning, Posey added a two-run double, and the Giants took a 5–2 victory over the third-place but still-dangerous Rockies.

After a trying August, the Giants were starting to jell once more. And everyone was contributing. When they beat the Rockies again the following day, the player who scored the winning run wasn't even in the ballpark when the first pitch was thrown.

Speedy outfielder Darren Ford, a call-up from Double A Richmond, had traveled across the country to join the expanded roster and made an immediate impact. He arrived in the second inning, made his major league debut as a pinch runner in the eighth, advanced easily on a sacrifice bunt, sprang to third on a wild pitch that only trickled a few feet from Colorado catcher Miguel Olivo, then sprinted home when Olivo threw the ball into left field. It was an unforgettable debut in a 2–1 victory—as if everyone who wasn't old enough to see Willie Mays could go back in time and experience the Say Hey Kid's explosiveness, if only for a moment.

In the postgame interviews, Ford's story got even better. It wasn't just his big-league debut. The quiet kid from New Jersey admitted it was the first time he'd ever stepped foot in a major league stadium.

Now the Giants had a modest winning streak and momentum. Most brightly, their rotation, after getting lectured by their general manager, was showing signs of a turnaround. Their rookie left-hander, Madison Bumgarner, already had flown past his previous high for innings in a season and had just turned 21 years old on August 1. The bull strong kid from North Carolina seemed to be throwing harder as he went along. And Lincecum, with the help of Ford's mad dash, broke his panic-inducing, five-start winless skid. Lincecum had gone up against Ubaldo Jimenez again, and this time he was equipped to pitch Colorado's ace to a standstill.

Meanwhile, the irrepressible Padres, who had lost three consecutive games just once prior to the All-Star break, were starting to run low on pixie dust. Their surprising starting staff finally had a bad turn through the rotation. The breaks that bounced their way all year started to go against them. On September 1 they lost their seventh in a row.

The Giants were embarking on a crucial, 10-game road trip that could brand them as contenders or pop their tires. The final stop would be Petco Park, for a four-game showdown with the Padres. The Giants merely hoped to be within striking distance by the time they touched down in San Diego.

The trip didn't start off well. The Giants lost the opener at Dodger Stadium behind an erratic Barry Zito, and the next day, they came out flat and trailed 4–0 in the seventh inning. Dodgers left-hander Ted Lilly hadn't allowed a hit since Rowand opened the game with a double. But Posey snapped Lilly's spell with a solo home run in the seventh. Edgar Renteria hit another homer to chase Lilly in the eighth. Burrell followed with a pinch homer off reliever Octavio Dotel. And after Ross beat out an infield single in the ninth, Juan Uribe crushed a two-run shot off country-sized closer Jonathan Broxton to turn a one-run deficit into a one-run lead.

The visiting dugout erupted in a mad celebration. The Giants had 33 comeback victories on the year, and this was the third in which they erased a deficit of at least four runs. But for pure shock value, nothing compared to this.

Four home runs. All in the seventh inning or later.

"It's funny to see guys who've been in this league 10 years, 30 or 35 years old, jumping around like little kids," Posey said.

Uribe was in a 2-for-22 slump before he lifted Broxton's slider over the left-field wall.

"I got chills running around the bases," Ross said. "I couldn't wait for him to get home so I could give him a double high-five."

Huff and Burrell decked each other like Rock'em Sock'em Robots in the dugout. Posey was so excited that he slipped and tumbled down the dugout stairs. Uribe simply strutted to meet his teammates, screaming at the top of his lungs.

Of course, there would be a torturous end. Wilson put runners at the corners with one out, but escaped to record his NL-leading 39th save. Everyone in road grays knew they had just seen something powerful, something special.

"Hopefully we do look back [on this game]," Bochy said.

As stirring as the victory was, the Giants understood that they weren't designed to win with home runs and improbable comebacks. Their blueprint began with their starting pitchers, and with Sabean's lecture ringing in their ears, the Giants' rotation was starting to lock it down again. The day after the home run heroics, Jonathan Sanchez threw first-pitch strikes to 19 of his 26 batters while posting his second consecutive quality start—something he hadn't done since April—and

Uribe went deep again in a 3–0 win. The Giants had captured the series at Dodger Stadium.

That same day the Padres lost their 10th consecutive games. The Giants had made up four games in six days. Now they were just one behind San Diego. And Sanchez's next start would come in the second game of the showdown series at Petco Park.

This time, Sanchez didn't fill up any reporter's notebooks.

"We're going to go there and try to do our business," he said, smiling. "That's all. Everywhere we go, we want to beat everybody."

He paused.

"Is that what you want to hear?" he said.

First, the Giants had to take care of business in Arizona. And they did, winning two of three. The biggest moment in the series came courtesy of Nate Schierholtz, the Giants' presumed starting right fielder when spring training began.

The season didn't go the way the Bay Area product had hoped, especially after the Giants added Ross and Jose Guillen to their stable of outfielders in August. Schierholtz hadn't started a game since July 23, and he made a monumental mistake at Chase Field when he got picked off first base as a pinch runner in the late innings of a scoreless game. But Schierholtz remained in the game, received another opportunity in the 11th inning, and his two-run triple sent the Giants to a 2–0 victory.

The Giants' other win in Arizona was even more spirit boosting. Lincecum not only pitched well but regained his Cy Young dominance, taking a perfect game into the fifth inning and a shutout into the seventh while striking out 11. It was the first time in two months that their ace had won consecutive starts.

The Giants entered Petco Park trailing in the NL West by two games. Sure, they had lost nine of 11 to these pesky Padres. But in their hearts, they believed they were the better team. This was the time to show it.

"We've faced them enough. We know what they've got," Huff said. "There shouldn't be any need to look at video all day. Strap it on, see it, hit it, and take some good, professional quality at-bats."

They took a week's worth of them in the series opener. Huff, Uribe, Posey, and Burrell each hit home runs to back Cain in a 7–3 victory—just the 20th time in Petco Park's seven-year history that a team hit four homers in a game.

They weren't wall scrapers, either. Burrell's shot was a mammoth drive down the left-field line that smacked the bricks on the top floor of the Western Metal Supply Co. building. Posey reached the second deck of the left-field stands. And Uribe's ball cleared the fence in right-center, landing in the sand box—a place right-handed hitters simply did not find, even in batting practice.

Next it was Sanchez's turn, although he wouldn't receive the same support that the Giants gave Cain in the opener. The left-hander pitched with extreme caution, knowing that the game could be lost on one mistake. His wariness was understandable; he had given up one hit and lost in this ballpark five months earlier.

Sanchez didn't have his best stuff but refused to give in. He walked seven batters in five innings but pitched out of trouble to keep the Padres from scoring. Huff helped Sanchez escape the fifth when he snagged Adrian Gonzalez's broken-bat grounder to start a difficult 3-6-3 double play.

The game featured just one run, and Huff willed himself into scoring it.

He yelped in pain after getting hit by a pitch on his elbow in the seventh, but literally ran away from trainers when they tried to examine it. Nothing would make him come out of this game.

When Burrell struck out, Huff gambled and took off with the pitch, stealing second base when he kicked the ball out of David Eckstein's glove. Then Huff took an even bigger gamble, burning every muscle fiber as he slid into third base on Guillen's ground ball to shortstop.

"Stupid decision," Huff said. "Sometimes they work out."

Bochy pinch ran Schierholtz for Guillen, who had been safe on short-stop Miguel Tejada's fielder's choice. It was a small but important move, because Uribe followed with a potential double-play grounder that Schierholtz disrupted with a takeout slide. Eckstein went flying as Huff crossed the plate.

The Giants' improving bullpen threw four scoreless innings, with Wilson getting the final five outs to secure the 1–0 victory. The Giants had scored the only run on a hit batter, a stolen base, a fielder's choice, and a ground out along with a takeout slide. It was the same maddening way the Padres had squeaked across runs against the Giants all season. Now the Giants were returning the favor.

"The Padres were playing flawless baseball against us early on," Wilson said. "Those were the first 11 games. These are the games that count."

For the first time since Sanchez's no-hitter a year earlier, the Giants had won consecutive games against the Padres. And now they stood in a virtual tie atop the NL West.

Technically, the Giants were percentage points behind San Diego, one back in the loss column, but try telling that to anyone in the visiting clubhouse. The Giants hadn't resided in first place since May 6. They hadn't played a postseason game in nearly seven years. First place was first place.

"If you need a breather or a day off, go to bed early," Wilson said. "You'll have to suck it up and play to win from here on out."

It wasn't just the players who were making a statement in San Diego. Thousands of Giants fans traveled south for the series, and at times Petco Park seemed like a road environment for the Padres. There were dozens of empty sections in the upper deck. It was clear that San Diego fans didn't believe in their surprising team, either. And their players noticed.

Closer Heath Bell posted on his Twitter page: "I wanted to know where are the padre fans????????? Not at the park."

The Padres realized they would have to generate their own momentum, and they did while pulling out a victory in the third game of the series. Tim Stauffer, a long reliever who proved successful as a late-season addition to the Padres' rotation, shut down the Giants as the Padres captured their own 1–0 win.

The Giants' coaching staff became furious with longtime umpire Jerry Crawford, who had a wide strike zone and lost his professional cool when players started riding him about it. The Giants also weren't happy with Padres catcher Yorvit Torrealba, a former backup in San Francisco who continued to play with a chip on his shoulder against them. Torrealba jockeyed for calls all game long, and when Posey tried to have a respectful conversation with Crawford between innings, the umpire gave the rookie a rather obvious dressing down. Nobody in the Giants' dugout could believe a 33-year veteran umpire like Crawford could be so unprofessional, especially when dealing with an earnest kid like Posey.

The Giants' loss ended emphatically with a strikeout–double play, as Torrealba gunned out Ford trying to steal second base. Torrealba and Bell rushed each other and bumped bellies, and the Padres stormed onto the field like they'd won the division.

Afterward, several Giants players and coaches smiled with odd satisfaction. They had just lost another 1–0 game to the Padres, but they saw something this time that gave them encouragement. Sure, the Giants had leapt for joy plenty of times after thrilling victories. But there was something over the top about the way the Padres hammed it up after this one. They seemed to be a team on tilt, perhaps too swept up by it all. Or maybe their players figured they'd better celebrate while they had the chance. In any case, the Giants didn't walk out of the ballpark feeling beaten.

With a chance to retake a two-game advantage, the Padres sent Latos to the mound in the series finale. He had been 2–0 with a 0.96 ERA in four starts against the Giants. Not only that, but he entered with an unbelievable streak of 15 consecutive starts allowing two runs or fewer, a major league record.

This time, the Giants felled the oafish right-hander—and Posey cast the first smooth stone. He stunned Latos with a two-run home run in the first inning, and the Giants went on to a 6–1 victory to regain a share of first place. Not only did Lincecum beat another ace, striking out nine in seven innings to win his third consecutive start, but he also slapped a two-run single.

The Giants had completed a highly successful road trip, capturing all three series while winning seven of 10. Yet unlike the Padres, they didn't belly-bump after the final out. They simply went through the handshake line like they were closing a business transaction. Lincecum affixed a dapper bow tie—a relatively new addition to his travel ensemble—and the Giants snapped their briefcases shut and headed home.

"I guess that's the way guys are on this team," Posey said.

The Giants had taken three of four in San Diego, making a statement against the little team that had bossed them all season. But they knew they hadn't achieved anything yet. The Rockies remained a factor, too, ripping off one of their patented September winning streaks to get them within 1½ games of the NL West coleaders. Everyone knew strange things happened when the Rockies started winning in late September.

Besides, the Giants had received crushing news early that Sunday morning in San Diego.

Torres, their inspirational little catalyst, hadn't felt right for more than a week. He woke up with such acute pain in his abdomen that he took himself to a local hospital. A few hours later, he was on the operating table having an appendectomy. The doctors used a minimally invasive laparoscopic procedure through the belly button. But normal recovery time was two weeks, minimum—pretty much the remainder of the regular season.

"It's a shame for that kid," Bochy said. "He's done an unbelievable job for us. I feel awful for him."

Rowand batted leadoff in the series finale at Petco and was 0-for-5. The Giants didn't have another attractive alternative atop the lineup. Torres had slumped in recent weeks, but that didn't make the news any easier to take. The Giants would miss Torres' glove, his legs, his tree-trunk bat, and his energy.

They were going home. Perhaps they'd find some of that energy there.

Chapter 8

Too Much Awesome

It almost seemed to sprout overnight.

Brian Wilson already had a water serpent tattooed on his left arm. He already styled his hair in a Mohawk. He already wore loud travel clothes, including an all-yellow ensemble that made him look like he got lost on his way to a Devo concert.

Now the Giants' eccentric closer was growing a rather bushy beard. And it was suspiciously dark.

Hockey players usually grew beards during a playoff push. Baseball players changed their hirsute habits with their moods, too, unless George Steinbrenner held any sway over them. So when Wilson's perma-stubble grew into something more, it didn't seem like it would become a character-defining trait. But by the middle of September, it was impossible to ignore the thing that had invaded his face. And fans started to wonder…is it a dye job? Is it even real?

Wilson wasn't Santa Claus, and this wasn't *Miracle on 34th Street*. Fans couldn't just tug on his whiskers. Finally asked if he'd combed in any Just For Men to darken his beard, Wilson answered in his own offbeat, roundabout way. "I cannot believe you are asking me that question," he said, full of mock outrage, and walked away.

That was classic Wilson. He could be witty, sarcastic, outlandish, or just odd. But he always delivered his lines with a half-bemused, half-annoyed look on his face. Sometimes it was a battle to maintain the deadpan, but he usually succeeded.

Wilson was in his third season as the Giants' full-time closer, and the fans knew all about his personality quirks. Some players went fishing in the Florida Keys or took the kids to Disneyland in the off-season. Wilson hopped on a flight to Mumbai and taught teenage cricketers how to throw a baseball.

For a time, he had his own reality show on a local cable network—*Life with Brian*. It flopped badly because, well, it was essentially a half-hour of him holding a shaky camcorder as he played Guitar Hero and ordered room service. He was a master of the one-line comeback, but the show didn't provide the interaction needed for his humor to work.

Not everyone understood Wilson's humor, anyway. He once maintained an active Twitter account but shut it down out of frustration when a reporter highlighted one of his late-night dispatches. Wilson had posted a message after 1:00 AM about getting harassed by "overaggressive males," presumably at a bar. The next day against the Arizona Diamondbacks, an afternoon game, he blew a three-run lead.

Suddenly embroiled in a Twittergate, Wilson claimed the whole thing was a joke that everyone took the wrong way. He pointed out that he also posted messages about engaging in hand-to-hand combat with Ninjas.

"Obviously, I'm not doing things like going toe-to-toe with a Ninja," he said. "Find me a Ninja, for one."

Wilson didn't blow many other three-run leads. He was serviceable as the Giants' closer in '08 and '09, recording 41 and 38 saves while converting 86 percent of his opportunities. He seldom made it easy on Bochy and the fans, though, often loading the bases before escaping or allowing a two-run lead to be cut in half. He averaged 1.34 base runners per inning over those two seasons—far higher than the elite closers in the game.

Yet his fellow players saw the save totals and rewarded him for the bottom line, putting him on the NL All-Star team in 2008. His peers selected him again in 2010 after he converted 22 of his first 24 save chances.

Before jumping on a plane to Anaheim, Wilson told reporters that he would be pumped up for any role in the NL bullpen.

"That would be epic if we had home-field advantage in the World Series…as Giants," he said, pausing for a reaction. He didn't get one. At the time, it was just another of Wilson's goofy statements.

But Wilson did help to secure home field for the NL, needing just 10 pitches to retire three hitters in the eighth inning. Dodgers closer Jonathan Broxton protected a 3–1 victory in the ninth—the NL's first win in the Midsummer Classic in 14 years. For the first time since the All-Star Game determined home-field advantage in the World Series, the NL pennant winner—whoever that ended up being—would receive it. The NL All-Star staff was so talented that Lincecum watched the entire game from the bullpen.

"It's funny to look up at the radar and see everybody throwing absolute thunder," Wilson said. "It's like, 'Good luck, hitters.' When it gets in the late innings, you're pretty much getting the cheeseball. Enjoy that, American League."

Wilson also debuted new footwear during his All-Star appearance— a pair of day-glo orange cleats that were bright enough to sear retinas. Wilson planned to keep them as his home cleats for the second half. But in late July, when Florida Marlins manager Edwin Rodriguez saw Wilson warming up in the bullpen, he sensed an opportunity to get in the reliever's head.

Wilson's shoes were no worse than the bright orange, 1970s jerseys the Giants wore for home Friday games. It was a team color, after all. But when Rodriguez complained to the umpires, they agreed the cleats violated the uniform code. Wilson was royally miffed when the league fined him $1,000. And he had a few sarcastic words for Rodriguez.

"The fact that he thinks these shoes throw 97 to 100 mph with [movement] might be a little far-fetched," Wilson said. "I guess we should have these checked. They're performance-enhancing cleats."

Wilson refused to let the Man win, though. The next day he and reliever Dan Runzler each grabbed a black marker and colored in portions of the shoes. According to the uniform guidelines, they had to be 50 percent black. Wilson made sure he covered up the bare minimum.

He called them his "Nike Air Sharpies."

Now into the stretch drive, Wilson's black-bearded appearance held intrigue from head to toe. And with the country beginning to pay attention to the Giants, he had an opportunity to share his unique personality with a larger audience.

Wilson made regular appearances via his home computer camera on *The Cheap Seats*, a program on Fox hosted by Chris Rose. On a show at the end of August Rose and Wilson were seven minutes into a goofy, stream-of-consciousness segment, talking about his Miniature Pinscher, Dubz, when a mysterious visitor walked through the background of Wilson's house. It was a rather large man who appeared suddenly from around a corner and sauntered down a hallway. He wore only black leather briefs, a harness that criss-crossed his bare chest, and a black mask that would be recognizable in certain fetish circles.

Rose almost had a heart attack during the live broadcast.

"What was *that!*" he exclaimed.

Wilson barely held it together.

"What was *what?*" he said.

Wilson continued to play dumb until Rose cued up an instant replay for him to watch. The pitcher chuckled with faux surprise, and then with a perfect nonchalance, he explained it was only his next-door neighbor, known simply as "the Machine." He comes over from time to time to borrow a cup of sugar, Wilson said.

"He doesn't say much," he added.

It was beyond strange. The next day in the Giants clubhouse, all anyone wanted to talk about was "the Machine." Who was he, really? One of Wilson's teammates? Was he a Giants fan? Would he make a visit to the clubhouse? Some folks had their suspicions as to the Machine's identity. But Wilson was just as evasive about his neighbor as he was when asked if he colored his beard.

A week after "the Machine" wandered through his house on live television, Wilson made another memorably unusual appearance, this time with ESPN talk-show host Jim Rome.

It was more absurdist performance art than interview. Wilson began by telling Rome he was "just living another day, my man," then proceeded to detail his morning. He finished the *USA Today* crossword puzzle in 2½ minutes—left-handed. He breakfasted on eggs, a croissant, and "some kind of weird sausage deal I didn't even think of attacking. Went bacon."

Rome mentioned that Wilson was a certified Ninja.

"Correct statement," he said.

How long did that take?

"I believe we discussed this," Wilson said. "It happened in a dream. It takes a lifetime, but only, I think, 12 minutes [in a dream] to complete the courses."

And what about those orange cleats? Why was he fined for them?

"Pffff," Wilson said, getting petulant. "For having too much awesome on my feet."

Rome loved it. His mantra to callers was to "have a take and don't suck." Yet he'd interviewed thousands of dull athletes who tripped over their words or were afraid to say anything remotely interesting. Here, finally, was a professional baseball player who was just as engaging off the field. Whether it was the ninth inning at AT&T Park or the studio of a talk show, you never quite knew what Wilson would do.

Wilson ended the interview by pulling out a gigantic 1980s, Gordon Gekko–style cell phone and answering a call. Of course, it was none other than "the Machine," telling him he had stuffed something in the pitcher's back pocket. Wilson reached behind him to produce the black leather mask that he'd been hiding the whole time.

"He doesn't have much to say, but I feel he just wants to be heard," Wilson said.

"Dude…that's crazy," said Rome, hastily ending the segment.

Wilson wasn't just offbeat. He was experimental music. The pair of interviews went viral on the Internet. He was becoming a cult hero. You couldn't tell if he was genuinely out to lunch or constantly in character. He was like Comedy Central host Stephen Colbert, but with more facial hair.

None of Wilson's act would be funny if he continued to blow three-run leads. But he was better than ever on the mound, often going four and five outs to record saves while still able to maintain his high-velocity stuff the next day.

As the Giants headed home on September 12, tied for the NL West lead following their 7–3 road trip, Wilson was 42-for-46 in save opportunities. The only blemishes on his record had come on a chalk-line double (by the Phillies' Jayson Werth in April), a broken-bat hit (the one by the Rockies' Carlos Gonzalez, which Ross misjudged), and two other games the Giants eventually won.

Wilson was setting career bests with 11.4 strikeouts and 3.3 walks per nine innings. His ERA had fallen from 4.62 in '08 to 2.74 in '09 and now stood at 1.79. Since the All-Star break, his WHIP was a much less adventurous 1.08. Not only did he keep racking up the saves, but they were a little lighter on the torture.

"When everybody on the team has confidence in you, it builds confidence within yourself," he said. "You take that positive arrogance to the mound. Do I want bases loaded with no outs? Yeah, I do."

Yet among many Giants fans, there remained an uneasiness about Wilson. They knew closers were a different breed, but he was from another planet. When a season was on the line, could they really trust him to make the pitch?

By now, Wilson didn't care if someone failed to get the joke, but it bothered him when anyone would question his seriousness on the mound. He used to beam with an odd sense of pride whenever Bochy would complain to the media that the ninth inning was taking years off his life. Now the Giants' closer was growing annoyed by the pithy comments.

There was a serious side to Wilson, too, and he flashed it for a brief instant every time he recorded the final out. He would turn his back to the plate, look upward, and cross his arms, pointing the index finger on his right hand. For the better part of his first season as a closer, he deflected all inquiries into its meaning. Eventually, some fans figured out that the gesture was the symbol for a mixed–martial arts clothing line called "One More Round."

"It has to do with the drive and determination that certain fighters have when their backs are against the wall," he explained. "It's, 'No matter how deep I am in this fight, no matter how badly burned I am, I've got one more round in me.'

"And to me, that relates to what I do on the mound. In the ninth inning your back is against the wall and you're probably facing the meat of the order. You can't back down, you can't give in, and that's exactly how I portray my inning—as a war, as a battle. So when I go out there, I'm fighting for my team. I don't care about any personal statistics, giving up runs or whatever. As long as I preserve the win, everything's okay."

Brian Wilson's tattoos, dark beard, and outrageous sense of humor worked together to form the mystique of the Giants' successful closer.

That wasn't all. Wilson attached two deeper, very personal meanings to the gesture.

It was a tribute to his father, Mike, a 22-year Air Force veteran who died of cancer when Brian was 17. And it was a tribute to the God that Brian had forsaken for taking his father away from him.

The fist inside his gloved hand represents the strength of God. And the raised index finger represents the strength of one man—himself—and how that man can do all things when he combines his own will with the power of his faith.

"Talent only goes so far, but faith gets you a little farther," Wilson said. "I take it as a reminder of why I'm out here. It's, 'Remember what kind of gift you have, and most of all, don't let your team down.'"

There was a time in the minor leagues when Wilson nearly quit on himself. The Giants had taken a chance on him as a 24th-round pick in the 2003 draft, knowing he threw hard but would need a year to recover from reconstructive elbow surgery. Young pitchers who underwent Tommy John surgery often made a full recovery, but it took dedication and commitment to a yearlong schedule of excruciatingly dull rehab exercises.

Wilson admitted it: he often blew them off.

He wasn't prepared for professional baseball and got crushed when he reported to Hagerstown, Maryland, in the Low-A South Atlantic League, finishing with a 5.34 ERA. But things began to turn around when a team chaplain had convinced him to leave a card game and attend a prayer group. Wilson was transformed. He made his peace with God and came to understand a simple truth.

"As soon as we're born, we're dying," he said. "So why not live all-out?"

He attacked his rehab work, transformed himself in the gym, and turned his body into weapons-grade muscle. Each confrontation with a hitter became a micro war. When he blew a save, he'd follow it with hours of corporal punishment the next day, sprinting up stadium stairs, running the track for miles, and pedaling so hard on a stationary bike that he'd nearly bust the fly wheel.

If the Giants lost a division with Wilson on the mound, it wouldn't be because of fear or fatigue. He had become a machine—without the mask.

Wilson wasn't the only weapon in the Giants bullpen. The entire group was coalescing, including Javier Lopez and Ramon Ramirez—the pair of unsexy trade-deadline acquisitions that caused so much consternation among fans. On their 10-game trip, the bullpen was 3–0 with five saves and had a 0.38 ERA in 24 innings.

No performance was more impressive than their extra-inning victory on Labor Day at Arizona. Bochy used Ramirez, Lopez, and Sergio Romo to face one batter each in the eighth inning and strand the tiebreaking run at third base. The manager still had Jeremy Affeldt and Santiago Casilla, who combined for five strikeouts while throwing nasty stuff in the ninth and 10th. When Schierholtz tripled to put the Giants ahead in the 11th, Wilson shut the door without incident.

Lopez, the sidewinding lefty, had a 1.10 ERA in his first 20 games as a Giant. He was neutralizing left-handed hitters, holding them to three hits in 33 at-bats while changing arm angles from one pitch to the next. Ramirez, despite a 4.46 ERA in Boston, had a 0.91 ERA in 19 games as a Giant and was holding hitters to a .181 average.

With those two trade additions boosting the club, the bullpen bailed out the rotation during its underachieving stretch in August. Relievers had compiled a 20–4 record since July 1. They were extending games and giving their teammates a chance to pull out victories. All these close and late games might have been pure torture, but the Giants had learned to win them.

The hitters were learning to trust the guy behind them, and the same was true in the bullpen. Romo, the young and outspoken little right-hander with the Frisbee slider, admitted he had been selfish earlier in his career. He worried only about putting up his zero for the day. Now he understood that sometime, pitching around a tough hitter was better for the team. The next guy would come in and watch his back.

"I sold out and bought in," Romo said. "We believe in ourselves, and that's not conceited. We understand we're pretty good. But now this is when the real grind starts."

The Giants entered the final two weeks of the season with a better, deeper, and hotter bullpen than anyone could remember in recent franchise history. And when the starters began to rediscover their form, the team appeared poised to go on a mighty roll.

In front of their euphoric home fans, they took sole possession of first place on September 16, manhandling the uninspired Dodgers in a 10–2 victory. It was fitting that Jonathan Sanchez pitched them there. The left-hander struck out a career-high 12 batters, he didn't issue a walk, and his bold prediction from August suddenly wasn't looking all too misguided.

Huff, whose wife gave birth to a son, Jagger, the previous day, played on no sleep yet cracked a tiebreaking, three-run homer in the third inning. "I didn't know how much I had in the tank, to be honest," Huff said. "Goes to show you sleep is overrated."

Sanchez was throwing with plenty of gas. Bochy waited until the team jogged onto the field in the eighth to take out the left-hander, assuring him a loud, standing ovation. The Giants were 11–4 in his starts since early July.

The last time out against the Padres, Sanchez had survived without his best stuff. Now he was facing a Dodgers team that was folding like an origami class at the senior center. And he pumped the zone, going right after them with fastballs, splitters, and curveballs.

"Anything I threw today was going to be good," Sanchez said. "I've never been in the postseason. I've never celebrated. That's what I want.

"We're better than just getting to the playoffs. We get there, I think we're going to be tough to beat."

It was an extra satisfying victory because it clinched the season series with their archrivals for the first time since 2005. The Giants won 10 of 18 despite getting overrun by the Dodgers in April and May.

The rivalry had some spice again, too, whether it was Dodgers third baseman Casey Blake mocking Wilson's post-save gesture a year earlier, or Vicente Padilla's beanball that broke Rowand's face in three places, or hotheaded center fielder Matt Kemp taking a threatening walk toward Lincecum after getting plunked. These two teams didn't like each other. But by the end of the season, the Dodgers weren't hitting and barely seemed to care. The "Beat L.A." chants were meaningful at AT&T Park once more.

As Tony Bennett's "I Left My Heart in San Francisco" wafted through the ballpark, a great many in the near-sellout crowd stayed and trained their eyes on the right-field arcade before heading out into the foggy night. The stadium workers hastily rearranged the flags that represented the standings. A cheer went up as they were raised. For the first time in seven years, the black banner fluttered highest in September.

The stadium workers had to keep those stepladders handy, though. The Padres reclaimed the top spot two days later, after the Giants lost their second consecutive game to the Milwaukee Brewers. For the first time in nearly a month, the Giants were assured a series loss.

The Giants offense, which had become too dependent on the long-ball ever since that magical, four-homer comeback at Dodger Stadium, had returned to earth. It wouldn't be long before they would bounce into their 154th double play, breaking a franchise record that stood for 71 years. They missed Torres' energy in the leadoff spot, too.

Not only had the Padres retaken first place, but the Rockies now stood even with the Giants in the loss column. The Giants trailed the Atlanta Braves by two games for the wild-card, too. And Lincecum was chippy at his manager, who was so desperate for offense that he lifted his ace for a pinch-hitter in the fifth inning against the Brewers.

"I don't think any of the guys in here want to go five and dive," Lincecum said.

Asked about the lack of run support, Lincecum answered honestly. "That's something we've dealt with for four years as a pitching staff," he said. "It's nothing new."

Lincecum said it in a matter-of-fact tone. There wasn't any mean edge in his voice. Yet these had to be heartbreaking words for Giants fans to hear. Because of their inconsistent offense, this amazing pitching staff could be deprived a chance to shine on the brightest stage. And now Lincecum was 14–10—a double-digit loser for the first time in his career.

The Giants didn't put runs on the board consistently. But unlike the previous year, they had guys who could hit it out of the park. And when they did, they didn't just squeak out victories, either.

They avoided getting swept by the Brewers and reclaimed first place with a 9–2 victory powered by Jose Guillen, who hit a grand slam as part of a six-RBI game. The flood of runs only highlighted the feast-or-famine nature of their lineup. Over their past dozen games they had scored nine, one, zero, 10, two, zero, six, zero, one, seven, one, and six runs. Beginning with that magical night in L.A., they had homered in eight of 15 games. When they went deep over that 15-game stretch, they were averaging 6.63 runs per game. When they didn't, they scratched out an average of just 0.86 runs.

The home run–fueled offense was great when it worked. But it only seemed to work once or twice a week.

"I do think there are times we're overswinging a little bit," Bochy said. "They all need to calm down offensively.... We don't need home runs. We need base hits. We need to keep the line moving and to get a hit when we need it."

Huff had driven in seven runs in his last 19 games—all on home runs. He also was riding a stretch that included 11 strikeouts in 22 at-bats.

"Everybody's gripping it so hard," Huff said. "It's the last thing you need to do this time of year."

The pressure was mounting. The Giants' pennant-race inexperience looked to be a factor. The hitters understood their playoff hopes would boil down to this: would they score enough runs to win?

"Our pitching is second to none in the league, if you ask me," Huff said. "Guys are trying so hard to make something happen. Well, you can make it happen with a walk. When we score 10 runs, it's because we got that big hit early. Guys calm down and relax. It shows when you're relaxed, you have fun and take good at-bats."

The Giants took off for their final road trip of the regular season, at Wrigley Field. They silently hoped the wind would be blowing out.

Instead, they managed one run over the first two games against the Cubs, although one of them was a 1–0 victory that might have elevated Posey to the NL Rookie of the Year award. Posey caught Cain and three relievers in a two-hit shutout, he hosed a runner at second base, and his home run to dead center accounted for the game's only run.

Afterward, third-base coach Tim Flannery told Posey to savor the moment. You never know how many chances you'll get to play in a pennant race, the coach said.

Posey, as respectfully as he could, disagreed.

"You hear people say, 'You don't know how many opportunities you'll have to get into the playoffs.' Well, I don't know if that's true," Posey said.

"God willing, if we're healthy, I think we have the guys to be there for a lot of years to come."

After the game, some prankster put a load of shaving cream in a folded towel, and the whole clubhouse erupted in laughter when Flannery emerged, just then realizing he had given himself a pie to the face.

"I can't wait 'til we get out of here," grumbled Flannery, "and coaches get their own shower room."

There would be no postgame shenanigans the following day, though. Randy Wells, the Cubs' middling right-hander, shut down the Giants while dealing them a 2–0 loss, and the hitters were on the verge of widespread panic. It was the eighth time in 13 games the Giants were held to one run or fewer.

"We're just not putting together smart at-bats," said Huff, who had flung his batting helmet in anger when he lined into a double play.

Meanwhile, the Giants' pitching had gone from merely good to historically good. It was the 16th consecutive game they held an opponent to three runs or fewer, tying the longest streak by a major league club in the live-ball era.

The Dodgers didn't have a streak like this with Koufax and Drysdale. The Diamondbacks didn't do it with Schilling and Johnson. All the Gibsons and Marichals, Dizzys, Daffys, Big Trains, and the Big Three—heck, even the Atlanta Braves' triumvirate of Glavine, Smoltz, and Maddux—none of those teams put together a staff-wide streak of dominance like the Giants were on now.

The Giants' hitters simply couldn't foul this up. The sense of responsibility—and urgency—was rising.

"It seems if we don't score early…you can just feel everybody tensing up, trying to hit a home run," Huff said. "It doesn't work that way. We've gotta work at-bats, see pitches."

The next afternoon Bochy and the position players gathered for a meeting. They didn't have a spacious, indoor cage or a roomy manager's office at their disposal. Wrigley Field was built in 1914, when most of the country still traveled by horse-drawn carriage, and the facilities reflected it. The visiting batting cage was a tiny space—a cave, really—underneath the right-field bleachers. The players filed through the ivy-covered threshold and crammed themselves inside.

Nobody would detail specifics of the meeting or who got up to speak. But that cave under the bleachers had the effect of a visit to the grotto at Lourdes. The Giants raised holy hell against right-hander Ryan Dempster in a 13–0 victory, with Uribe hitting a grand slam and a two-run home run in the second inning alone. His six-RBI inning was the biggest by a Giant in 40 years.

Sure, it helped that the wind was howling out. But that didn't seem to assist the Cubs against Bumgarner, who struck out nine in his seven innings. For the 17th consecutive game, the Giants held an opponent to fewer than three runs. It now ranked as the longest streak since the 1917 Chicago White Sox.

The streak was about to be tested at Coors Field.

Lincecum had simmered down over the quick hook from his previous start. The decision to pinch-hit for his ace hadn't blown up in Bochy's face, because the bullpen followed with four scoreless innings. And if anything, it might have been good to ease up on Lincecum's pitch count as he readied for the two most important starts of his Giants career.

In the past Bochy had no problem pushing Lincecum. In 2008, with the Giants out of contention, Bochy let Lincecum throw 132 pitches in search of his first career shutout to boost his Cy Young credentials. Lincecum's bid failed, but when he was in position again three starts later, Bochy let him throw a whopping 138 pitches to get it.

Over the previous five major league seasons, only two pitchers (Livan Hernandez and Jason Schmidt) had thrown that many pitches in a start.

Lincecum did take home the Cy Young hardware, but his 3,680 pitches thrown in '08 were the most in the NL. He threw almost as many, 3,438, the following season. And when his fastball began to lag, it was all too easy to bring up those old doubts about his size and durability.

Bochy was managing Lincecum differently now, though. He hadn't thrown more than 123 pitches in a start and was averaging just more than 100 per outing. Even in the first half, when Todd Wellemeyer was a train wreck as the No. 5 starter, Bochy and Righetti didn't use days off to jigger the rotation and move up Lincecum. All five starters simply received the extra day of rest. Given how the rotation was pitching in September, the strategy appeared to be paying dividends.

Lincecum had taken Sabean's lecture to heart. He spent more time between starts working to strengthen his legs and core. He returned to playing long toss. He poured his mental energy into preparation instead of apprehension.

"It's digging for something extra," Lincecum said. "It's time to get wins now. That's my mind-set: put the rest of the season behind me and focus on what I can do."

Bochy loved what he was seeing from Lincecum in September. Not only was he pitching with purpose and confidence again, but he had an ornery edge to him that he'd only flashed on occasion in the past. Like Randy Johnson going after his fifth Cy Young Award, Lincecum pitched like he was dissatisfied.

"I'm just trying to take that bulldog mentality out there that I used to have," Lincecum said. "Just shove it up your…whatever, you know what I mean?"

For the first time all year, Lincecum was keeping up that mentality on the four days between his starts, too.

"Oh, it hit him," Bochy said. "I think he knows now. But I'll say this: he's already taken responsibility for putting in more time and effort into his workouts. He's been spending more time in the weight room. He's got a routine. But that has to carry throughout the off-season, too."

Lincecum's September resurgence involved more than stronger legs and a brighter outlook. He also began to mix in a slider that he began throwing while playing catch with Cain. It put one more pitch in hitters' minds—and made his disappearing change-up all the more effective. He was back to pounding the zone and challenging hitters. When he struck out 11 at Arizona on September 7, he didn't walk a batter. It was the first time he hadn't issued a walk since the April 5 season opener at Houston.

Along the way, Lincecum reached the 200-strikeout mark for the third consecutive season, a feat that only two other Giants—Hall of Famers Juan Marichal (1963–1966) and Christy Mathewson (1903–1905)—had accomplished since the turn of the 20th century.

Lincecum was pitching like a playoff ace, and he kept it rolling through his final two starts of the season. At Coors Field, he took a perfect game into the sixth inning and ended up allowing just two hits over eight. Burrell came through in the clutch again, hitting a two-run homer in the seventh as the Giants won the series opener 2–1.

It was an especially satisfying win, and not only because it knocked the dangerous but fading Rockies 4½ games off the pace. In the hours leading up to the game, all the talk was over the Rockies' humidor, a temperature-controlled room in which they stored baseballs to keep them from drying out in Denver's thin air. There had been rumblings for years that perhaps the Rockies might slip in a few livelier, non-humidor balls when their hitters were at the plate, perhaps explaining why they hit so much better and won more games at home. Sabean didn't accuse the Rockies of cheating, but with the season at stake, he raised his concerns to league officials. They agreed that more transparency was a good thing.

Beginning with the second game of the series, umpires would be charged with overseeing the chain of custody of baseballs from humidor to ball bag.

On the mound, cameras caught a tight shot of Lincecum, scowling as he called for a new baseball. The words he spoke were easy to decipher: "F—ing juiced ball bullshit." It didn't seem possible that Giants fans could hold any more love for Lincecum in their hearts. Now they did.

After the game, Lincecum ran into Colorado shortstop Troy Tulowitzki in the hallway to the weight room.

"We couldn't even get you with our juiced balls," joked Tulo, a huge smile on his face.

The next day, the umpires must've reached into the humidor and grabbed Titleists by accident. The Giants and Rockies played one of those Coors Field specials from the mid-1990s, trading salvos into the 10th inning. Tulowitzki and Carlos Gonzalez, arguably the two hottest hitters in the NL, both made diving defensive plays and got the knocks to send the Rockies to a 10–9 victory. Tulowitzki hit a tying, two-run double off Wilson in the eighth, then he doubled in Gonzalez, who scored all the way from first base on a ball that got away from Burrell in left field.

The Giants pitching staff's historic run had ended at 18 games, and the team had absorbed another soul-crushing loss at Coors Field. But the Giants had become conditioned to washing off defeat here, and besides, Torres had rejoined the starting lineup and hit a homer in his return. The Giants had one more road game remaining on the 2010 schedule and Cain on the mound.

Cain refused to entertain the thought of defeat. Not only did he pitch the Giants to a 4–2 victory and a series win, but he got within five outs of the second no-hitter in Coors Field history. Uribe double-clutched a ground ball that was scored an infield single, and Melvin Mora followed with a home run in the eighth inning. But Bochy trusted his laconic right-hander to finish off the complete game. And for the seventh time in 11 days, there was a lead change atop the NL West. After taking two of three in Chicago and doing the same in Denver, the Giants finished their road schedule with a 43–38 mark—their first winning record away from AT&T Park since 2004—and they held a half-game edge over the Padres.

There was one week remaining in the season, and the Giants had the comfort of knowing they'd be home for the duration. First, they would play three games against the Diamondbacks, and then, as fate demanded, the Padres would arrive for the final series of the season.

When the Giants came home, they found their waterfront ballpark at Third and King Streets had been transformed. Unlike the Padres, whose fans never really invested themselves in the playoff drive, the Bay Area had thrown all its attention and energy behind the Giants. Fans held aloft all manner of "torture" signs. They wore Panda hats and Lincecum wigs. They embraced the Giants not just because they were contending, but also because they identified with this team of castoffs and oddballs.

The Giants didn't scare you when they walked off the bus. Their ace was too pale and skinny, their third baseman was too plump, and their closer was a 28-year-old eccentric with too much awesome on his feet and too much lumberjack on his face.

But this had become San Francisco's band of misfits. And a new chant began to echo through Willie Mays Plaza.

"Fear the Beard."

Chapter 9

Home Stretch

Nobody wanted them.

Aubrey Huff's phone had been silent all winter. Another team paid Pat Burrell to disappear. Cody Ross was given away. Andres Torres and Juan Uribe arrived as minor league free agents.

The Giants' lineup was full of former Pirates and Rays. They were a collection of castoffs—players nobody valued.

To this island of misfit toys, the Giants added two rookies who didn't think, act, or play like rookies. Madison Bumgarner walked straight out of North Carolina horse country. Buster Posey seemingly walked out of the New Testament.

Young and old, new and newer, borrowed and yet so well assembled—the Giants were one good week away from winning the NL West.

And it drove Mat Latos crazy.

The Padres had led the division nearly wire to wire. They boasted the NL's best record for most of the summer. Sure, they had traded for Ryan Ludwick and Miguel Tejada, but for the most part, they were the same club that broke camp together in the spring. They might have been underdogs nobody picked to win. But at least they weren't soldiers for hire.

In his uniquely dim worldview, that's how Latos saw the Giants—as a group of mercenaries, dishonorably gathered from the farthest reaches of the land. The Giants hadn't been together since spring training. They *couldn't* be a team in the same sense the Padres were, could they? And yet here they were, seizing the lead in the NL West and threatening to walk off with the division title like marauders in the night.

"Baseball works in funny ways," Latos told sportsline.com in the season's final week. "The only way I could honestly put it is, we could be like the Giants and go and change our whole lineup, put guys with 'San Francisco Giants' across their jerseys. We didn't. We added two guys. We've been the same team all year. We haven't just gone and grabbed guys from other teams."

Latos had the facts right, but not the context. It's true, the Giants picked up hitchhikers as they rumbled down the road. But to them, it didn't matter that Burrell had been released or Ross was dumped by the Marlins on waivers or that a rookie, Posey, was making every important decision behind the plate. Their clubhouse was loose enough to integrate new players and tough enough to keep crushing losses from lingering in memory.

San Francisco was a city of tolerance and acceptance. And so was their baseball team.

"We can't have outcasts here," Wilson said. "On this club, everybody pulls for each other. When we get a new guy, he's a part of our family, and we'll treat him like part of the family."

Giants players scoffed at Latos' criticism, barely dignifying it with a response. They knew the comments were coming from a frustrated kid who felt his season slipping away.

Latos had dominated all year but suddenly was winless with a 10.13 ERA over his last four starts. And his immaturity issues were as well documented as the repair bill for Dave Flemming's sunroof.

"We grabbed guys?" one Giant said. "Maybe those guys should've grabbed more."

The Giants entered their final, six-game home stand with everything they needed to wrap up the division. They had five healthy starting pitchers, four of whom were on hot streaks. They led the major leagues in strikeouts and were about to break the single-season franchise record they had set one year earlier. Their unbelievable bullpen had a 1.11 ERA in September, and unlike the Padres, they weren't leaning on the same three or four relief arms every night.

The Giants were back home, too, where they had a tangible advantage. The marketing slogan for the season—"It's Magic Inside"—elicited snickers when it was revealed in the spring. But now it seemed appropriate. The stands looked like Halloween with splashes of black and orange and fake beards wherever you looked. It wasn't just loud inside the quaint retro ballpark at Third and King, either, there was a confidence and belief behind the cheers, and it reverberated through concrete and steel. The Giants had momentum, talent, confidence, attitude, and energy from their fans.

They weren't a perfect team. They had obvious flaws. But over the grind of a six-month season, they had proven something to themselves: they could overcome them.

The "Giants Baseball: Torture" theme connected deeply with the fans. But one former player understood the true meaning of the term better than anyone.

Willie McCovey, the Giants' beloved Hall of Fame first baseman, had lived nearly all his life with debilitating back and knee pain. He underwent dozens of surgeries over the years and needed a motorized cart and crutches to reach his suite at AT&T Park. Yet the 72-year-old legend still came to spring training every year, still arrived at the ballpark early to shoot the breeze in Mike Murphy's office, and still followed almost every home game from his private box.

"Stretch" had been noticeably absent for most of the summer, though. He couldn't attend his annual charity golf event. When Posey got within one game of matching McCovey's rookie-record hitting streak, Willie Mac wasn't there to see the kid try.

McCovey's back had locked up so severely that he required another operation, and when doctors opened him up in July, they were shocked at the amount of damage to his vertebrae. The surgery took 12 hours and required 18 pins. Stretch would be hospitalized for almost two months.

His rehabilitation would be long, painful, and grueling. His physical therapists recommended he set a goal to push him through. And he had one: to be on the field during the final home stand, when the Giants presented the Willie Mac Award to their most inspirational player.

Usually it was McCovey who inspired the team. This summer, the team would inspire him.

McCovey never was one to waste breath complaining. During his playing career and after it, he remained always gracious, humble, and gentle, even though he barely received the recognition he deserved.

He wasn't seen as the best player on his team; he batted behind the brilliant Willie Mays, after all. He wasn't the greatest player to come from his hometown of Mobile, Alabama; Hank Aaron was from there, too. But McCovey received respect from those who mattered most—opposing pitchers. They intentionally walked him 45 times in 1969, a major league record until Barry Bonds broke it in 2002. Only Bonds and Hank Aaron drew more intentional walks in their career than McCovey.

In so many ways, the Giants' story in San Francisco was McCovey's story. In an era without the wild-card, the Giants often finished behind the Dodgers, their hated rivals, who had Koufax and Drysdale leading the way. Those Giants teams from the 1960s were recognized for their greatness and their concentration of Hall of Famers. But they did not reach the pinnacle.

Despite a dynastic load of talent, the Giants of the Mays-McCovey era only played in one World Series—in 1962 against the New York Yankees. It ended with a thrilling Game 7 that should have ranked as one of the most memorable in baseball history, every bit as dramatic as Bill Mazeroski's home run for the Pirates in 1960, Joe Carter's drive to win it for the Blue Jays in '93, Luis Gonzalez's jam shot for the Diamondbacks in 2001, or Edgar Renteria's euphoric single as a 21-year-old rookie for the 1997 Florida Marlins.

But people remember successes. They remember images of home-plate celebrations and joyful jaunts around the bases.

And while Game 7 of the 1962 World Series ended with a purely struck line drive, it wasn't a game-winning hit. With the tying and winning runs in scoring position, McCovey drilled Ralph Terry's pitch— and Yankees second baseman Bobby Richardson was in the perfect position to snag it.

All McCovey could do was try to hit the ball hard. And he did. The Yankees still won 1–0.

Some weeks later legendary cartoonist Charles Schulz, who lived in Sonoma County, spoke for Giants fans everywhere through his beloved *Peanuts*. The first three panels were identical: Charlie Brown and Linus, glumly leaning their chins in their hands. In the fourth, the round-headed kid wails, "WHY COULDN'T McCOVEY HAVE HIT THE BALL JUST THREE FEET HIGHER?"

A month later, Schulz penned a nearly identical strip. This time Charlie Brown blared out, "OR WHY COULDN'T McCOVEY HAVE HIT THE BALL EVEN *TWO* FEET HIGHER?"

During that 1962 World Series, the ongoing story was the heavy rain that kept pushing back the games. As it turned out, a World Series championship in San Francisco would be delayed longer than anyone could have imagined.

"I remember thinking we would be back the next year," said Felipe Alou, their star outfielder, leadoff hitter, and future manager. "We all knew we had a great team."

The Giants posted a winning record in eight consecutive seasons after 1962, reaching the 90-win mark five times. They did not make the postseason once during that span. In fact, they would make the playoffs just once in 24 years, bowing out to the Pittsburgh Pirates in the 1971 NLCS. McCovey hit .429 with two home runs in those four games.

In 1980 the Giants organization decided to recognize the club's most inspirational player with an annual award, as selected by their fellow teammates. They called it the Willie Mac Award. It remained the single highest honor a Giant could receive. Gold Glove first baseman J.T. Snow had won it twice. So had right-hander Mike Krukow, now the club's TV analyst. Bengie Molina was the only other two-time recipient.

These current Giants had no shortage of inspirational candidates. It would be one of the closest ballots in history, and because it was the 30th anniversary of the first award, the organization was gathering as many former winners as possible for the on-field ceremony.

As the final weekend approached, McCovey's doctors weren't sure whether he would be strong enough to attend. He had gone months without being able to stand up or get out of bed. But just a few days before the ceremony, the therapy seemed to start working. Stretch would make it.

When he appeared on the field and slowly made his way across the infield grass, the sellout crowd showered him with applause and more than a few tears. The scene was every bit as emotional as the 1999 All-Star Game in Boston, when all the game's greats paid tribute to a wheelchair-bound Ted Williams.

"Just to be out here for the game is enough motivation for me," McCovey said. "It's a lot different than watching from TV in a hospital bed, let me tell you."

Former Giant and Hall of Famer Willie McCovey (left) congratulates Andres Torres on winning the 2010 Willie Mac Award on October 1, 2010. The award is selected by teammates to honor their most inspirational player.

An even louder cheer followed when McCovey leaned into the microphone and announced this year's winner. It was Andres Torres, their improbable little dynamo who persevered through a decade of professional baseball before blossoming as an impact player in the big leagues. And now Torres' incredible story held eerie parallels to the Robert Redford character in *The Natural*, right down to his injured side. Torres was in such tremendous shape that he'd flown through his recovery from an appendectomy to get back on the field in 10 days. He hit a home run in his first start. Later in that game, when he made a headfirst slide, he ignored the pain.

He was an inspiration, all right. And he received McCovey's vote, too.

"This is a blessing," said Torres, after apologizing to the crowd for his English.

For all the positive vibes at AT&T Park, there remained a nervous energy among the tortured fan base when the final homestand against the Diamondbacks and Padres began. And nothing made the fans more nervous than the way Bochy had decided to align his starting pitchers. There had been a public push for Bochy to adjust the rotation and move Lincecum back a day so that he, and not Zito, would pitch the Friday series opener against San Diego. Instead, the coaches took the opposite approach. They moved up Lincecum's start, sending him to pitch on normal rest Wednesday—the middle game of the Arizona series.

It was easy for Giants fans to get all lathered up over pitching decisions.

In 1993, the final playoff season before the addition of the wild-card, the Giants won a staggering 103 games but needed to beat the Dodgers in the regular season finale to force a one-game playoff with the Braves atop the NL West. Rookie manager Dusty Baker selected 21-year-old Salomon Torres to start instead of veteran Scott Sanderson; the kid didn't make it out of the fourth inning, and his name became forever synonymous with one of the most crushing moments in franchise history.

In his 10th and final season as the Giants' manager, Baker made another fateful decision. In Game 7 of the 2002 World Series he went with Livan Hernandez instead of choosing Kirk Rueter on short rest, even though the Angels had hit Hernandez hard earlier in the series. The Angels romped again and denied the Giants their first title in San Francisco.

Shortly before Baker's divorce from the Giants became official, the charismatic manager told the *San Francisco Chronicle* that perhaps it was best he move on.

"It's glaringly apparent that whenever we lose, it's because of something I did to make us lose," he told the newspaper.

Bochy never had Baker's cool-cat persona, nor was he a beloved figure with fans to begin with. Now he was going to let Zito, the weakest link in the rotation, pitch in the final weekend against the Padres. It was not a popular decision, to say the least.

But Bochy made one other tweak to his rotation. He moved up Cain a day, too, aligning him to pitch the series opener against the Padres. Zito would have the Saturday game, and Jonathan Sanchez would be ready for Sunday's season finale.

Bochy's decisions often had an unspoken confidence attached to them. Everyone in the clubhouse understood what he was doing, even if he couldn't come out and say it.

Bochy was lining up his playoff rotation. He effectively told his players: we're clinching this thing, and we're going to be ready for what's next.

Plus, by moving up Lincecum, the Giants also would have their ace fully rested should they be forced into a one-game playoff.

Entering the final weekend, though, a one-game playoff was the last thing on the Giants' minds.

They took care of business against the Diamondbacks, and their pitching staff dominated again, sweeping the Snakes by scores of 4–2, 3–0, and 4–1. Sanchez reached the 200-strikeout mark in the opener, Lincecum fanned 11 in seven innings, and Bumgarner fended off the Diamondbacks just long enough to end personal frustration and win for the first time in nine career home starts.

Sandoval, whose season-long slump and weight problems had turned him from a .330-hitting marvel into a platoon player, put aside his burdens and had two big hits in the series—including a home run that splashed between two kayaks in McCovey Cove. Torres, whose side remained sore after he rushed back from his appendectomy, looked fully recovered as he tripled and hit a tiebreaking homer. Burrell had one more huge home run to support Lincecum, connecting for a three-run shot.

Lincecum ended his tumultuous regular season with a thunderous, standing ovation. In a bit of theater, Bochy trotted to the mound and allowed Lincecum to keep the ball after a two-out walk in the seventh inning. Lincecum responded by throwing one of his disappearing change-ups that froze Chris Young and sent the crowd into a frenzy.

"He asked how I was doing," Lincecum said. "I said I was great. I just…I wanted it."

Lincecum finished with an NL-best 231 strikeouts, making him just the third NL pitcher since World War II to lead the league in three consecutive years. Randy Johnson (1999–2002) and Warren Spahn (1949–1952) were the others.

His 3.43 ERA was nearly a run higher than the previous year, so he wouldn't take home another Cy Young. In fact, he'd finish 11th in the balloting. But more importantly, he had a 1.94 ERA after September 1.

The Giants had their ace back, and just in time.

"Certain months, obviously, I struggled, but I think the biggest month for me was bouncing back here, when we needed it the most and when it matters the most," Lincecum said. "All these guys helped me get through this. Everybody's done their part to help me get back to where I needed to be."

While the Giants swept the Diamondbacks, the Padres continued to take on water. They dropped three of four to the Cubs, who were playing hard under interim manager Mike Quade—and perhaps didn't appreciate the Padres wearing their 1984 throwback jerseys during the series.

Suddenly, the Giants led by three games with three to play. Their magic number was one. Even if the Padres somehow managed to sweep them on their home turf, they'd still have Lincecum as a failsafe in a potential one-game playoff.

"But you just knew," Bochy said, with a groan. "We never make anything easy."

This was Team Torture, after all.

Cain seemed to be the perfect choice to punch the Giants' playoff ticket. He was coming off his near no-hitter in Colorado, he was the club's longest-tenured player, and everyone admired his ironwood toughness. Cain would take the mound on his 26th birthday, which didn't dissuade Bochy from lovingly referring to him as the "old goat on the staff."

The old goat could not play the hero. Cain's fastball was straight, and the Padres were ready. They hit three home runs off him to take a 6–4 victory and extend the drama. At least the Giants could take solace knowing they rallied back enough to force Padres manager Bud Black to use all his frontline relievers in the late innings. Closer Heath Bell pitched for a third consecutive day. Perhaps that would be a factor later in the weekend.

Now it was Zito's opportunity, and the story seemed to write itself in a different way. If the longest-tenured Giant couldn't slam the door, maybe their highest-paid player could touch off the celebration and finally earn a place in franchise history that didn't include mention of his $126 million contract.

Lincecum battled self-doubts and tinkered to reinvent himself in August, but that was the story for Zito over most of his four seasons as a Giant. Even when he got on a confident roll, like his 6–0 start to begin the season, it didn't take long for the fans to turn on him when an outing began to unravel. They didn't trust Zito in a big game. This was his chance to prove his worth, to remind everyone on this side of the bay that not long ago, he was a big-game pitcher with the A's who beat aces like Johan Santana and Roger Clemens in the postseason.

But that script was torn in half, too.

Zito did the worst thing he could possibly do. He pitched scared. He issued two bases-loaded walks in the first inning as his teammates stood powerless behind him. It sucked the life out of China Basin, and the Padres held on for a 4–2 victory.

It set up one of the wildest final Sundays in pennant-race history. Not only could the Padres tie for the NL West title with one more victory in San Francisco, but both teams remained alive in the wild-card race, too.

The Atlanta Braves and Padres entered Sunday with identical records, meaning a San Diego victory and a Braves victory over the Phillies could forge a three-way tie for two playoff spots. In that unprecedented instance, the Giants would be forced to travel to San Diego for a one-game playoff to decide the NL West, and then the loser would fly to Atlanta to face the Braves in another sudden-death game for the wild-card.

There was an even crazier scenario, if Atlanta lost, in which the Giants and Padres could have clinched on the same field—the Giants as the wild-card team and the Padres, who held the tiebreaker, as NL West champs.

For the Giants, a chalk-dust cloud of calculus could be reduced to this: beat the Padres in game No. 162, clinch the NL West, pop corks.

Even the rookies knew to keep it simple.

"You know what? It feels the same as it's felt the last month," Posey said. "We've got to go out and win a game. It's probably felt like that since September 1."

Bochy sent another of his veiled messages in a closed-door meeting. He told the players to bring only the clothes on their backs to the ballpark on Sunday.

Left unspoken: we'll win, and we aren't going anywhere.

Cain and Zito couldn't get it done, but the final act offered the most delicious pitching story line of all. It featured none other than Sanchez, the hasty prophet, and Latos, the self-styled expert on team chemistry.

The Giants had begun Latos' four-game losing streak when they beat him September 12 in San Diego. But nobody had forgotten that he outdueled Sanchez in a pair of 1–0 victories earlier in the season. On the very same mound at AT&T Park in May, he finished an infield hit away from throwing a perfect game. He remained an intimidating presence.

The night before the game, Sanchez repeated to teammates what he couldn't say in public. He guaranteed the Giants would beat the Padres. And they wouldn't look back.

But when the game was scoreless in the third inning, Sanchez did something even he couldn't have predicted on his boldest day. He stroked a pitch to the deepest part of right-center field and coasted into third base with a triple. It was the sudden icebreaker the Giants needed.

Freddy Sanchez, the former Pirate playing in his first pennant race, hit an RBI single up the middle. And Huff, who played so many throw-away games for losing teams in Tampa and Baltimore, smoked a first-pitch double that escaped Chris Denorfia's dive in center field. Each hit drove in a run.

Posey added a solo home run in the eighth inning to make it 3–0 and send a buzz through the crowd. It was the 59th anniversary of Bobby Thomson's Shot Heard Round the World. Posey's homer didn't clinch the pennant by itself, as Thomson's did, but it felt as if the Giants couldn't lose now.

The Giants' stout bullpen already had helped untangle one jam, when hard-throwing Santiago Casilla entered in the sixth and stranded both of Sanchez's runners. Casilla had been an unspectacular pitcher with the A's earlier in his career, but learned a spike curve from a team-mate in the Dominican League that winter. The Giants signed him to a minor league contract that spring. And he had become a dominant short reliever.

But Casilla needed someone to bail him out, too, after allowing a pair of runners to reach in the seventh. Ramirez, the quiet addition from the Red Sox, threw a 3–2 cutter to strike out Miguel Tejada and preserve the shutout.

All the way down the stretch the relievers had picked each other up. They were unscored upon in their final 24 innings of the season, and had a 0.90 ERA after September 1. With a summer's labor on the line, they had each other's backs one more time.

The ninth belonged to Wilson, and he did not prolong the torture. He worked a 1-2-3 inning, striking out Will Venable to end it.

Posey, the stoic rookie, leapt up in pure elation as the Giants piled upon each other. They weren't getting on a flight that evening. They weren't going anywhere. They were staying home—and celebrating as NL West champions.

Wilson let out a furious yell, made his signature post-save gesture, and turned back to meet the young catcher, who jumped into his tattooed arms.

"That's the first time I've seen some absolute, unadulterated craziness out of the guy," Wilson said. "I thought he was going to punch me, and I was totally accepting of it. I was finding a reason not to thank him for punching me, actually, if he did."

Burrell was the first player out of the dugout, running out to tackle Wilson—and then delivering a punch to Huff. Even the hardest body blow wasn't going to wake them from this dream.

Mike Murphy finally could unfurl the plastic sheets that had been rolled up atop the lockers all weekend. The Giants could break out the champagne that stood good and chilled. But before they doused each other in an eye-stinging haze, Bochy wanted his players to perform an errand. He pulled aside Burrell, the leader of his misfits, and asked him to gather the players for a lap around the field. These fans had poured out their souls to support their team. It was time to share this victory with them.

"Anything you say, skip," Burrell nodded.

Pablo Sandoval, bouncing along madly, moved to the front—taking charge of this not-so-light brigade—and players extended their hands to thousands of hoarse-voiced, towel-waving fans.

"Some fans weren't letting go," said Lincecum, whose next assignment would be Game 1 of the NL Division Series against the wild-card Atlanta Braves. "You can see how much they invested in our season.... I'm just stuttering my words right now. I'm so excited to celebrate this and push forward."

The Padres, eliminated after leading the division most of the season, slumped away. They had squeezed everything they could out of their roster, won dozens more games than anyone had predicted. Bud Black would be named NL Manager of the Year in spite of the way their season ended.

They beat the Giants 12 times in 18 games. It wasn't enough.

"I was right," said a champagne-soaked Sanchez, who posted a 1.03 ERA in his last seven starts. "I believed in the team, you know? We're always together. Look at our team. Look at everybody. We have everything we need to win."

Sanchez saved his biggest talk for the mound. He walked five and didn't make it out of the sixth inning, but once again, he refused to give in. He did everything he could to win.

"You know what? This is one of those games that defines your career," Posey said. "For him to come out and have the poise he had...Wow. You could tell he had it. I didn't see nerves. It was more pure focus."

The Giants were heading to the postseason for the first time in seven years, and so much had changed since then. This wasn't a team dominated by one surly slugger. The Bonds window had closed, but a different one had opened, bringing so much fresh air with it. And all of Northern California was ready to jump through and join them.

Even as Sabean took waves upon waves of criticism for not replacing Bonds with a fearsome slugger, the GM refused to break up his home-grown rotation. Now these pitchers looked capable of taking the Giants deep into October.

"In the past we lived and died with one superstar player," Sabean said. "There aren't any superstars on this team. There might be a couple rising stars, but our organization is built on pitching. I can't say enough for our scouts and player development people, especially Dick Tidrow.

"And quite frankly I've got to thank Peter Magowan and even Bill Neukom for keeping me around for two tours of duty. A lot of organizations wouldn't have allowed us to soldier on and have some continuity. They were proven right."

Wilson, who so respected the Giants' legends and traditions, said all along that he didn't want to break the late Rod Beck's franchise record of 48 saves in a season. He knew how much Beck meant to the people who played with him and fans who cheered him. With Beck's mullet and Fu-Manchu blowing in the breeze and his arm dangling, Beck was the every-man ballplayer. He was on their level. Years later, when he was reviving his career for the Cubs' Triple A team in Des Moines, he lived in a trailer behind the stadium. He wouldn't just sign autographs for fans, he'd invite them in for a beer.

On the final day of the regular season, Wilson recorded his 48th save. He would share the record with Beck. It was just one more perfect way for this 162-game season to end.

"As far as I'm concerned, he still has the record, and I'll stand beside him," Wilson said.

Beck would've fit right in with this team. They were about to stage one hell of a party.

Lincecum, stopped in the dugout by Comcast reporter Amy Gutierrez, couldn't contain his euphoria. He was on live television and the interview was being carried on the stadium big screen to a ballpark that remained full of fans. But Lincecum didn't care about that.

"Are you ready for your champagne shower?" he was asked.

"F— yeah!" he said.

It was the most memorable F-bomb dropped by a Giant on live television since the 1987 team clinched the division and Will Clark, in just his second season, shrieked in that high-pitched, Louisiana voice of his as he shook up another bottle of champagne.

"WHOOO! We did it, that's goddamn right.... I've been waiting a long time for this...since the f—ing amateurs!"

Clark had lifted that team with his sweet swing, competitive fire, and notorious Nuschler scowl. Now Giants fans had another supremely gifted young player, Posey, who portrayed a different kind of confidence on the field. And you could tie this team's turnaround to a single event—the decision to trade Molina and entrust their pitching staff to a rookie who didn't start catching until his sophomore year of college.

The Giants were 40–38 on the day they traded Molina. They went 52–32 the rest of the way. But unlike Will the Thrill, Posey didn't test the censors amid the celebration.

"Naw, naw. Not me," said good ol' Buster, standing off to the side. "I'm just happy for all these guys in here, probably more than for myself."

Huff surveyed Posey wiping the champagne from his eyes and laughed.

"Screw him, man!" Huff yelled. "First year in the big leagues and he makes the playoffs. I don't want to hear it."

After all those years at the bottom of the AL East, all those years of false hope and meaningless Septembers, all those years of playing for himself because he had no other choice, Huff could call himself a major league winner.

And the Giants could call themselves NL West champions. They were going to the postseason. And a certain piece of skimpy red underwear was coming along.

Huff nailed it: the Rally Thong went exactly 20–10, just as he promised.

Chapter 10

A Nickel for Your Thoughts

In his 14 years as a professional ballplayer, Bruce Bochy never had a comfortable spring training.

He was the 25th man on the roster, the third-string catcher. His place on the team wasn't secure until the moment the first pitch was thrown on Opening Day. Sometimes a team decided to carry that extra pitcher or add another left-handed bat. Bochy would be the victim of those decisions. So much of his future was out of his hands.

He wasn't the only one left hanging until the last minute. His wife, Kim, was raising their two sons. She had accompanied him no matter where he played, even if it was a winter league stop in Venezuela and they only had a frying pan and a barely functioning water heater in their hotel room. Bochy knew better than most: the whims of management affected real people and real families.

It was an experience that Bochy didn't forget when he entered a coaching career, first in the minor leagues, then elevated to manager Jim Riggleman's staff in San Diego, and finally, as a big-league skipper himself.

Bochy didn't spend all day coddling his star players. He'd spend most of batting practice moving around the infield and outfield, checking in with as many of his "little boogers" as he could. It might be a small-talk question about their family, a comment on the previous night's game, or even a minor scolding over a poor decision on the base paths. There were times when he'd call a player in his office for a more serious discussion, but he didn't make a scene over it. Some managers needed to show their players who was boss. Bochy didn't see the point in that, nor did his ego demand it.

He didn't need to put on airs to relate to the players. He just did.

Bochy took the same approach in his twice-daily dealings with the media. He answered questions as honestly as he could, but very seldom would he try to send a message to a player through the newspaper. If a strategic move backfired, he wouldn't spend five minutes explaining all the reasons why his thought process was sound. He'd only do that if he wanted to show everybody how smart he was, and he didn't spend much time worrying about things like that.

Nobody likes to be savaged in the press, but Bochy paid only scant attention to the prevailing opinion of columnists, pundits, or fans. He was accountable to the people who mattered most—his staff, the organization, and his players—and that was enough.

With his slow, baritone grumble, you might mistake Bochy for being as dimwitted as the Billy Bob Thornton character in *Sling Blade*. Yet you'd be mistaken. When the cameras clicked off and the notepads were put away, Bochy would show you his dry, cutting sense of humor.

Often his best jokes were at his own expense, usually pertaining to his famously large head. His size 8⅛ cap was the largest that the New Era Company made for anyone in the big leagues.

One time at old Veterans Stadium in Philadelphia, the ever-creative Phanatic was lampooning the Padres as they were announced. When Bochy's name boomed over the PA system, the mascot grabbed his head like it was too heavy for his neck to support, and fell to the turf. All the players in the Padres dugout laughed, then they turned a wary eye to Bochy. They saw he was laughing harder than anyone.

All through his playing career, Bochy wore the same catching and batting helmets because he couldn't find a replacement that fit him. Every time he changed organizations or rode the Triple A shuttle, he'd have to paint his helmets to match his team colors. Once he threw his helmet in a burst of frustration in the dugout and it split down the middle. He had to glue it back together.

In the minor leagues, whenever he had a game-winning hit, his teammates used his helmet to ice down a whole six-pack. He's heard the old joke too many times to count: "What would you rather have—a million dollars or Bochy's head full o' nickels?"

Helmet maintenance aside, the itinerant baseball life never bothered Bochy. He was accustomed to a transient existence, following his father, Gus, a U.S. Army Sergeant Major, all over the world. The third of four children, Bochy was born at an Army installation near Bussac, France. Before he graduated high school, he had lived in the Panama Canal Zone, South Carolina, northern Virginia, and Melbourne, Florida.

Years later, when Kim finally persuaded him to go on a European vacation, they drove into the French countryside and visited the town of his birth. They didn't find any evidence of an Army facility, and the locals raised their palms in confusion. When he returned home, he told his sister, Terry, what had happened.

"Turns out we went to the wrong Bussac," he said.

Bochy did more watching than playing during a nine-year big-league career with the Houston Astros, New York Mets, and San Diego Padres. As a 25-year-old third-string catcher in 1980 with Houston, he received just 28 plate appearances and didn't score a single run all season. But he found a comfortable existence in San Diego, where he was the Padres' backup catcher for five years, including their trip to the World Series in 1984.

The urge to manage first struck him in San Francisco, of all places. He was squatting in the bullpen at Candlestick Park when he broke his hand while warming up a pitcher. It was Opening Day 1987, and he was 32 years old.

"I had a lot of time to reflect while on the disabled list," he said. "I was coming to the end of my playing career. I thought managing was something I would love to do."

Two years later Bochy was filling out lineup cards at the Padres' Class A affiliate in Spokane. Shortly after that, he ended up on Riggleman's big league staff.

For all its surf culture, perfect weather, and swaying palm trees, San Diego is a big-time military town. There are seven bases or installations nearby. The Top Guns scream overhead at Miramar, and Marines march across Camp Pendleton. It's a regular spectacle at Padres games when hundreds of camouflage-clad Marines, in boot-stamping unison, file into a section of the upper deck. File-in, file-out is a way of life for so many in San Diego.

But Bochy remained a fixture there. He spent a total of 24 years in the Padres organization, from the time he signed as a 27-year-old catcher to his 12th and final season as manager. The small-market Padres won four NL West titles on his watch, often with talent-depleted rosters.

Bochy had borrowed his temperament from his manager in Houston, Bill Virdon, who kept an understated, even keel. You always knew where you stood with Virdon, who was honest with his players. Bochy also borrowed a bit from Dick Williams, his fiery manager with the Padres, who obsessed over details and fundamentals.

Bochy brought something unique to the bench, too. So many ex-catchers had become successful managers because they understood how many hundreds of little decisions go into winning a ballgame. Bochy had that background. But he also had spent a lifetime warming up pitchers in the bullpen. He understood that relief pitchers are more comfortable when they have set roles and a clear expectation for when they're going to enter a ballgame. He also knew they had a finite amount of bullets, and it didn't do any good to waste them. If Bochy warmed you up, chances are you were going to pitch.

Bochy also understood and respected the grind of a 162-game season. As much as the fans or media wanted to quit on struggling players, Bochy knew he'd have to rely on that guy to make a contribution down the road. A winning team needed its entire roster to stay ready, both physically and mentally.

Bochy had set ideas about running a game, too. While not an adherent to advanced metrics that were changing the way teams valued players, Bochy agreed with the *Moneyball* devotees on a few things. He was loath to give away outs, for example. Bochy's teams usually ranked near the bottom in sacrifice hits. He'd put runners in motion, but usually to stay out of the double play. He liked the three-run home run and he played for big innings. Sure, there were times a team needed to manufacture a run. But to play ultra small ball was to tell your men, "Listen, I don't think you're good enough to score a four-spot. So we're going to bunt that runner over and hope for one hit."

For a similar reason, Bochy also hated the intentional walk. He didn't like telling his pitcher that he didn't have faith in him to retire the next hitter—even if that hitter was Barry Bonds in his prime. It's one of the reasons that Bonds hit more home runs against the Padres than any other team.

Bochy lost a lot of games to the Giants in those years, but it wasn't just Bonds who made an impact.

The Giants had another a secret weapon against the Padres, although he didn't step foot on the field. Pat Dobson, a former major league pitcher who won 20 games for the Baltimore Orioles in 1971, was one of Sabean's most trusted advisors and as good an advance scout as anyone in baseball. It was the Padres' misfortune that he lived in San Diego. "Dobber" saw the Padres more than any other team, and his reports on them were like getting the answer key to the world history midterm.

The Giants always seemed to position themselves perfectly in the field to make the play. Their pitchers could find the hole in any swingin' Friar. At the plate, their hitters knew what pitch sequences the Padres were likely to throw.

Dobson seemed to be made of iron. He never missed a day of work and never got sick. But he hadn't felt well for a few weeks in November 2006, and at the urging of his wife, he went for tests at a local hospital. He was diagnosed with leukemia, and shockingly, he died the very next day. He was 64.

Not long after that, another member of Sabean's inner circle, former major league infielder Ted Uhlaender, was diagnosed with multiple myeloma. Uhlaender had made progress in his fight against the disease when he succumbed to a heart attack in February 2009. He was 68.

Uhlaender owned ranches in Colorado and Kansas, was an avid horseman, and once walked into the baseball winter meetings in Dallas with muddy cowboy boots because he was literally in the middle of a cattle drive, moving a herd down to Austin. He was so well respected in Denver that his memorial service was held at Coors Field—even though he had been working for an NL West rival.

If Dobson knew the Padres' every tendency, Uhlaender had the Rockies scouted just as well inside and out. Having written up thousands of players, the two men were able to provide a frame of reference for anyone who stepped in a batter's box or lifted a leg on the mound. Their human knowledge was a resource more valuable and irreplaceable than any statistical model you could hope to create.

They were just as quick with a joke and could break up the room. Dobber and Teddy together, especially, were a powerful comic team.

For Sabean, the losses were coming in waves. A few months before Uhlaender passed, Sabean's mentor, Joe DiCarlo, had died at the age of 73.

DiCarlo was the ultimate character. He had a thick Jersey accent and worked as a Yankees scout for decades. A Giants series at Shea Stadium wouldn't be complete without the sight of little Joe in the summertime steam, a wet towel around his neck, cracking wise. He had been an immeasurable help to a young Sabean, who climbed up the chain to become the Yankees' scouting director. When Sabean went to San Francisco, DiCarlo followed him there. He had worked for the Giants the last 13 years of his life.

One of Sabean's greatest strengths was his ability to delegate and have faith in his staff. And he listened when Dobson made one final recommendation a few weeks before he passed away.

The Giants had been looking for a manager to replace the dignified Felipe Alou, whose contract wasn't renewed after the team had stumbled through two losing seasons in 2005–2006 while Bonds recovered from knee surgeries.

While announcing that Alou would not return in '07, Sabean described the ideal replacement as "somebody who runs the game at a high level, who is thought to be prepared and actually can make a difference in a game.... You want people who carry their lunch pail and punch the clock, so anybody who can create that type of environment would be attractive."

Sabean thought that Lou Piniella, another familiar face from his days with the Yankees, could be an ideal fit, and he doggedly pursued him. Piniella hated to let Sabean down, but the Cubs were coming hard after him, too. Piniella looked at the rosters of both clubs and had to be honest: the Cubs were in better shape to contend in the near term. He took himself out of the running for the Giants job.

Sabean interviewed Manny Acta, the Mets' bright third-base coach who came highly recommended. He talked to former Giants left-hander

Bud Black, who was a well-regarded pitching coach in Anaheim under Mike Scioscia. Sabean gave due consideration to Ron Wotus, who was a highly successful minor league manager and served ably as the Giants' bench coach under Alou and Dusty Baker.

Then he heard from Dobson that Bochy might be available. Bochy had one year remaining on his contract, but the Padres had brought Sandy Alderson on board as club president, and there were strong indications they wanted to go in a different direction. They weren't going to fire Bochy—he was making too much money and they weren't going to pay two managers at once—but in a lunch meeting at Del Mar Country Club that felt more like a colonoscopy, Alderson suggested to Bochy that it would be an excellent idea if he pursued other opportunities.

Bochy was floored. The Padres were coming off their second consecutive NL West title. He had hoped to begin negotiations on an extension. Instead, he was being told to get lost—and in a lily-livered, passive-aggressive way, too.

It wasn't just a personal affront to Bochy. It also was a professional slight. He believed in being honest and upfront with his players. Now the small-market Padres, which he had led to four division titles and a World Series appearance in his 12 seasons, couldn't be honest with him.

Dobson told Sabean: "I don't know what's happening there, but this is a guy you want to hire."

Dobson had taken note of how Bochy ran a game. He liked the way his teams always seemed loose and yet accountable to each other. Dobson loved how Bochy managed a pitching staff—a quality that would be needed in the next Giants manager as the organization sought to rebuild behind its young rotation.

The Giants also needed somebody with enough stature who could handle the one-year migraine of Bonds' march to the all-time home run record and the daily media storm that would accompany it. An egotistical manager would be ruinous with Bonds around. Bochy had the self-assurance to handle an impossible situation and the accomplished résumé to maintain authority.

And so Bochy, a military brat since birth, packed his duffel bag yet again.

"You know, I couldn't feel more comfortable now," he said, on the day he was introduced as the Giants' manager and pulled a snug black cap on his head—size 8, the biggest anyone could find on short notice. "I would not have made a change if I was uncomfortable with where I was going. San Francisco is the right fit. I'm not going to have any problems turning the page."

Of course, he was asked about the Padres. Every time, he took the high road. With clipped answers, he said he appreciated everything about his time there but he was moving forward. After a while, the questions stopped.

Bochy turned into more than just a capable manager for Sabean. They became tremendous friends, as well, and so did their wives. When Sabean's wife, Amanda, went into labor, Kim assisted in the delivery and was asked to become a godmother to the baby boy.

Sabean's inner circle, which had suffered so many losses in recent years, became a lively place again. He and Bochy stayed long after games, talking over scenarios, roster moves, and pitching matchups. Unlike Dusty Baker, who often became impulsively defensive when Sabean asked about a decision in a game, Bochy relished the opportunity to talk ball. He and Sabean didn't always agree, but they stayed on the same page.

In the Bay Area, though, Bochy was not a popular choice to replace Alou. He wasn't new and exciting like Acta. He wasn't the loyalty pick, as Wotus would've been. His charisma wasn't the kind that showed up in a 10-second sound bite or within quote marks in the newspaper.

Manager Bruce Bochy integrated a roster filled with castoffs and eccentrics, whom he called his "Dirty Dozen," and guided them to the Giants' first World Series championship in 56 years.

Giants fans were desperate for a new direction after years of broken-down veterans. They wanted Bochy to stuff his lineup with young players and remain patient if they fell into deep slumps. They knew Bochy's reputation for preferring veteran players in San Diego and considered him the wrong field manager for a rebuilding club.

The blogosphere nearly imploded when Neukom gave two-year extensions to Bochy and Sabean after the '09 season, even though the results on the field warranted the move. The team finished 88–74, breaking a streak of four consecutive losing seasons and making a 16-game improvement from the previous year.

For all Bochy had accomplished as a major league manager, there weren't many in the Bay Area who thought of him as a particularly astute person. But those perceptions began to change with a single event in 2010.

It was the night of July 20 at Dodger Stadium, and even by rivalry standards, it had been a nutty game. The Dodgers' Matt Kemp had glared at Lincecum after getting hit by a pitch. Later in the game Dodgers lefty Clayton Kershaw plunked Rowand, drawing an immediate ejection for the pitcher as well as manager Joe Torre. Bench coach John Schaefer already had been ejected for arguing balls and strikes, so the team was left in the hands of hitting coach Don Mattingly.

When the Giants loaded the bases in the ninth inning against struggling closer Jonathan Broxton, Mattingly went to the mound to go over the infield defense. He began to walk off the mound, then turned around when first baseman James Loney asked a question.

Bochy sprang from the dugout as fast as his bad knees and arthritic hips allowed. He immediately cited Rule 8.06(b), arguing that Mattingly made a second mound visit and that Broxton would have to be removed from the game as a result.

Crew chief Tim McClelland agreed with Bochy's interpretation, and a dumbfounded Mattingly accepted his rookie-ball mistake. Left-hander George Sherrill entered with minimal warmup time, and Torres ripped a two-run double to center field. The Giants took a 7–5 victory, and although Bochy didn't receive credit for a win or a save in the box score, his sharp actions were acknowledged as a major factor.

It wasn't the first time Bochy called the Dodgers on Rule 8.06(b). With the Padres in 2006, he caught then–Dodgers manager Grady Little on a double-back visit with Brad Penny on the mound. Little was forced to take out his starting pitcher, and the Padres won that game, too.

After he hoodwinked Mattingly, Bochy sought to deflect credit.

"Well, I saw it. I was watching," he said. "I knew they had to make a change. The umpires got it right, but it still takes Andres delivering there."

When the teams met at AT&T Park on August 1, Bochy tried to get in the Dodgers' heads again. He asked plate umpire Joe West to check the end line of the batter's box, where Dodgers third baseman Casey Blake had kicked the chalk away. Bochy asked West to use Blake's bat to measure the end line. It was one of those infractions that hitters get away with all the time, wasn't it?

"It's illegal," Bochy said plainly, with a hint of a smile. "It's been brought up before on our side, too."

Cameras caught Kemp on first base, scowling with clear annoyance over the brief delay. But perhaps the head game worked just as Bochy had hoped. A moment later Cain picked a distracted Kemp off first base.

There seldom was a detail on the field that Bochy missed. A few years earlier at Miller Park he noticed that his backup catcher, Guillermo Rodriguez, who'd just been promoted following a long career in the minor leagues, was zipping his throws back to the mound with a little too much gusto. Bochy was afraid Rodriguez might sail one over the pitcher's head. So he asked veteran second baseman Ray Durham to slide over a few steps, just to be safe.

Durham, never known as a heady player, dutifully followed his manager's orders. In fact, he followed them so well that he kept backing up throws when the Milwaukee Brewers didn't have anyone on base. Finally, when Bochy noticed Durham backing up a throw from the umpire, he had to intercede.

"Ray, listen, I appreciate the effort—really, I do," Bochy said, as gently as possible. "But you know, when the umpire throws it, it isn't a live ball."

Bochy's leadership might have been most valuable when his teams were struggling. It was rare for him to call team-wide meetings, and when he did, they usually lasted as long as your average beer commercial.

On September 18, 2006, in Bochy's last year in San Diego, the Padres lost one of the most stunning games in regular season history. They gave up four consecutive home runs in the bottom of the ninth at Dodger Stadium, then lost 11–10 on Nomar Garciaparra's two-run shot in the 10th.

Bochy simply came to the ballpark the next day like nothing had happened. He told stories in the dugout and kept everyone loose. The Padres beat the Arizona Diamondbacks that night, and won 10 of 13 down the stretch to win the NL West.

Now Bochy could claim five NL West titles in his career, after capturing his first with the Giants.

But when his Giants entered the 2010 pennant stretch, and the Padres were in the midst of their 10-game losing streak, Bochy decided his boys needed a jolt of confidence. So on September 3 he closed the visiting clubhouse at Dodger Stadium for a pregame meeting. Minutes later the players filed out for batting practice with smiles on their faces, leading to any number of theories.

Did Bochy wear the Machine's mask? Did he put on the Rally Thong? Or both?

It was neither. Bochy wheeled in a television on a cart, like a fifth-grade science teacher, and flipped on the scene from *Braveheart* in which William Wallace, portrayed by Mel Gibson, steels his Scotsmen for battle.

Bochy added no postscript. The players got the message. In fact, they would exclaim, "*Freedom!*" in the postgame handshake line the remainder of the season.

Now the Giants had won the season-long battle, finishing September with an 18–8 record and outlasting the Padres to win the NL West on the final day of the regular season. It was Bochy's fifth career postseason team—more than any Giants skipper could boast since the legendary John McGraw.

But Bochy had decisions to make. As a player, he dreaded every cutdown day. Now he had to whittle his 40-man roster down to 25 for the postseason. Bochy respected everyone's effort and contributions. But now he had to tell some players who'd battled their asses off all season that they wouldn't be on the team.

Some of the decisions were obvious. Zito was the only pitcher in the rotation with postseason experience, but he also was the unquestioned weakest link in the rotation over the second half. The Giants' No. 4 starter would be lined up to pitch a potential Game 4 at Atlanta, and Zito hadn't won in 13 road starts since May 5. He was coming off that inexcusable game against the Padres, when he had a chance to lock down the division and instead walked in two runs in the first inning.

Meanwhile, Bumgarner was just 21 years old and in uncharted territory in terms of workload, but he kept throwing harder and locating better as the year went on. He had a 1.18 ERA in his last six starts, and he'd been even better on the road.

In the regular season Zito probably would've gotten the benefit of the doubt. But this was the playoffs. And Bochy was about to show all of San Francisco that he manages a little differently in the postseason.

He left Zito off the roster.

"Barry is such a good teammate and a stand-up guy," Bochy said. "I think it's fair to say the other four are throwing a bit better right now...."

Believe me, it's tough when you [leave off] a guy who's a big reason you are here."

The team's next two highest-paid players, Rowand and Renteria, were on the bubble, too, but Bochy decided to keep them.

Bochy had started Renteria on October 1 in the opener of the Padres series, because he wanted to see if the veteran shortstop was healthy. In the postseason, Bochy knew he could trust a veteran like Renteria with a big at-bat or a bouncing ball hit in his direction. Someone who owned a walk-off hit in Game 7 of the World Series would know how to control his emotions in that environment. Sure, Renteria looked physically done for most of the year, but Bochy knew the veteran shortstop would be an asset at some point in the playoffs.

Besides, Renteria had recent history against Braves closer Billy Wagner—a heroic, two-run home run off him in the April 9 home opener. It tied the score, and the Giants went on to win 5–4 in 10 innings.

Rowand also made the roster by virtue of his history against the Braves pitching staff. He was 11-for-23 off right-hander Derek Lowe, a postseason veteran who would oppose Lincecum in Game 1. Rowand also was 8-for-21 against Tim Hudson, who was scheduled to go for Atlanta in Game 3.

Most of those numbers came a lifetime earlier, when Rowand was in his prime years with the Chicago White Sox. He clearly wasn't the same hitter now. He had a .123 average since August 4 and received just four at-bats in the last 15 games of the season. But he contributed a pinch home run during the final Padres series that nearly sparked a comeback victory. And Rowand owned a World Series ring, too, with the 2005 White Sox.

Bochy had one more decision to make. He had pushed hard for the Giants to acquire Jose Guillen from the Kansas City Royals in August, even though the outfielder would be joining his 10th major league team and had a well-documented history as a problem in the clubhouse.

It was a testament to their manager and the welcoming nature of the club that Guillen didn't cause any noticeable problems with teammates in his short stint with the Giants. Bochy even went so far as to call him "a good team player" on the day the Giants acquired him—a description that probably won't be Guillen's epitaph.

Guillen did provide a reward on rare occasions, most notably his six-RBI game against the Brewers to help the Giants avoid a sweep in mid-September. But that was his last good act as a Giant. His neck was bothering him again, and Bochy kept running him out there anyway, starting him in 15 of the final 16 games of the season.

It had become clear that Bochy had a better right-field option in Cody Ross, whom the Giants had claimed from Florida, ostensibly to keep him away from the Padres. Ross was a high-energy athlete whose defense was far superior to Guillen's in right field. Ross filled in admirably while Andres Torres recovered from his appendectomy, batting .344 with three home runs over a nine-game hitting streak. When Ross came off the bench in the opener of that final series against the Padres, he had two doubles among his three hits.

The Giants didn't have to announce their NLDS roster until the morning of Game 1 at AT&T Park. And when the lineup cards were posted, Ross was in right field. Guillen was a surprising omission from the roster.

It hadn't become public knowledge yet, but some time in late September federal investigators had busted Guillen's wife when she signed for a package that contained 50 preloaded vials of human growth hormone, according to the *New York Daily News*. The feds had been monitoring the supplier and seized the shipment at San Francisco International Airport, then posed as a delivery service to set up the sting. This was nothing new for Guillen. He was named prominently in the

Mitchell Report for having shipments of anabolic steroids sent to Oakland Coliseum during a brief stint with the A's in 2003.

When the investigation was reported during the World Series, Bochy insisted that Guillen's neck pain was the reason the outfielder didn't make the roster. But the *New York Times* quoted sources close to the investigation saying that Major League Baseball learned of the bust just prior to the start of postseason play, and that the Giants had been advised to take Guillen out of the picture.

Whatever the reason, Guillen had dropped from sight by the second game of the NL Division Series, never to be seen near the team again. Ross would start in right field the rest of the postseason. It turned out to be a blessing in more ways than one.

The roster wasn't the only conundrum that weighed on Bochy's mind. He didn't have the benefit of a set lineup like the Yankees or Phillies. He mixed and matched his personnel, rode the hot hand, played educated hunches, and often platooned to get ideal matchups. Torres, as amazing as his season had been, remained a much weaker hitter from the right side. The same was true of Sandoval, whose playing time had been cut significantly over the previous two weeks.

Sandoval would be Bochy's most difficult lineup decision.

The Kung Fu Panda remained ultra popular with fans, who snapped up furry, black and white hats faster than vendors could fill their baskets. Yet his season had been such a colossal disappointment—and not just because his average fell from .330 to .268, his homers dropped off from 25 to 13, and his slugging percentage plummeted 150 points.

Sandoval had become unreliable at third base, too. He entered the season a few doughnuts shy of morbidly obese after a highly publicized "Camp Panda" fitness boot camp failed to deliver lasting results. He couldn't field a half-dozen practice grounders without panting in exhaustion. He wasn't moving as well to his left or right, and although he once had a highly accurate arm, he'd lost some agility. His footwork suffered, and he was throwing wildly as a result.

When the Giants visited Atlanta in August, Sandoval had gotten thrown out at third base after Lincecum tried to advance him with a sacrifice bunt. Bochy had assumed that Sandoval missed the sign and got a late jump. When he went back to look at the replay, he was shocked at what he saw. Sandoval hadn't missed the sign. He was just that alarmingly slow.

Yet you had to root for Pablo. He maintained his sense of fun on the field, often blowing bubbles while fielding ground balls. He remained the loudest, towel-waving cheerleader in the dugout. He was the mastermind behind all the coordinated handshake rituals, and he constantly chattered words of support in two languages.

In that heated game at Dodger Stadium, when Matt Kemp glared at Lincecum and took two threatening steps toward the mound, Posey was slow to react from behind the plate. But Sandoval sprinted from his position, protecting Lincecum with the devotion and determination of an attack dog. The Panda remained fiercely loyal to his teammates, and he had a big heart.

Behind the scenes, the Giants also knew that Sandoval had a difficult season from a personal standpoint. He and his wife had divorced the previous year. Now he was fighting for custody of his two-year-old daughter, Yoleadny. He took a three-day personal leave after the All-Star break to attend court proceedings in Venezuela.

If that weren't enough, Sandoval received more jarring news in September, when the house he had been renting in San Bruno, just south of San Francisco, had to be evacuated because of a gas explosion that killed seven people and destroyed more than 50 homes. Sandoval's house was just outside the destruction zone, but his mother, who didn't drive, had to leave with only the clothes she was wearing. The Giants were playing in San Diego at the time. When Sandoval returned to San Francisco, he still smelled gas in the house. He walked out and never returned.

With the playoffs about to begin, Bochy decided to put his faith in Sandoval. But if the Panda missed another sign or threw to the wrong base, if he let the pressure of the postseason build up and let the game get too fast, then Bochy would have to make a change.

Bochy knew he couldn't afford to make a mistake—not when he'd be matching wits with Atlanta's Bobby Cox, the major league manager he most admired. Cox, 69, was finishing his 21st and final season in a run that saw the Braves win five pennants and a stunning 14 consecutive division titles.

"I revere this guy so much," Bochy said. "We all venerate this guy because of what he's accomplished, and I'm glad he's in the playoffs. I know we have our hands full playing them."

Cox might have done his best job in his final season, coaxing just enough victories out of an injury-ravaged team to win the wild-card.

The Giants and Braves were mirror images. As usual, Atlanta had three exceptional starting pitchers in Lowe, Hudson, and young Tommy Hanson, to go along with a nasty bullpen that matched the Giants in every respect.

They knew torture in Atlanta, too. Sure, the Giants completely overhauled their Opening Day lineup during the season, with only Huff and Sandoval at the same positions. But the Braves were forced into a similar makeover because of injuries to Martin Prado and Chipper Jones. They had traded their inconsistent starting shortstop, Yunel Escobar, for veteran Alex Gonzalez. Their only constants from Opening Day were Brian McCann, the catcher whose double won the All-Star Game for the National League, and Jason Heyward, the super-talented rookie right fielder who ended Buster Posey's high school career.

Like the Giants, the Braves simply hoped to scratch out a couple of runs—string together a few hits or pop one out of the park at the right time—to support a very good pitching staff.

Both teams entered with their claws sharpened, too, after battling to their 162nd game to reach the postseason.

"I know you have to play your best ball to beat this team," Bochy said. "You're not going to surprise Bobby over there. You know you've got to be ready for anything, be on your toes."

The team that pitched better and made fewer mistakes in the field would win. It was Lincecum's time to prove he could handle the pressure of being a postseason ace.

In the middle of the NL West champagne celebration, after the Giants' families were allowed to join the revelry, Chris Lincecum sipped his beer and jabbed his elbow into a friend's chest.

"Don't worry," he said. "Timmy's got this."

Chapter 11

Held in Check

The Giants were on the eve of their playoff opener with the Braves, but all anyone wanted to talk about was Phillies ace Roy Halladay.

The right-hander already had thrown a perfect game during the regular season. Now he had thrown a no-hitter in his first career playoff start as the heavily favored Phillies took the advantage in their Division Series with the normally potent Cincinnati Reds.

This was big stuff. It was the first no-hitter in the postseason since Don Larsen's perfect game for the Yankees in the 1956 World Series.

Lincecum, looking half-asleep during his mandatory trip to the interview room, was asked if he'd watched any of Halladay's game.

"Yeah, I mean, all the TVs were on showin' it, so…yeah," he said.

Asked for a reaction, Lincecum was disinterested.

"Great for him, but obviously we're concerned with ourselves," he said.

Lincecum had his own difficult opponent to face. As incredibly as the Giants' ace had pitched in September, Atlanta's Derek Lowe took home the NL Pitcher of the Month award after going 5–0 with a 1.17 ERA in his final five starts. The sinker specialist had regained command of his breaking ball, he was a veteran of six postseason teams as a starter and reliever, and he'd be making his 11th playoff start. Lowe also had a history of pitching exceptionally well on short rest—something Lincecum might not be able to match.

The Giants also knew they were under pressure to get off to a hot start in this NL Division Series. They held home-field advantage, but unless they swept the first two games at AT&T Park, they'd be forced to win at least one out of two at Turner Field—where the Braves' 56–25 home record was the best in the majors.

Lincecum kept saying all week that he had to treat it like any other start. One batter into the game, he had to step off the mound, take a deep breath, and truly believe it. Omar Infante had hit a sharp double to left field, and a buzzing crowd at China Basin fell fearfully silent.

"You've done this a thousand times," Lincecum told himself. "We've been in these situations. It's another game and just treat it like that."

In the biggest, most frenzied environment of his life, Lincecum calmed himself down and got Heyward to fly out. Then he struck out Derek Lee and Brian McCann, and walked off the mound to a thunderous ovation.

The Giants' playoff journey did not begin with a wayward step. Tens of thousands of orange rally rags twirled in the stands.

By the end of the second inning, it was clear that Chris Lincecum wasn't blowing smoke. Timmy had it, all right. He threw 14 pitches in that inning, nine of them for strikes—every single one of them a swing and a miss.

Lincecum felt in rhythm on the mound. He and Posey, for all their early lumps working together, had become a seamless duo. They were the first all–Golden Spikes Award battery in major league history, and here they were, fulfilling all their promise and potential.

Lincecum threw his fading change-up, mixed in his slider and spotted his fastball while retiring 19 out of 20 batters following Infante's double. He and Posey switched to more fastballs in the later innings, sensing the Braves were either late or tentative.

"Their swings were telling me what I needed to throw," Lincecum said. "The game will show you.… And I've got Buster back there helping me, so that makes it twice as easy."

Lowe wasn't making it easy on the Giants, either. But they received a break in the fourth, courtesy of the umpires. Posey hit a leadoff single, and Bochy, hoping to stay out of a double-play grounder, started the rookie with a two-strike pitch to Burrell. It was a decision that should've backfired. Burrell struck out, McCann made an accurate throw, and replays appeared to show that second baseman Brooks Conrad applied his high tag before Posey reached second base. But umpire Paul Emmel had the only opinion that mattered.

It was Posey's first stolen base in the major leagues. And the kid was too much of a Boy Scout to lie.

"I guess it's a good thing we don't have instant replay right now," Posey would say afterward. "Beautiful slide, wasn't it?"

Then Braves manager Bobby Cox made a very questionable move. After Lowe struck out Uribe for the second out, Cox ordered an intentional walk to Sandoval, who had flailed at three pitches in his first at-bat. He wanted the matchup with Ross, a player he knew well from facing him in the NL East with the Florida Marlins.

Cox got the ground ball he envisioned. But it was well placed, if not well struck. Infante, who had become the third baseman just weeks earlier because of Martin Prado's injury, allowed the ball to scoot under his glove. It was so slowly hit that left fielder Matt Diaz couldn't reach it in time to make a play on Posey, who scored easily.

Ross was credited with a single. Cox disagreed with the scoring decision.

"We made the right move," Cox said after the game, tersely. "We made an error. He made the pitch and got a ground ball. We kicked it."

Tim Lincecum was not rattled by Omar Infante's double to start Game 1 of the NLDS. He mixed change-ups, sliders, and fastballs to find his rhythm and overwhelm Atlanta in a 14-strikeout performance.

Meanwhile, Lincecum kicked it into overdrive. Even though he wasn't throwing in the mid- to upper 90s any longer, the Braves couldn't catch up to his heat. He didn't allow a second hit until McCann doubled in the seventh and advanced on a ground ball. With the tying run 90 feet away, Lincecum calmly pumped a first-pitch fastball, and Diaz flied out to end the inning.

A 1–0 lead never looked so insurmountable. Lincecum retired the final six hitters in order, striking out four of them, and finished with 14 strikeouts in a two-hit shutout.

It wasn't Halladay's no-hitter, but it was every bit as dominant, and perhaps more. None of the Giants relievers made so much as a cleat mark on the bullpen mounds.

Romo got as far as unbuttoning his jacket in the eighth inning before Lincecum set down pinch-hitter Eric Hinske.

"They said to go warm up, and I'm thinking, 'Why?'" Romo said. "Hey, I was a fan today. I was entertained from the first pitch to the last pitch. I've never seen that before, especially in the magnitude of a game like this.

"Holy cow. [Lincecum] had his A-plus game today."

Against the Braves, an organization steeped in tremendous pitching talent, Lincecum performed with Tom Glavine's accuracy, John Smoltz's fearlessness, and Greg Maddux's serenity.

If either Lincecum or Posey had become unglued in their first post-season game, if either showed any lack of mental preparation or had frayed nerves or allowed any thoughts of inadequacy to creep between their ears, the Giants would've lost. Plain and simple.

Instead, working with Posey was like, well, a contact high.

"Just a relaxed feeling, telling each other we've done this before, no big deal, come out and play the game," Lincecum said. "Throwing to Posey has been so great for me. The guy is a student of the game. He just wants to get better, help us get better."

Unafraid of the Braves' slow bats, Lincecum ended the game with a 92 mph fastball that Derrek Lee, deeply pondering the breaking stuff he'd seen all night, powerlessly watched fly into Posey's mitt.

As the crowd roared and surged with approval, Lincecum only gave an understated pump of his fist and a back-tap bro-hug to Posey. He was a puddle of still water as a stadium reverberated around him.

Nine innings. Two hits. A walk. Fourteen strikeouts. All performed in the eye of an orange hurricane.

No biggie.

Lincecum still had his game face on when he walked into the interview room following the 1–0 win. He could have seized the moment to mock his doubters or delve back into his struggles in August. He had no interest in any of that. He simply wanted to get out of the room as quickly as possible.

"Things feel like they're in the right place," he said. "I think I kept my emotions in check, and I was pretty poised out there."

It's just as well that Lincecum was so understated in the interview room. Nothing he could say would be any louder or more impressive than the performance he had just unleashed. It was like watching Michael Jordan score 69 against the Cleveland Cavaliers or Jerry Rice gliding for 215 receiving yards in the Super Bowl.

It might have been the greatest postseason start in Giants history. Lincecum destroyed the Giants' postseason record of 10 strikeouts, last accomplished by Jack Sanford in Game 5 of the 1962 World Series at Yankee Stadium.

Lincecum generated 31 swings and misses—the most by any major league pitcher in a game all year. The next closest was Brandon Morrow—coincidentally, the pitcher the Mariners had taken ahead of Lincecum in the 2006 draft. Morrow had made the Cleveland Indians swing and miss 25 times in a start on May 5.

"I don't know how many he struck out, but it was more than fingers on my hand," Cox said of Lincecum. "His breaking stuff is always out of the strike zone. Easier said than done. 'Don't swing at it.' It's almost impossible."

Lincecum's 14 strikeouts were the third-most in a shutout in major league postseason history, trailing only Bob Gibson (17) in 1968 and Roger Clemens (15) in 2000.

According to "game score," a stat that attempted to account for the overall dominance of a pitching performance, Halladay's no-hitter was a 94 out of 100. Lincecum scored even higher, with 96. They were ranked as two of the seven greatest starts in postseason baseball history, and they had come on back-to-back days.

Already, the breathy hype began to build: how about Lincecum versus Halladay in Game 1 of the NLCS?

It was not a hypothetical on Lincecum's mind. Not yet, anyway. A day after his start against the Braves, he was still trying to grasp what he'd accomplished.

"You soak it up a little bit," he said during a quiet moment in the dugout tunnel. "You have a little appreciation, maybe a pat-yourself-on-the-ass kind of thing. But then you're getting ready for your next start."

Why such an understated fist pump when the game ended?

"You know, it was almost like the game wasn't over for me," he said. "I was in that mentality where if another batter steps to the plate, I want to be ready for it. You could even see I was surprised to get the ball from Buster when he threw it at me. It's been so long since I've thrown a complete game. I forgot all about that."

Lincecum's lifetime coach and father, Chris, the only person whose belief in him never wavered an instant, had an even harder time processing the moment. "It was one of those situations where he's got to pinch himself a little bit, I think," Tim Lincecum said of his dad. "It's hard for him to believe what's been going on this year and the last couple years. It takes a little perspective to teach him to be supportive and just be a fan."

He was a blubbering idiot?

"Yeah," Timmy said, smiling. "Yeah, he kind of was."

One night later, the Giants were stunned silent. They were six outs away from winning Game 2 and taking command of the series behind their impenetrable bullpen, which had ended the season with 24 consecutive scoreless innings.

But the Braves rallied for a 5–4 victory, evening up the best-of-five series and accomplishing everything they had hoped when they landed in San Francisco. They split on the road, and now they could clinch the series by defending their home turf.

It was a game that scared the Giants in more ways than one. In the first inning Posey and Sandoval collided as if they ran red lights at an intersection. They were chasing a foul pop and neither heard the other calling for the ball. Both remained on the grass for several seconds— Posey holding his shoulder, and Sandoval trying to get some breath back in his lungs. The ballpark fell silent.

Both players remained in the game, but Posey's ribs were sufficiently sore that he went for precautionary X-rays afterwards.

The fiercest punch to the midsection was yet to come.

The Giants had built a lead on Burrell's three-run home run in the first inning off Hanson, and Cain pitched brilliantly while holding the Braves to an unearned run in 6⅔ innings. Cain also chipped in an RBI single after Ross hit a double in the second inning.

Cain didn't seem to levitate above the rubber like Lincecum did in Game 1. But he was almost as effective, throwing his fastball on the fringes while scattering seven hits. He walked off the mound to a standing ovation after Infante hit a two-out single in the seventh, and with the crowd chanting "*Po-sey's bet-ter*," Javier Lopez froze Heyward on a slider to end the inning.

But Atlanta led the NL with 46 come-from-behind victories in the regular season, and they threatened when Lee and McCann hit consecutive singles off Romo to begin the eighth.

Bochy attacked the flickering rally with a pressure hose. He bypassed all options and went straight to Wilson, asking his well-rested closer to convert the first six-out save of his career.

The move was questioned in the national media and on the TBS broadcast, but everyone in the Giants' dugout understood that Wilson was well equipped for this. He had pitched two innings or more 12 times in his career, and 10 of his saves in 2010 had been assignments of four outs or more. It was the most by a major league closer since the Red Sox's Jonathan Papelbon in 2008.

Melky Cabrera was no match for Wilson's fastball, but the outfielder managed to hit a tapper to third base. And like Ross's roller a day earlier, Cabrera found a weak seam in the Giants defense.

Sandoval, who had become so unreliable at third base, confirmed Bochy's worst fears. He rushed his throw, pulling Huff off first base, and Cabrera was safe as a run scored. It was 4–2, and after a sacrifice bunt moved the tying runs into scoring position, Wilson made his one mistake of the inning. He left a fastball at the belt to Alex Gonzalez, who lashed it for a double to tie the game.

Wilson had seen Gonzalez struggling to catch up to fastballs from Lincecum and Cain. He and Posey felt they could blow it past his bat. But Gonzalez was ready for it.

It wasn't the only second-guess that Posey would have to wash off in defeat. The Giants nearly won the game in the 10th inning after Renteria surprised the ballpark with a perfect bunt against Wagner, the hard-throwing Braves closer he had victimized for that home run way back in April. Renteria was thinking about duplicating that home run swing on the first pitch, and took a huge rip at it. But he missed, and with Troy Glaus now playing out of position at third base following a double-switch, Renteria abruptly changed his strategy. He laid down a perfect bunt. It was a brilliant bit of small ball.

Torres followed with a sacrifice bunt, and Wagner screamed in pain as he bounded off the mound to field it. He had strained a muscle in his side and limped off with the help of trainers. Months earlier Wagner had signaled his intention to retire after the season. Now he had ripped his oblique muscle, an injury that would take weeks to heal. He had thrown his last major league pitch.

The Braves brought in erratic reliever Kyle Farnsworth, who hit Freddy Sanchez on the hand with a pitch and walked Huff to load the bases. Posey stepped to the plate, and the crowd stood, fully anticipating a walk-off hero act from the unbelievable rookie catcher.

But Posey grounded into a double play, ending the inning. And the Giants' bullpen blinked in the 11th. Ramirez left a pitch in Rick Ankiel's happy zone, and the former pitcher crushed a high drive into McCovey Cove. It was the second splash home run in a postseason game at China Basin. Barry Bonds was the only other player to do it.

"To be honest with you," said Ankiel, "I wanted to go from the batter's box to the dugout. I didn't want to run the bases. I wanted to be with the guys."

Cox wasn't there to greet him. He had been ejected for arguing a play on the bases in the second inning. It was one final hat toss in a feisty career that included a major league record 158 ejections in the regular season.

The Giants had absorbed so many tough losses over the season—the longest game in Coors Field history, the 10-run comeback and eventual loss to the Reds, the 12-inning back-and-forth defeat at Colorado—but this would be tougher to wash off than any of them.

"I didn't get the job done," Posey said. "I take pride in being in that situation, and plain and simple, I didn't get it done."

Huff stepped in front of the rookie, saying the failures were team-wide.

"We got the lead early and went into cruise control," he said. "If we get another run or two, there's a chance they fold. We've got to right that ship and have better at-bats when the game is on the line."

Romo thought about those two hits he allowed in the eighth. Wilson shook his head and simply said a loss like that couldn't happen. Sandoval played an abysmal game on both ends. He looked off-balance and over-anxious at the plate while going 1-for-4, his error probably cost Wilson the game, and his collision with Posey nearly caused disaster, too.

There was one bit of good news as the Giants traveled to Atlanta: Posey's X-rays came back negative. So did a scan on Freddy Sanchez, who thought his hand might have been broken by Farnsworth's fastball.

Now the Giants would get on a plane and face another postseason ace, Hudson, who had induced more double plays than anyone in the National League. The Giants had bounced into more than any team in the NL. It seemed destined to be another low-scoring, one-run game.

Chapter 12

Southern Discomfort

On the workout day before Game 3, Bochy kept fielding the same two questions. And he kept dodging them.

Would he start Sandoval again, after such a miserable Game 2? And now that there would most assuredly be a Game 4 in this series, would he replace the rookie, Bumgarner, with Lincecum on three days of rest?

Bochy said he hadn't decided on his Game 4 pitcher. But he dropped a hint about Sandoval's status. "Yeah, we've talked about putting Fontenot in there…and that could happen," he said.

He couldn't have made it any clearer without hiring a skywriter. Sure enough, Mike Fontenot, who had been acquired from the Cubs in August, started at third base. Freddy Sanchez's bruised hand was good enough to start at second base.

When the Giants played their four-game series at Turner Field in August, their pitchers were out of sync, and the Braves took advantage of their mistakes. Now it was the postseason, where every weakness would be exposed. The softest spot in the bullpen, the hardest hands on the infield, the poorest outfield arm—any shortcoming would be laid bare.

Bochy knew Sandoval had become a liability. So the manager gave himself one fewer trouble spot on the field.

The Braves didn't have that option. After all those second-half injuries, they barely could fill out their infield. Troy Glaus had played a total of two innings at third base all season, but he ended Game 2 there. And Brooks Conrad had to play second base.

Everybody knew that Conrad, a former A's minor leaguer who had been a valuable pinch-hitter for Atlanta, was an erratic second baseman. Conrad already had made an error in Game 1, and from the outset of Game 3 at Turner Field, he was having problems yet again. He booted a ball in the first inning, although the Giants failed to score when Uribe grounded out with the bases loaded. Conrad's glove struck again in the second inning, and this time it cost the Braves on the scoreboard. Fontenot had led off the inning with a triple, making Bochy look smart for starting him. Then Ross followed with a pop fly that clanked off Conrad's glove in shallow right field.

Fontenot came home on the error. It was the only run the Giants would score off Hudson, who didn't allow another runner into scoring position until Torres stole second base in the seventh inning.

Meanwhile, the Braves had almost as little chance against Jonathan Sanchez as they had against Lincecum in Game 1. The left-hander took advantage of the afternoon shadows by throwing plenty of curveballs, first locating the pitch for called strikes, then extending the zone with it as the Braves went fishing.

Sanchez took a no-hitter into the sixth inning, when Hudson bounced a single up the middle. Sanchez still appeared strong with a 1–0 lead in the eighth, after Alex Gonzalez led off with a single. Conrad's misery continued when he popped up a sacrifice bunt, bringing Glaus to the plate as a pinch-hitter.

Bochy decided he wanted the right-handed matchup, even though Sanchez had thrown a manageable 105 pitches. He brought in Romo. The skipper got thoroughly outfoxed.

Bobby Cox burned Glaus in favor of pinch-hitter Eric Hinske, a dangerous left-handed batter. It was the worst possible matchup. Hinske had three pinch-homers in the regular season. Romo had allowed six home runs, the most among Giants relievers. Although Romo got two quick strikes, he made a mistake that Hinske lined just inside the right-field pole.

Hinske raised an arm as he rounded first base, and Turner Field thundered. The press box began to shake, and longtime Braves reporters grabbed the countertops as they looked around to make sure the ceiling tiles weren't about to fall down. In all the playoff games they covered in this ballpark, they'd never experienced anything like it.

In an instant, the Braves led 2–1, Sanchez's incredible start was wasted, and the Giants were three outs away from trailing in the series and fighting for their lives the following day.

"That's not a good feeling when you make a change and they hit a two-run homer," Bochy said. "But the 'pen has done a great job all year…. They hit the home run they needed, but what was important is how we handled it."

Righetti went out to visit Romo. He had to yell over the crowd's roar.

"He told me these next two outs are important," Romo said. "Our guys were heartbroken, but they knew we still had a chance. It's tough to get three outs in this league, and basically, we were ready to rock."

Romo snapped off a couple funhouse-mirror sliders to get two fly outs and end the eighth. The Giants faced long odds. Atlanta was 73–3 when leading after eight innings. But the Braves didn't have Wagner, their injured closer, and young Craig Kimbrel didn't always know where his 98 mph fastball was going. With one out in the ninth, Bochy called on Travis Ishikawa, his starting first baseman a year earlier who had been forced to accept a bench role.

Bochy and third-base coach Tim Flannery nicknamed Ishikawa "Smoky." It was a reference to Smoky Burgess, a God-fearing catcher with the Pittsburgh Pirates who found a career as a specialist off the bench and once held the record for career pinch-hits. Flannery's uncle, Hal Smith, had played with Burgess in Pittsburgh. The quiet backup catcher didn't smoke, drink, or swear—and neither did Ishikawa. They were alike in more respects than one.

Ishikawa did what any good pinch-hitter would do. He forced Kimbrel to throw strikes, and when the pitcher wasn't able to split the plate, Ishikawa walked to first base.

Torres had the same idea, but he took a called third strike down the middle. The Giants were down to their final out, and it was up to Freddy Sanchez to extend the game.

Sanchez wasn't just playing with a sore hand. In the final two weeks of the regular season he strained his rotator cuff while trying to turn a double play. Bochy had to talk him into playing a game at Colorado— "If you can't make a play on defense, I'll take the blame for it," the manager told him—and both parties got lucky. Sanchez only had to make one throw during that game, and his lobbed lollipop to first base was sufficient to record the out.

It was fair to wonder about Freddy's toughness. Reporters weren't happy about his off-season shoulder surgery that stayed secret for more than a month. In the spring, Sanchez kept saying he was ahead of schedule in his rehab, even when it became clear he was going to start the season on the disabled list. In early May Bochy phoned Sanchez while the team was in Miami. The manager all but demanded that Sanchez begin his minor league rehab assignment. That way, Bochy figured, at least Sanchez couldn't stall indefinitely. The longest a rehab assignment could last in the minor leagues was 20 days.

Sanchez surprised everyone when he got off to a hot start upon finally joining the Giants in late May. But then he disappeared for long stretches in the second half.

This was a guy who expressed legitimate sadness to be leaving Pittsburgh when the Giants acquired him at the trade deadline in 2009. Sure, he won a batting title when he hit .344 in 2006. But would he be afraid of failure when it mattered? He was 1-for-11 thus far in the postseason. Maybe he simply wasn't a winner.

Now he was the only batter standing between the Braves and a series-altering victory.

He swung through the first two pitches.

But you don't win a batting title without trusting your hands, and with the Giants down to their final strike, Sanchez trusted himself. He hit a chopper up the middle to extend the rally and move the tying run into scoring position.

Then it was Huff's turn. Like Sanchez, he was in his first postseason. He also looked overwhelmed at times while going 2-for-11 with a pair of singles.

But Huff had studied tough left-hander Mike Dunn, whom he faced twice earlier in the series. He figured he'd get a slider, and he'd just have to fight it off. He managed a flare to right field that fell in front of Heyward.

"Longest medium fly ball I've ever hit," Huff said. "I didn't think it was ever going to get down."

Huff couldn't have picked a better time for the first postseason RBI of his career.

Ishikawa sprinted home ahead of the throw, and the only noise in the Turner Field came from the Giants' dugout. Lincecum had scurried like a mouse from one side to the other, trying to get a clear view of home plate as Ishikawa crossed it. Lincecum jumped in the air and the television microphones clearly picked up his exclamation:

"F— YEAH, SHUT UP!"

The moment wasn't lost on Ishikawa: he wore No. 10. And the date was 10–10–10.

"Everyone kept telling me I was going to have a big day," he said, smiling broadly.

The Giants had tied it, and the Braves' night was about to get a lot worse. Posey followed with a ground ball up the middle that looked like a routine out for the second baseman. But Conrad made his third error of the night, allowing it to skip under his glove as Sanchez scored the go-ahead run.

Conrad could only stare straight ahead in disbelief, later saying his impulse was to "dig a hole and go sleep in there." It was the worst day of his professional life. Baseball history was replete with unforgettable goats, going back to Merkle's Boner in 1908. Now Game 3 would be forever known as the "Brooks Conrad Game."

But it wouldn't have happened without clutch, two-out singles by Sanchez and Huff—the biggest hits in their baseball lives. Now the pair of playoff rookies could settle down and settle in. Maybe the Rally Thong had power, after all. Or maybe it had more to do with mettle and belief.

Wilson retired the Braves in the ninth to nail down the 3–2 victory, and the craziest line in the box score was this: Sergio Romo, winning pitcher.

"There's a reason why I love and hate this sport," Romo said. "It's unbelievable. There's ups and downs that you can't explain, things come out of the blue. And, hey man, I got a win in the postseason.

"I love my team. I do. From the bottom of my heart."

It was the 157th postseason game in Giants history. It was the first time they rallied from behind to win in the ninth inning.

"Personally, I don't care how we did it," Ishikawa said. "We're one win away. It's really, really exciting. My legs are still shaking a little bit, to be honest with you."

Cox had gotten the matchup he wanted against Bochy in the eighth inning, Hinske had hit the home run of his life—and yet the Braves still found themselves down to an elimination game.

"Well, we had this one won," Cox said. "We gave up a walk, a base hit, and a base hit.... We're not the best team in baseball, okay? We can win games and compete against anybody. But we can't afford to make mistakes."

Especially with the Giants' rotation giving the Braves no quarter. Jonathan Sanchez struck out 11 in his 6⅔ innings. Before this series, no Giant had struck out more than 10 in a postseason game. Now, with Lincecum and Sanchez, they'd done it to the Braves twice in three games.

Atlanta was hitting .165 with 37 strikeouts in the series.

The Braves already had decided that Derek Lowe would pitch Game 4 on short rest. Everyone assumed the Giants would do the same with Lincecum, if they were facing elimination. Now there was no question the Giants would pitch Bumgarner, and save Lincecum for a potential Game 5.

Unbeknownst to anyone at the time, Bochy had decided to go with Bumgarner in Game 4 no matter what. Bochy had spoken to Lincecum, who insisted he could handle the assignment on short rest. But coaches were concerned with a raw spot on the middle finger of his pitching hand, where his nail had cracked. He had been throwing his slider more frequently, and it tended to exacerbate the problem. They didn't want the small blemish to bloom into a major issue.

Besides, Bochy had confidence in Bumgarner. He liked the kid's confident, sometimes ornery demeanor on the mound. It was apparent to anyone who watched him that he wasn't intimidated by any hitter or any environment. He had a 1.91 ERA in 10 road starts.

Bumgarner didn't need to be told he would get the ball in Game 4.

"I was planning on starting until I was told I wasn't," he said.

When the year began, nobody could have predicted that Bumgarner would be on the mound for the Giants in a playoff game. His spring was a total disappointment to coaches and to Sabean, and it became obvious that he hadn't done any throwing over the winter.

Bumgarner was one of the top prospects in the minor leagues and had amassed a 1.65 ERA on three levels over two seasons on the farm. He had resisted early efforts by coaches to tweak his mechanics, and because his statistics were so overwhelming, club officials couldn't hold him back. Prospect watchers noted with alarm that he'd lost velocity by the middle of 2009, struggling to hit 90 mph at Double A Connecticut. But his deceptive, sidearm delivery was as syrupy as his North Carolina drawl, and minor league hitters simply couldn't see the ball out of his hand. Combine that with his fearlessness and ability to throw strikes with his fastball, and he continued to dominate at every level.

The Giants called him up for the first time in September 2009, hoping he could serve as another left-hander out of the bullpen as they remained on the fringes of contention. Mostly, they wanted to give Bumgarner a taste of the big leagues, believing it would serve him well when they introduced him into their rotation the following year.

But it became apparent early the next spring that Bumgarner wasn't ready. When journeyman Todd Wellemeyer had a few clean exhibition starts, the Giants didn't hesitate to send out Bumgarner with a few weeks remaining in camp.

Bumgarner had walked eight in 11 Cactus League innings, and his fastball was just 87 to 89 mph for most of the spring. Nobody could figure out what happened to the flashy prospect who came up from minor league camp the previous March and threw 95 mph while striking out the Dodgers' Manny Ramirez on three pitches.

There were other factors, though. Bumgarner had been granted leave early in the spring when he received news that his half-sister, Dena, had accidentally overdosed on pain medication following a recent hospitalization. She was engaged to be married, and her 16-year-old son was among her survivors.

Madison Bumgarner overcame a poor spring and personal hardship to arrive at the mound in the postseason, where the rookie's composure served him well in Game 4 of the NLDS against the Atlanta Braves.

Dena and Madison grew up in the same house and were close. The Giants originally termed Bumgarner's leave a family situation, but he was willing to discuss the details with reporters because he hoped everyone would send their prayers to his family, and to his mother, Debbie, in particular.

"She's taking it really rough," he said. "Dena was a good girl. Her family's going to miss her."

Two hours after his flight landed back in Arizona, Bumgarner was throwing off a bullpen mound. He would dedicate the remainder of the season to Dena's memory, and although it might be too late to get in shape to crack the Opening Day rotation, he vowed to push his way back into the team's plans as soon as possible.

At Triple A Fresno, though, Bumgarner made headlines for a different reason. He had allowed his competitive streak to run wild one night, arguing when an umpire called a runner safe following a pickoff throw. Bumgarner had to be restrained from making contact with the umpire, and when he reached the dugout, he flung a baseball into center field. The Pacific Coast League suspended him for three games.

Although Bumgarner was agreeable and soft-spoken off the mound, the Giants knew he had a temper when he stood on the rubber. One time at Double A, he threw behind a hitter and received a warning. After the inning was over, a coach asked if he'd done it intentionally.

"Yeah," Bumgarner said.

"Why?" the coach asked.

"Because he swung too hard," the pitcher replied.

It wasn't long after Bumgarner's Triple A suspension that the Giants needed him in the big leagues. Wellemeyer's spring magic ran out almost as soon as the season began, although he did manage to find a way to beat the Phillies in a game in April.

When Wellemeyer strained his quadriceps while trying to beat out a double-play grounder June 10 at Cincinnati, the injury almost seemed merciful. Bumgarner, who had made steady progress at Fresno, was an immediate upgrade in the No. 5 spot. In July, when the Giants swept the four-game series in Milwaukee that turned around their season, the big left-hander played a major part in it. He threw eight shutout innings, limiting the Brewers to three singles in a 6–1 win at Miller Park.

And when Brewers left-hander Randy Wolf threw off-speed pitches to Bumgarner, the kid clearly was bent on returning the favor. He brushed back Wolf once, then dropped in a slider to strike him out.

It was his first big-league victory, and even though he was 3½ weeks away from his 21st birthday, his teammates lured him into the shower for a dousing of Milwaukee's finest liquid refreshment. Bumgarner was 20 years, 340 days old—the youngest Giant to win a big-league game since Cain, who was exactly one day younger when he broke into the victory column in 2005.

Bumgarner had a special kinship with Posey. They both came from small towns in the South. They both dealt with the pressure of being a No. 1 draft pick. They both married their high school sweethearts. Their fathers even held similar jobs, working in the food distribution business.

Posey had caught Bumgarner in the minor leagues. He knew how to keep the lefty's temper in check.

"I've always said he's a guy who goes out and competes every time," Posey said of Bumgarner. "Even if he doesn't feel good or doesn't have his best stuff, he'll do what he can to give you a chance to win."

When Bumgarner and Posey worked together for the first time at Dodger Stadium, neither rookie was intimidated by the hostile, rivalry-tinged atmosphere. Both used the same word to describe the experience.

"It was fun," they said, almost in stereo.

In a start at St. Louis in August, Bochy was struck by the way Bumgarner went right after Cardinals slugger Albert Pujols in each at-bat. Pujols hit a home run in their final confrontation, but the Giants had a 6–1 lead. By staying aggressive, Bumgarner had done the right thing.

"I'll try to do the same thing in the playoffs," Bumgarner said at the time. "I want to have that intensity every day now. I want to go out there and be intense, throw strikes, and treat every game like a playoff game."

As the Giants got deep into the pennant stretch, Bumgarner was well beyond his professional high for innings in a season, but it didn't seem to matter. He was throwing harder and harder as the year went on, hitting 94 and 95 mph. There was a time when the Giants thought of piggybacking Wellemeyer with the rookie, perhaps alternating starts to alleviate some of the workload. But when Wellemeyer returned from the DL in August, he appeared in just one game, giving up hits to all four batters he faced. Then he was gone for good.

Bumgarner chalked up the improved velocity to his mechanics. He didn't want to listen to minor league coaches as a headstrong 19-year-old who had dominated hitters his entire life. But now he was starting to incorporate some tweaks to increase the extension in his delivery. He continued to work on a straight change-up that Righetti had taught him in the spring. And he wasn't taking days off between starts, either. He was sticking to a running and throwing program.

"I'm learning more about my mechanics as I go," he said. "I never had a reason to mess with them before."

The Giants had taken Lincecum, Bumgarner, and Posey with their first-round picks in successive years—a string of jackpots that would be the envy of any organization. Lincecum and Posey were making an impact in a playoff series. Now it was Bumgarner's chance.

"We have all the confidence in the world that Madison will go out there and give us everything he's got," Bochy said. "This kid has no fear."

Bumgarner was the only member of the rotation that hadn't pitched in Atlanta when the Giants visited in August. But his entire family came from North Carolina for that series, and teammates joked that his kin were "rednecking up" the Ritz-Carlton.

"They've never seen so many pickup trucks in the valet circle," left-hander Jeremy Affeldt said with a good-natured laugh.

Posey's hometown of Leesburg practically shut down for that series in August, too. A Methodist church chartered a bus to take parishioners up to Atlanta. His former grade-school teachers drove across the state to see him play. Folks from Tallahassee made the trip. Everyone in Leesburg was proud of any association they had, however tenuous, to their Buster. They simply wanted to touch the hem of his garment.

Posey didn't give them much to cheer during those four games, though. With his body banged up and his legs heavy, he was 1-for-10 in the series and didn't start the last game.

Now back at Turner Field for the playoffs, Posey was getting a different reception from Braves fans. They heard Giants fans chant "*Po-sey's bet-ter*" whenever Jason Heyward came to the plate in San Francisco. It was all too easy for Braves fans to turned the chant around.

Posey wasn't offended in the slightest. He hadn't considered Atlanta his turf, anyway.

"This is kind of a different world than where I grew up," he said.

By the end of Game 3, the "*Heyward's better*" chants were impossible to justify. He was 0-for-12 with seven strikeouts in the series. Posey was 5-for-12 with two runs and a double.

And while Posey and Barry Bonds were completely different personalities, it turned out they had something in common. They both took great satisfaction in getting booed on the road.

"Yeah," said Posey, with a proud smile. "I loved it."

The story leading into Game 4 was on the Atlanta side, where Conrad, a shattered player after his three-error game, lost his place in the lineup. It was a move the Braves simply had to make. Even the Giants pitied

Conrad. Burrell didn't know him well, but felt compelled to walk over during batting practice and offer a few words of encouragement.

The Giants took the field knowing that in the worst-case scenario, they'd still have Game 5 at home—and Lincecum on the mound. That didn't mean this series would be won easily, though.

In fact, Game 4 might have ranked as their most torture-filled night of the season.

Bumgarner didn't dominate and looked to be in significant trouble when the Braves loaded the bases in the second inning. But he refused to give in and successfully pitched out of trouble.

"His composure was unbelievable," Posey said. "I came out to talk to him once, and he just kind of smiled and said, 'I'm all right.' When you see that, you know you're probably in for a good night."

The Braves led 1–0 through five innings, with their run scoring on a sacrifice fly. The Giants worked a few long at-bats against Lowe but couldn't scratch him. Once again, the Braves' ace was stepping up on short rest. The Giants only had one base runner in the first five innings, and that was because Torres reached on an error. He was promptly thrown out trying to steal.

It was Ross, the No. 8 hitter the Florida Marlins had foisted onto the Giants, who came through. He connected for a solo home run in the sixth that broke up Lowe's no-hitter and tied the game.

The Braves responded in the bottom of the inning. Bumgarner threw a good curveball that appeared to break off the plate, but McCann found a way to pull it down the line for his own solo shot that pumped belief into the stands at Turner Field and put the Braves back in front.

"This was just the sixth [inning]," Huff said. "The other day, they hit it in the eighth. I almost puked then, but I was fine with it this time. We knew how these games would go."

The Giants were scarred over from a decade's ration of torturous games. They were conditioned to them. And at a time when so many teams would panic, they remained patient.

Outside of one swing, they hadn't damaged Lowe all game. But they had driven up his pitch count, and now he was beginning to tire. Huff drew a one-out walk in the seventh and Posey reached on an infield dribbler.

Cox went out to talk to his battle-tested ace. The crowd roared when Cox allowed Lowe to face one more hitter.

It would turn out to be the last important decision of Cox's respected career—and he got it wrong.

Lowe tried to get Burrell to bite on a borderline pitch, but he missed too far off the plate and lost him on a walk that loaded the bases. Sidearm right-hander Peter Moylan entered to face Uribe, who hit a ground ball to shortstop Gonzalez. In his haste to try for a double play, Gonzalez threw high to second base, and the Braves failed to record an out as Huff scored the tying run.

Left-hander Jonny Venters struck out Rowand for the second out, but Ross stepped up yet again. He flared a single to left field that brought home Posey and put the Giants ahead 3–2. Burrell was thrown out trying to score from second base.

The Giants still had to record nine more outs against a wounded but dangerous team that had come back the previous night. This time, Bochy kept Romo in the bullpen and sent out Casilla for a second inning.

McCann singled, and pinch runner Nate McLouth moved into scoring position on a ground-out, but Lopez entered and bailed the Giants out of yet another huge spot. He struck out Heyward to end the eighth inning and strand the runner.

Heyward was 2-for-16 in the series with eight strikeouts. He didn't score a run, nor did he drive one in.

Posey was better, all right.

The final three outs belonged to Wilson, whose black beard glistened on the mound. This was the moment so many Giants fans had dreaded while watching his roller coaster act over the years. A postseason series was in his hands.

Conrad came off the bench to pinch-hit in the pitcher's spot. There would be no final redemption for him, as he flied out to center field. But Wilson pitched carefully to Ankiel and Hinske, two players who already had proven they could tie the game with one swing.

Wilson had developed certain rules as a closer. He treated the ninth inning like a zero-sum game. If he lost spectacularly on a three-run homer to a fringy hitter, he would be pissed beyond belief. But he could live with himself. When facing a dangerous hitter, though, he wasn't going to give in.

He walked Ankiel. And he walked Hinske.

In the dugout, Wilson's teammates couldn't bear to watch. They turned away like it was a horror movie. Huff buried his head in the water cooler. Burrell felt like he was suffering a panic attack.

Wilson nearly walked Omar Infante, too, but he struck out while failing to check his swing.

Wilson wanted the matchup with Melky Cabrera, knowing that his ground ball to Sandoval in Game 2 should've been an out. He attacked Cabrera again and induced more weak contact to third base. This time Uribe was there, and although his laser-beam throw was wide, Ishikawa played Twister while keeping his foot on first base.

And then…

"Pandemonium," Wilson said. "It was, 'Where am I? Who's going to hit me? Do we even do that right now? I don't care. I'm going to jump around.'

"Let's do this."

The Giants spilled onto the field, mobbing Wilson and celebrating a series in which the injury-ravaged Braves gave them everything they could handle. Each game, even Lincecum's dominant effort in the opener, could've turned on one pitch.

"We were fortunate to have come out on top," Bochy said. "We know it."

The Giants had won twice at Turner Field, beating the team that had the best home record in the NL. All four games in the series were decided by one run. The Giants outscored the Braves 11–9. It was pure, rapturous torture.

"I don't know how you can be a fan of this team sometimes," Huff said.

Bochy had an opposing view.

"If you're a baseball fan, you had to love this series," the manager said.

There was just one bittersweet element for Bochy. Bobby Cox, the man he so revered in the opposing dugout, had managed his last game in a major league uniform.

Less than a minute after umpire Jerry Layne signaled the final out, the crowd began chanting "Bobby, Bobby" while standing and applauding. Cox came waddling out, his eyes glassy, and gave a 360-degree wave. The massive video board in center field began showing images from his many years at the helm.

The Giants had just survived a fingernail-scraping series and were releasing all their tension and elation in a mosh pit with Wilson at its center. But in one of those rare, organic moments, they understood what was happening. And they ceased their celebration.

The Giants turned as a team toward Cox and joined in the applause, doffing their caps and paying respect to a career baseball man who, like their own skipper, never had to tip a spread to send a message.

Everyone played hard for Bobby Cox. There was no better compliment to pay a manager than that. He found a way to be candid but still fiercely loyal to his players, to be a character without drawing attention to himself, to be feisty without being disrespectful and to be warm without being maudlin.

In the postgame interview room, Cox stopped for a moment to compose himself.

"Grown man shouldn't do this," he said, sniffling.

It was a totally different scene in the visiting clubhouse. The Giants had arranged to fly back to San Francisco after the game, but they weren't going to cut short their victory celebration. Players blasted each other with champagne and crumpled full cans of beer over their heads.

Neukom, the Giants' buttoned-down owner, finally found Ross and vigorously rubbed his bald head while screaming jibberish nobody could understand.

It was hard to comprehend any of this. Posey and Bumgarner had become the first all-rookie battery to win a postseason game since Hugh Bedient and Hick Cady of the Boston Red Sox bested the New York Giants' Christy Mathewson in Game 8 of the 1912 World Series.

Yep. It was so long ago, there was a Game 8.

Dave Flemming grabbed Lincecum for a live interview amid the clubhouse madness. By now, anyone with a microphone should've known better.

"Guys tell you what this is like, but you don't know until you experience it," Lincecum said.

"And what is it like?"

"A lot of swearing, a lot of screaming—and a lot of alcohol."

Lincecum had a mischievous gleam in his eye when Flemming asked him to survey the scene.

"I don't know what the f— to say, I'm so f—ing pumped up right now," Lincecum yelled.

"Okayyyyy," said Flemming, pulling the microphone away. "Let's save those words for later, Tim."

The party continued to rage on the all-night flight back to San Francisco. Soon enough, the Giants would face a sobering thought: the Phillies, the team with the best record in the National League, awaited them in the NLCS.

It would be Lincecum versus Halladay—a matchup for the f—ing ages.

Chapter 13

Bulls and Whistles

The Giants returned home to find a city smitten with them.

This team took years off your life and made you chew your fingernails to the nubs. But there was something about their drive and determination. The dugout was full of players who were approachable, loose, and personable, too.

Sure, they were eight victories away from the first World Series in the San Francisco Giants history. But nobody who watched this team all season dared to start thinking too far ahead. The Giants couldn't win with Mays and McCovey. They couldn't win with Barry Bonds or Will the Thrill. It would be too much to believe this hastily assembled group could succeed where so many greater, more talented teams had not.

Maybe if they didn't think about it, maybe if they simply focused on the next game, it might actually happen.

The Giants could beat anyone on a given day, right? They already defeated Roy Halladay back in April. They knocked off the Phillies' No. 2 pitcher, Roy Oswalt, all three times they faced him before the Houston Astros traded him in July. And they knocked around left-hander and former World Series MVP Cole Hamels in August, too.

It wasn't impossible to believe the Giants could beat the mighty Phillies, was it?

According to the experts, it was. On ESPN.com, all 10 panelists took the Phillies to win the series. Only three of them gave the Giants enough respect to predict the series would go seven games.

More than ever, the Giants would need "Don't Stop Believin'" to become their mind-set. Journey's classic power ballad had been adopted by plenty of sports teams over the years—heck, even the Dodgers played it in the eighth inning of every home game—but the song rightfully belonged to the Bay Area. And the Giants were taking it back.

Former Journey lead singer Steve Perry was a lifelong Giants fan who grew up in the San Joaquin Valley. When the Dodgers started showing him on the big screen during their nightly sing-along, Perry protested by sneaking out of his seats before the eighth inning began. Now the Giants were making their playoff run, and Perry had become a regular sight at AT&T Park, thrashing around from a club-level suite as he spurred on the crowd.

This being the Internet era, fans could make statements beyond hand-painted signs. A Giants devotee named Ashkon Davaran became a local sensation after he rewrote the lyrics to "Don't Stop Believin'" to serenade the Giants, complete with references to the Rally Thong, Kung Fu Panda, and Will the Thrill. He shot a low-budget video outside AT&T Park and involved dozens of fans. It scored a million hits on YouTube within a week, and the players got a huge kick out of it.

The Giants had to keep on believing. They would open the NLCS against Halladay, a pitcher who was coming off a no-hitter and later would become a unanimous choice as the NL Cy Young Award winner, ending Lincecum's two-year reign.

The Phillies' biggest advantage, though, was their experience. They had won the World Series in 2008. They made it back the following season. And they were motivated to become the first NL team to win three consecutive pennants since the 1942–1944 St. Louis Cardinals.

They persevered through injuries that would have wrecked less talented clubs. But unlike the Braves, who held together their playoff infield with duct tape and Brooks Conrad, the Phillies had injured stars Ryan Howard, Chase Utley, and Jimmy Rollins back in their lineup.

They had three legitimate aces to match the Giants. And the Phillies also scored the second-most runs in the National League. Only the Reds scored more, and the Phillies had just held them to a .124 average while sweeping Cincinnati in their division series.

"You're not wondering: are you good enough to win?" Rollins said. "With experience, you're not going to panic or worry about the ups and downs. You know guys are going to execute."

Burrell knew better than anyone what the Giants were up against—and what they'd hear from the stands. He received a standing ovation in August when the Giants went back to Citizens Bank Park, his first time in the stadium as a visiting player. Then he hit a home run and was booed the rest of the series.

If their heavily favored opponent didn't succeed in getting inside the Giants' heads, the Philadelphia fans were bound to try.

"You don't get to the World Series two years in a row without being good, and they know they're good," Burrell said. "Obviously, we'll probably be the underdog. But for this team to accomplish what it has, I think we're all proud and we'll give it our best shot.… I'm not going to take anything away from what we're doing. We're a hell of a team, and we're coming in pretty confident."

If the Phillies were the equivalent of the Gas House Gorillas, the Giants had their own little Bugs Bunny on the mound. Lincecum was fine playing the underdog role. It suited him his whole life. Now he represented a whole team of players who weren't the right size or shape, and who'd already been counted out.

Lincecum had the Wascally Wabbit's cartoonish change-up, too.

"I don't think it's proving anything to anybody," Lincecum said. "We all know what we're capable of, what we have to do. Score more runs than the other team."

By now, Lincecum's blister issue had become public knowledge, although everyone on the Giants side downplayed its significance. It had calloused over, the right-hander said.

But everyone wondered if Lincecum could pitch on short rest, if needed. The Giants automatically assumed they would see Halladay on short rest, perhaps getting him a third time if the series went the distance. Halladay had thrown 43 complete games since 2005. Only one other major leaguer—CC Sabathia, with 25—had thrown half as many. He had a 2.69 ERA in six career starts on three days of rest.

As Charlie Manuel, the Phillies' homespun, easygoing manager put it: "Big Roy is Big Roy."

Lincecum was not in Halladay's weight class, nor would the Phillies' fearsome hitters swing consistently late on fastballs as the Braves seemed to do. Howard had three career homers off Lincecum, more than any active player. Even Carlos Ruiz, the Phillies' No. 8 hitter, finished the season with a .302 average and .400 on-base percentage.

The Phillies always provided a measuring stick of sorts for Lincecum. He never forgot his major league debut against them, when their ringing contact rudely told him that he'd have to make adjustments against big-league hitters. He was no longer a rookie relying on a searing fastball and big, easily recognizable curve that usually broke out of the strike zone. Now he had that tight little slider to go along with that nearly unhittable change-up. And he was coming off the game of his life.

The Phillies players were respectful of the Giants and Lincecum in their public comments—perhaps too much, in Manuel's view. They had a long layoff following their sweep of the Reds, and they didn't hit so well in that series, either. Manuel didn't want his hitters to keep praising the Giants' pitching so much that they'd psych themselves out.

"We can score on anybody," Manuel insisted. "We can score on the Giants."

Bochy kept the same playoff roster from the NLDS. He decided to stay with Fontenot at third base over Sandoval. He also kept Ross in the No. 8 hole, even though the right fielder finished the season on a hot streak and had three huge hits against the Braves.

Now it was time to find out if anyone could hit Halladay.

To the delight of the home crowd in South Philly, Halladay retired the first six Giants in order, striking out two. He certainly looked sharper than Lincecum, who recorded three well-struck fly-outs in the first inning, then gave up a leadoff double to Howard in the second. It took every bit of skill and composure for Lincecum to strike out Jayson Werth, then retire Rollins and Raul Ibanez on two more fly-outs to maintain the scoreless tie.

Halladay faced the bottom of the Giants' lineup in the third. That's where Ross resided, still surprised not only to be on a playoff team, but in the starting lineup. Just two months earlier, he assumed he'd finish out the year with the Marlins, then see if they'd tender him a contract for the following season.

Ross was the final addition to the Giants' cast of castoffs in late August, and his career path certainly matched the against-all-odds spirit of the group. By the time he was 25, the streaky hitter had 2,559 at-bats over seven minor league seasons and just 44 in the major leagues.

Ross was kicking around the Detroit system in 2005 when the Dodgers acquired him for outfield depth. They called him up in '06, and he memorably had a two-homer, seven-RBI game at Pittsburgh. It was the best day of his baseball life.

Four days later he had one of his worst. The Dodgers designated him for assignment. They needed roster space for a backup infielder because Jeff Kent—who'd been hit by a pitch in a game against the Giants—was questionable to play. Kent ended up missing one game.

That's how much the Dodgers thought of Cody Ross.

The Cincinnati Reds didn't think much better of the excitable, 5'9" outfielder. They had picked him up from the Dodgers, but he broke a finger in his first game with his new team. After almost a month on the disabled list, Ross made it back for one more game before the Reds realized they didn't have use for him. Ken Griffey Jr., who missed the beginning of the season, was back in the lineup and their outfield was full. Before long, the Reds needed a roster space for someone else, too, and sold Ross' contract to the Marlins.

Ross already had been traded for players you've never heard of— Steve Colyer and Ben Kozlowski. Now he had been dealt for the dreaded "cash considerations."

But going to Florida turned out to be the career break Ross needed. He finished the '06 season by hitting 11 home runs in 250 at-bats for the Marlins—including a three-homer game against the Mets in which he drove in seven runs yet again—to earn himself an everyday role for the following three seasons.

Ross struck out too much, and his on-base percentage wasn't much to look at. But he hit 22 home runs in 2008 and 24 in '09, along with 37 doubles. His extra-base hits came in grapefruit-sized clusters. And when he heated up, he could carry a team.

Seen from afar, Ross could make the wrong impression with opponents. It was a popular opinion that the Marlins played the game with a little bit too much panache, and Ross wasn't shy about celebrating a home run. He had a reputation as a bat flipper who'd watch his shots as he skipped out of the box. That might be tolerable for superstars, but Ross didn't belong in that category. He also wore excessive streaks of eye black, something that started out as a joke between Dan Uggla, his best buddy in Florida, and himself. Ross was having fun. For some players who subscribed to the old school, he was having a little too much fun.

But those who knew Ross had a completely different impression of him. He might be excitable, but he wasn't cocky or brash. He was polite and affable, he stopped to sign autographs for fans and treated reporters with respect. The Marlins' clubhouse had its share of fractures, especially when star shortstop Hanley Ramirez showed up late or loafed after a ball. But Ross didn't belong to cliques or make any enemies.

Even his annual mug shot, the one that always appeared on video boards when players stepped to the plate, showed him with a wide, almost hyper-looking toothy grin.

His new Giants teammates gave him a nickname: "Smiles."

Given his upbringing, Ross was lucky to have all his adult teeth. He grew up in Texas and New Mexico, the son of a chiropractor by day and cowboy by night, and he loved everything about the rodeo. His father, Kenny, a former safety on the University of New Mexico football team, competed all throughout the West on the rodeo circuit, roping and wrestling steers. Little Cody tagged along, all decked out in his overalls, colored scarves, and face paint. He competed in an act called Kindergarten Rodeo, too. Dozens of kids would chase calves around the dirt ring, trying to grab the ribbons tied to their tails—a sort of Wild West Easter egg hunt. Kids received cash prizes for every ribbon they returned, and Cody often had more than he could carry.

He'd do his share of mutton busting, too.

But more than anything, little Cody wanted to be a rodeo clown. He loved their moxie and daring. He loved the way they protected fallen riders.

"I guess I thought that riding the bull was too dangerous," Ross said. "But actually, being a rodeo clown is probably a little more dangerous than that. You have to protect the guy from getting stepped on and run over. I just liked the way they were, maybe it was the mentality they had—no fear. That was probably the reason I was so drawn to them."

All that eye black made sense after all. So did Ross' fearlessness on the baseball field. Once in Florida he got hit in the mouth by a pitch after squaring to bunt. He spit up blood at home plate. The next day, he was back in the lineup—and hit a two-run homer.

"He thinks he's 6'13"," Kenny Ross once told the *Ft. Lauderdale Sun-Sentinel.* "It used to really upset him when somebody would say, 'You know, you're really not that big.'"

It didn't seem like a big deal when the Giants were awarded Ross on a waiver claim on August 20. They liked the player, but they already had a roster stuffed with outfielders. Sabean acknowledged that his prime motivation was to block Ross from going to the first-place Padres, who were in need of an outfielder after Tony Gwynn Jr. broke a bone in his hand. The Giants were lower in the standings at the time, so they were awarded the claim ahead of the Padres. They figured the Marlins would pull back Ross and he'd remain with Florida for the rest of the season.

But for a low-payroll club like the Marlins, Ross had become expensive through arbitration—his salary was $4.5 million in 2010—and his power numbers were down. The Marlins already had decided that they weren't going to tender Ross a contract for 2011. They said they wanted to give a younger player, Cameron Maybin, an everyday look in the outfield. (Strangely enough, Florida traded Maybin to the Padres after the season.) Ross had $1 million left on his deal, which the Marlins could use elsewhere. And besides, they liked his effort and enthusiasm. Giving him a shot to play in a pennant race? That seemed like the neighborly thing to do.

At first, Ross didn't see it that way. He wasn't ecstatic about leaving the Marlins.

"You play your heart out for this organization, and the next thing you know, you're gone," he told Florida reporters. "That's the game. That's the tough part. But there's a bigger plan for me, and I'm excited to get on that team. It is going to be a fun rest of the year for me."

The Giants were unprepared for the Marlins' decision. They scrambled to find a roster space, asking trainer Dave Groeschner if he had any candidates for the disabled list. Right-hander Guillermo Mota, the last man standing in the bullpen, went on the DL with something called "IT band syndrome" in his leg.

On the day they received Ross, the Giants strictly viewed him as a two-month rental. He was a solid defender at all three outfield positions and had an .864 OPS (on-base plus slugging percentage) against left-handed pitching, suggesting he'd make a nice fit in a platoon. But you don't pay more than $5 million for a platoon player.

Ross ended up being more useful than the Giants could've imagined. They needed another outfielder in late September when Torres went down with his appendectomy. Then came Guillen's slump, his painful neck injury, and the legal entanglements that kept him off the playoff roster.

Ross almost wept when Bochy pulled him aside to tell him the news: he'd be the Giants' starting right fielder in the postseason.

And against Halladay, the meanest steer in the National League, the 5'9" outfielder who dreamed of being the guy in the barrel and painted face stood his ground. He dropped the barrel on Halladay, all right, smacking a home run that landed in the suddenly silent left-field bleachers.

It was as if Rocky Balboa fell to the canvas. Halladay hadn't allowed a hit in nearly three weeks. He was mortal after all, and the Phillies fans came to a sudden realization: the Giants had a shot to win this NLCS opener.

The Phillies had their own dangerous No. 8 hitter, and Ruiz took Lincecum deep in the bottom of the third to tie the game. But Halladay wasn't the same the rest of the night. The Giants scratched him for two hits in the fourth without scoring, and when Ross stepped to the plate again in the fifth, he did the unimaginable. He turned on another of those nasty cut fastballs and got enough to send it over the left-field wall.

In San Francisco Giants history, only Jeff Kent, Rich Aurilia, and Will Clark had a multi-homer game in the postseason. And now Cody Ross joined that group. He was in one of his hot streaks. He was carrying his club.

"Nice garbage find for us, huh?" Huff said.

Ross probably wouldn't have been a Giant if DeRosa hadn't ruptured his wrist early in the year. He probably wouldn't have been a Giant if David DeJesus didn't break his hand against the wall in Kansas City as Sabean stood ready to make a deal in July. Ross probably wouldn't have been a postseason starter if Guillen didn't have a sore neck and a rap sheet.

Yet Ross, the most accidental Giant, had belted not one but two home runs off Halladay, a pitcher who was supposed to be untouchable.

There wasn't any way to see this coming. Ross entered the game 3-for-16 off Halladay with no walks and two strikeouts. He had been in the Marlins' lineup in May when Halladay threw his perfect game at Florida. Ross grounded out twice and popped to short on that day.

Now Ross was every bit as legendary a Giants postseason hero as Dusty Rhodes, whose string of clutch hits off the bench helped the Giants win the 1954 World Series. Like Ross, Rhodes had blue-collar ambitions outside of baseball. When his career ended, he worked on a tugboat in New York Harbor for more than two decades. When he passed away in 2009, longtime Dodgers announcer Vin Scully told the Associated Press that the mere mention of his name brought a smile

Cody Ross hits his first of two home runs off pitcher Roy Halladay in Game 1 of the NLCS in Philadelphia. This homer in the third inning broke Halladay's three-week hitless streak and launched Giants fans' hopes that the pitcher—and the Phillies—could indeed be defeated.

to his face, reminding him of the time when "all Rhodes led to the World Series."

The Giants' new incarnation, "Dusty" Ross, had given them a 2–1 lead against Halladay in the fifth inning. But there was plenty of time for the Phillies to rally, and their braying fans had focused their lens on Lincecum.

They held up signs bearing messages like "Wanna smoke?" and "Hippie trash" and "Go fix your teeth." When he stepped to the plate in the third inning, a few fans began to wolf whistle at him like horny construction workers. It was their unique comment on Lincecum's long hair, and it rapidly spread through the ballpark. By the end of Lincecum's first at-bat, it sounded like 40,000 mockingbirds were flapping around him, defending their nest.

This was not a new taunt in Philadelphia. Flyers fans used to do the same thing to Jaromir Jagr, their hated rival with the Pittsburgh Penguins, who had some seriously long death-metal frizz spilling out of his helmet.

"You're fighting more than just the Philly team," Lincecum said after the game. "It turns into the whole Philly atmosphere. You know you're going to get that coming in here. It just makes the environment that much more fun, that much more special, and a lot more pressure."

Lincecum's other reaction: "I was thinking I must have a really nice butt."

He knew the fans were trying to knock him off his game, and, hey, give them points for creativity. But it didn't work.

Lincecum nearly became unhinged in the third inning, though, after Ruiz led it off with his tying home run. Halladay followed with a surprising single, and Shane Victorino grounded into a double play, which was most fortuitous because Placido Polanco followed with a ringing double.

Lincecum was starting to nibble with his fastball, perhaps sensing those negative vibes from August creeping back in. When his 3–1 pitch to Utley wasn't called, Lincecum stepped off the mound, held out his palms, and appeared to use a profanity at umpire Derryl Cousins.

The next batter was Howard, who owned those three homers off Lincecum in addition to that rocket-shot double in the first inning. One more mistake would be disastrous.

Bochy saw the oncoming crash and made a rare mound visit. He didn't coddle Lincecum so much as bark at him, and then he continued barking the whole way back to the dugout—this time, presumably, sending a message to Cousins.

Lincecum threw a high fastball that ticked off Posey's glove for a passed ball, advancing both runners. But Howard had waved through the pitch. Now Lincecum had Howard set up for that disappearing change-up, and it was impossible to lay off.

Lincecum couldn't have made that adjustment as a talented rookie or perhaps even as a Cy Young winner the previous two seasons. But his struggles this year had made him a little tougher on the mound. And he scrapped his way out of a dangerous jam.

After Ross's second home run put them ahead, the Giants caught a break while adding to their lead. Burrell hit a double that Ibanez failed to catch on the warning track in left field, scoring Posey. Bochy inserted pinch runner Nate Schierholtz, who scored easily when Uribe followed with a single up the middle to make it 4–1.

"I'm thinking there's no way we're going to make it this easy," Huff said. "Two pitches later, it's 4–3 and I'm thinking, 'That's about right.'"

The game tightened up when Lincecum gave up a two-run homer to Jayson Werth in the sixth. But Bochy let his ace hit in the top of the seventh, and that move paid off, too. Lincecum responded with a quiet, 11-pitch inning.

Lopez, the side-armed lefty, neutralized Utley and Howard in the eighth, leaving the final four outs for Wilson. He allowed a single to

Werth in the eighth and hit Ruiz with a pitch in the ninth, but struck out the other four batters he faced. The dominant pitching matchup between Halladay and Lincecum only partially materialized, but when all the jabs were tallied, the 4–3 decision belonged to the Giants.

It was another one-run victory. The Giants weren't winning going away. They just kept on winning.

"We like the odds stacked up against us," Wilson said. "If all the odds say we're going to lose, then what do you have to lose?"

In his postgame interview Bochy called his team "the Dirty Dozen," a reference to the World War II movie in which a rogue Army major played by Lee Marvin recruits a collection of convicts and mental defectives for a suicide mission behind German lines.

"We have some characters here, you know, whether you want to call them castoffs or misfits," Bochy said. "I compare them to the Dirty Dozen. That's the way they play, but they've coalesced into a team that goes out there to win."

They were a team that had everyone's attention now.

The Giants had wedged themselves into the postseason by winning one series after another in September, and they took the same mind-set into the NLCS: split in Philly, win two of three in front of the home crowd, then split in Philly again.

But now, after winning Game 1, it was time to think greedy. They knew they could get to Oswalt. And Bochy had juggled his rotation before the series began, moving up Jonathan Sanchez, his second-hottest pitcher, to take the ball in Game 2.

Sanchez was 4–1 with a 1.01 ERA after September 1, and he was coming off an 11-strikeout outing in Atlanta. He also dominated when he pitched in Philadelphia in August, holding the Phillies to an earned run on two hits in eight innings. He was a little less prone to the home run ball than Cain, who would pitch Game 3 in more spacious surroundings at AT&T Park.

Moving up Sanchez made sense from every angle.

"This kid's matured and showed so much better composure and poise on the mound," Bochy said. "At times he's been his own worst enemy. It looks like he's gotten over that and he's pitching with a lot of confidence, and that's why we have him going."

The Giants liked everything about the way Sanchez had been pitching. He began a tradition in the regular season finale against San Diego, staying on the mound after handing over the baseball and waiting for his replacement to arrive from the bullpen. Sanchez wanted to deliver some fighting words.

"We got this," he said. "Let's go. We'll get this done."

Sanchez did it again in his NLDS start at Atlanta, when Romo entered and allowed that two-run homer to Eric Hinske. But, hey, it was loud at Turner Field that night.

"I don't think he heard me," said Sanchez, smiling.

The Giants also made a lineup change shortly before Game 2. Uribe had jammed his wrist on a slide into second base the previous night and was too sore to play. Edgar Renteria would start at shortstop—only his second start in a month and his first of this postseason. Fontenot remained at third base, with Ross moving from eighth to sixth in the order.

Greed was not good, however. Oswalt overwhelmed the Giants in the simplest way possible, throwing fastballs on 70 of his 111 pitches—the most heaters he'd thrown in a start all season. He mixed in a few 65–mph curveballs seemingly for kicks while improving to 5–0 as a postseason starter as the Phillies took a relatively easy 6–1 victory.

"He had the good one today," Huff said. "It was getting on your hands. He's got that bowling ball fastball, and he went after guys."

The Giants' only run came on yet another Ross home run. His solo shot in the fifth inning marked the third consecutive playoff game in which he'd broken up a no-hitter.

215

"Amazing," Huff said. "We're fouling 'em off. He's hitting 'em."

But other than Ross' home run, Oswalt did not allow a runner in scoring position until the eighth inning. And by then, the Giants had made enough mistakes to seal their fate.

Sanchez never had a chance to settle, throwing 35 pitches in the first inning while walking three batters. Several of those pitches could have been avoided if Fontenot hadn't allowed Polanco's pop-up to drop in front of the mound for an error.

Sanchez issued a bases-loaded walk to Rollins in the first but limited the damage when he struck out Ibanez. He managed to hold it there long enough for Ross to tie it in the fifth, but the Phillies took the lead right back on Shane Victorino's double and Polanco's sacrifice fly.

The Phillies busted it open in an ugly, four-run seventh inning, with Rollins clearing the bases on a double off the wall against Casilla. Two of the three runners had been intentionally walked ahead of Rollins, but Bochy couldn't sidestep everyone in the Phillies' lineup.

Huff made a mental mistake earlier in the inning, too, when he cut off Torres' strong throw from center field to the plate. It appeared that Oswalt would be out easily—he had barreled through a stop sign, something he wasn't used to seeing in his tiny hometown of Weir, Mississippi—but the ball never reached Posey. The Phillies also had executed a double-steal that seemed far too easy.

It was the first truly wretched, breakdown-filled inning the Giants had played all postseason.

Rollins had been 2-for-17 in the playoffs after an injury-ravaged year. Now the former NL MVP from Alameda was showing signs of life. So too were the Phillies. The wolves were whistling.

"This is one when we come off the field in the ninth and walk up those stairs, we have to forget about it," Ross said. "We're upbeat and we're ready to go home again."

Chapter 14

A Lot of Happy

The NLCS shifted to San Francisco for Game 3, and with their opponent suddenly revitalized, the Giants needed all the support they could get.

They received it—in three dress-sized boxes sent to 24 Willie Mays Plaza, ATTN: Aubrey Huff.

Huff's Rally Thong had gotten so much publicity that the underwear company, totally unsolicited, shipped him dozens of men's thongs in every size and color. He became a giddy, thong-flinging Santa Claus on the day of Game 3, distributing them to all his teammates. He walked into Bochy's office, too, and tossed one at the skipper.

"I don't think anybody wants to see me in one," Bochy deadpanned. "And I don't really enjoy seeing Aubrey in his. But he's proud of his body, and he likes to walk around in [the thong], and he gets a lot of laughs. And it keeps the guys loose."

Huff didn't enjoy talking about his butt floss during media sessions. It was a clubhouse thing, not really meant for public amusement. But now it had become a phenome-thong. A sailboat owner even fashioned a giant red thong out of a bedsheet, marked it with Huff's No. 17, draped it across the mainsail, and parked the craft in McCovey Cove.

"It's just something to kind of loosen the guys up when it started, and it turned out to be kind of a nice run," said Huff, when asked about the thong in the interview room during the Atlanta series. "I couldn't stop and…

"I'm wearing it right now, if you're interested."

He squirmed in his chair, an impish smile on his face, as the room filled with laughter.

"Kinda get used to it," he said. "You know what I'm saying?"

Whatever knickers Bochy chose to wear, he had them in a twist. For the first time in the postseason, the Giants would face a left-hander, Cole Hamels, and that presented no shortage of head scratchers.

Leadoff hitter Andres Torres, for all the inspiration he had provided during the season, hadn't done nearly as much damage from the right side. And Torres was coming off a miserable Game 2 against Roy Oswalt in which he kept swinging at high heat while striking out in all four at-bats.

Torres was stepping into all the mental traps that can befall a player in his first postseason. He was letting the game get too quick. He was overthinking every part of his swing. And the Phillies knew how to exploit it.

"I just need to concentrate more," said Torres, giving an interview that sounded more like a therapy session. "I get distracted by so many things. I am staying positive. I just need to…I can't jump at the first pitch. I need to see pitches."

Fontenot's brutal defensive game had Bochy considering Sandoval as the starting third baseman again. But the switch-hitting Kung Fu Panda hadn't figured out his right-handed swing all season, either. He had become a platoon player down the stretch.

So Bochy inserted the two Giants who had been least popular with fans all season. Center fielder Aaron Rowand and shortstop Edgar Renteria barely played at all in September, and neither was a sure bet to make the postseason roster for the Braves series. But they had experience that Bochy valued. Rowand, who hadn't started since September 16, would get a chance to face Hamels, his former teammate. And Renteria, who'd been banged up all season, was Bochy's surprising choice to lead off.

At least Uribe's MRI exam checked out. He still had inflammation in his wrist after jamming it in Game 1, but he lobbied to play, and the training staff cleared him to start at third base.

The most surprising player to take the field that day was none other than Barry Lamar Bonds. The Giants had assembled mini reunions of players from their previous playoff rosters to throw out ceremonial first pitches, and this time it was the 2002 team. After Shawon Dunston, Robb Nen, and J.T. Snow took the field, Bonds bounded out of the dugout, fired up the crowd by doing a few jumping jacks in his oversized jersey, doffed his cap, and blew kisses. He knew this was the one place where he'd always be cheered, and he soaked it up.

The home crowd did not have much else to cheer in the early innings, though, as Hamels set down the first nine hitters in order. But Renteria lined a leadoff single to right field in the fourth inning, and he clapped his hands as he pulled into first base.

Renteria had collected so many of those crisp, opposite-field hits over his career, but so few in two seasons as a Giant. For the first time in four games, someone other than Ross had gotten the team's first hit.

Freddy Sanchez bunted Renteria into scoring position, and after Burrell worked a tough, two-out walk, Ross stepped to the plate.

The Phillies had spent considerable energy studying Ross's at-bats from the first two games of the series, trying to come up with a plan against him. He wasn't just in a hot streak. Something mystical was happening here. After his two-homer game against Roy "Doc" Halladay, it was noted that Ross's name, spelled backward, was *ssory doc*.

Hamels noticed that Ross was turning on those down-and-in fastballs designed to jam him. Hamels even mentioned it in his interview session the previous day: he wasn't going to throw Ross anything down and in.

But Ross was in such a zone that it didn't matter where you threw it. He lunged at an ankle-high fastball on the outer edge, somehow looped it over the third baseman's head, and Renteria scored easily. Hamels spat out a few curse words in frustration, feeling he had made the pitch he wanted.

"He's hitting pitches that most normal people can't hit," Hamels said. "If he can hit that through the regular season, we'll be very impressed, but that's what happens when guys are hot. They can hit anything.

"I don't know too many guys who can lift that up over a third baseman; most guys normally hit it into the ground. You have to tip your hat. That's kind of the way baseball plays out sometimes."

"He's right," Ross said. "It's probably a pitch I shouldn't have swung at.... Somehow I hucked it down the line."

By the end of Game 3, Ross was hitting .444 in the NLCS with three home runs and four RBIs. He had four of the Giants' five homers in the postseason, had knocked in seven of the team's 19 runs, and had broken up three no-hitters—each time by going deep.

Call him Babe Ross or Cody Ruth or the New Dusty Rhodes. The upbeat, energetic outfielder from New Mexico was taking the bull by the horns. And in the crowd, it was all smiles.

Hamels would endure more frustration before he could escape the fourth inning. He threw another bastard pitch—an outside change-up—that Huff managed to yank for a single that scored Burrell. The Giants added a third run in the fifth inning when Rowand pounded a double and scored on Sanchez's spinning, two-out infield single.

It was only the Giants' fifth hit of the game, and aside from Rowand's double, none of them were struck especially hard. They wouldn't get another hit, either. But their homer-or-bust offense had a rare and magnificently efficient night. Of the four base runners who advanced into scoring position, the Giants plated three of them.

The most magnificent performance, however, belonged to Matt Cain.

The Phillies had confidence against anyone's fastball, and they knew Cain could become a little too aggressive with his heater at times. He was 0–3 with a 6.23 ERA in five career starts against them. This was a matchup they liked.

But Cain backed them off the plate with hard stuff inside, then spent the rest of the game tricking them into lunging at knee-high fastballs on the outer edge. He worked the Phillies horizontally, too, changing eye levels while pitching up in the zone.

The Phillies came to hunt pitches, but Cain kept moving the target. He worked ahead in the count most of the game, and when he fell behind, he refused to give in. He walked three and hit two batters, but most of those misses seemed strategic.

Even when Hamels tried to give Cain an out in the third inning, squaring to sacrifice after Carlos Ruiz's one-out single, the curly haired right-hander was unyielding. He threw up and in to Hamels, turning a bunt attempt into an act of self-preservation. Hamels recoiled as he fouled off the bunt on his way to a strikeout. The next hitter, Shane Victorino, got brushed back by an inside pitch, too. It fluttered the front of his jersey, and he angrily slammed his bat as he jogged to first base.

No way did Cain want to hit Victorino. Now he had to face Chase Utley, who owned a .467 average with three home runs in 15 at-bats against him. But Cain and Posey executed a perfect sequence: a drop-in curveball for a strike, then three consecutive change-ups—all low and away. Utley grounded out. He was 0-for-4 in the game, twice stranding runners on base.

Cain had to escape one last jam in the seventh inning after hitting Ruiz and walking pinch-hitter Ross Gload with two outs. Bochy went out to the mound. He did not take the baseball.

"There was no doubt I wanted to keep him out there," Bochy said. "But you have to check on him. That's all I was doing. And he had that look. He was great. So he stayed out there."

Cain knew he'd get just one more hitter, and the last thing he wanted to do was leave a mess for the bullpen. Victorino ran the count full before grounding out.

"A couple of times I thought I had his fastball," Victorino said. "But I missed. I can say all I want that 'I just missed, I just missed.' But he came out on the winning end, and that's all that matters."

Cain had earned the right to walk off the mound, and that's exactly what he did. He didn't leap or jog. He took no pleasure in the moment with a roundhouse punch or even a fist pump. He simply gave a firm handshake to Posey, who waited for him at the rail with an admiration so palpable, the rookie catcher might as well have asked for an autograph.

That last pitch to Victorino?

"It was just a heater," Posey said. "A heater in. And he executed the pitch."

The Giants bullpen executed the rest. Even though Charlie Manuel split up his left-handed bats, putting Polano in between Utley and Howard, it made no difference. Lopez threw more of his baffling sidearm stuff to retire all three hitters in the eighth, and Wilson got a double-play grounder from Ibanez to end it.

The Giants won 3–0. They led the series once more.

Cain had become the first Giant to throw at least seven shutout innings in an NLCS game since Dave Dravecky tossed a two-hit shutout against the St. Louis Cardinals in 1987. Even more amazing, it was the first time the Phillies had been shut out in 50 postseason games—a streak that dated to Game 5 of the 1983 World Series, when Scott McGregor won the clincher for the Baltimore Orioles.

It was the seventh time in the Giants' seven postseason games that they received a quality start. And what the heck, it also marked the first time in these playoffs that they won a game by more than one run.

They had Renteria and Rowand to thank for that. Both maligned Giants contributed huge hits.

"I'm a little biased because I love Edgar," Rowand said. "You won't find a better professional. I told him when we clinched the NL West, 'It's been a real privilege to play with you.'

"This guy doesn't miss anything. He's been in a lot bigger moments than we've been in so far, and he's come out on top. So you don't worry about him. You know he'll give you a great opportunity to win games when he comes up in that spot."

Rowand hadn't said much all season about his reduced role, even though everyone in the clubhouse knew he wasn't happy with it. He took more swings in the cage than anyone, and when he would get into a slump, his answer was to work even harder and take even more swings. There were times that former hitting coach Carney Lansford had to lock the indoor cage to keep Rowand from using it.

Nobody ever questioned Rowand's dedication, work ethic, or self-sacrifice. He played at one speed, and often it came with a price. His nose always will be a bit crooked because he shattered it in 2006 while crashing into the center-field wall at Philadelphia. He held onto the ball, too.

But his first two years as a Giant hadn't ended well. He knew he'd have to adjust his training habits as he got older, so he bought an Italian racing cycle and rode it all over Nevada's Red Rock country over the winter, ticking off more than 2,500 miles. He'd start out before dawn, ascend 100 miles through a mountain pass, and be ready to start the ascent down before 7:00 AM. Alone on the open road, he had a lot of time to breathe the crisp desert air, commune with a landscape straight out of a John Ford picture, and think about his career.

He did not envision being a bench player by May and a fifth out-fielder by the end of the season. But he steadfastly refused to say much of anything when reporters asked about his reduced role. In the after-glow of Game 3, however, he offered a small thought:

"You know," he said, "it's a lot easier when we're winning."

Rowand took every question at his locker, but he didn't look too comfortable after standing there for 15 minutes or so. Huff, returning from the shower, took note of this.

"Dude, you okay?" Huff said.

"I just got out of the cold tub," Rowand said. "I'm shivering. My jaw is locking up."

"Well," said Huff, "media ain't been over there all year. So church it up, bro."

Perhaps Huff could've tossed Rowand a blanket. But all he had was a box of thongs.

Even before the Game 3 victory, Bochy said he intended to return Torres to the lineup in Game 4 against right-hander Joe Blanton. But Bochy seldom let a player sit after a good game, and so he changed his mind, and Rowand earned himself another start. Besides, Torres had looked out of his element all postseason; he was 3-for-26 with 12 strikeouts and just one walk.

There was one other lineup change. Uribe's wrist remained obviously sore as he went hitless in three at-bats. So Sandoval, the prodigal Panda, returned to third base after being benched for five consecutive playoff games.

"We think it's the right thing to give him the night off," Bochy said of Uribe. "I could tell with his swinging. I talked to him today, and he admitted it's still bothering him."

But Uribe would have a part to play in Game 4. So would Torres. And so would Game 2 starter Roy Oswalt, as crazy as that would've sounded.

The Giants and Phillies were about to stage a back-and-forth classic—one of the wildest and most entertaining playoff games in recent memory.

There were blown leads, huge at-bats, clutch hits, mistakes, redemption, Buster Posey, awe, electricity, wonder, genius, Posey, belief, more Posey, and in the end, a supernova of joy on the shores of McCovey Cove.

Of course, there was a little torture, too.

The Giants led 2–0 after four innings, sparked by their rookie battery. Posey drove in both their runs on a single in the first and a double in the third, while Bumgarner struck out five of the first nine hitters he faced.

But the Phillies reminded everyone why they scored so many runs during the season. They were seeing Bumgarner for the first time, and they seemed to examine him like a dissection frog while taking pitches the first time through the order. The next time through, they shortened up their swings.

They entered the fifth inning hitting just 2-for-21 with runners in scoring position in the series, but they finally sustained a rally. Ben Francisco and Carlos Ruiz led off with singles—the first back-to-back hits for the Phillies since the third inning of Game 1—and Blanton's sacrifice advanced them.

Victorino followed with a single up the middle that scored Francisco and Ruiz followed behind him. Rowand, whose throws from center field usually were more exuberant than accurate, got off a perfect one. Posey flashed an illusionist's hands while skillfully picking the short hop and applying the tag to prevent Ruiz from scoring.

Posey had learned so much about catching since strapping on his first chest protector just four years earlier. But a play like that was something that simply couldn't be taught.

Bumgarner was laboring, though, after working so many full counts in the early innings. So when Utley followed with a single, Bochy didn't hesitate to go to the bullpen for Casilla.

The Giants still led 2–1, but their run of quality starts in the postseason had ended. For the first time, the bullpen would have to get the majority of the outs.

The move didn't work out, as Casilla hung one of his spike curves that Polanco stroked for a two-run double. Not only did the Phillies now lead 3–2, but they were threatening to land a knockout punch after Howard was intentionally walked and Jayson Werth was hit by a pitch.

Casilla's wild ride was far from over. He threw a pitch that took a crazy bounce off the plate and popped all the way over the backstop netting, scoring Polanco and putting runners at second and third. Surprisingly, Bochy stuck with the right-hander, even though he was facing Rollins—who had hit the damaging, three-run double off Casilla in Game 2.

This time, Casilla got even. He threw a perfect, two-strike curveball that froze Rollins. And when plate umpire Wally Bell flat-out missed calling it for a third strike, Casilla was unfazed. He came back with another, this time striking out Rollins to keep it a two-run deficit. It ended up being one of the most important outs of the night—and it wouldn't be the last time in Game 4 that a reliever rewarded Bochy's faith.

The Giants immediately cut the deficit to 4–3 while rallying back for a run in the bottom of the fifth.

Torres, who had entered along with Casilla on a double-switch, led off in the No. 9 spot and did the most difficult thing imaginable. He forced himself to stay calm, trust his eye, and take pitches out of the strike zone. He drew a leadoff walk, and when Polanco let Renteria's potential double-play ground ball deflect off his chest, allowing Torres to slide safely into second base, the Giants took advantage of the break.

Huff cashed in the chance with a single up the middle. Torres, now back to full speed for the first time since his appendectomy, slid between Ruiz's shin guards and found the plate.

Blanton's night was finished. Both starting pitchers were gone before completing five innings, and strangely enough, both of them had been taken out with the lead. This would be a bullpen game, and although they still trailed by a run, the Giants liked their chances in that fight.

It seemed an odd choice when Bochy stayed with Casilla for another inning, but the right-hander retired the side in the sixth. And now another of Bochy's decisions was about to turn golden.

Sandoval was about to come through.

The Kung Fu Panda had been so impatient and unwatchable at the plate for most of the season. The swings became more and more desperate as he tried to raise his numbers and rescue his average. All the clichés applied: he was trying to hit a five-run home run. He was trying to get two hits in one at-bat.

Yet Giants fans continued to wear their panda hats in large numbers, perhaps just as in love with the furry concept as the player. Sandoval seldom got booed after an ugly strikeout, no matter how bad it looked.

Unfortunately for the Giants, he had been at his worst when they needed him the most. A terrific clutch hitter in his first full season, the Panda hit just .208 with runners in scoring position in 2010. He hadn't knocked in multiple runs in a game since August 24. He wasn't brooding or sullen, but he wasn't quite his happy-go-lucky self, either.

Injured veteran Mark DeRosa lockered next to Sandoval and became one of his chief motivators. DeRosa played on six playoff teams over his career, and was a starter on Cubs and Cardinals clubs that reached the postseason in each of the previous three years. He owned a .358 average in the playoffs. Yet only once in six tries did his teams escape the first round. He made it to the NLCS just once, as a young role player for the 2001 Atlanta Braves, who were beaten in four of five by the Arizona Diamondbacks.

Now the Giants were two victories away from the World Series, and DeRosa thirsted to be out there. But he also was humble enough to admit that his wrist surgery might have been for the best.

"You know what? We're a better team for me going down," said DeRosa, fully aware that Burrell and Ross might not have become Giants if he remained the everyday left fielder.

DeRosa was lauded for his intelligence, character, and leadership abilities. He was the starting quarterback for two seasons at Penn, including an undefeated run to the Ivy League title in 1994. Now he was learning something new about the team dynamic.

"I've always worried about myself and trusted my teammates were going to be all right," he said. "But now you see it from a bigger scale.... I'm determined to help these guys however I can."

Back in August DeRosa told Jonathan Sanchez about the way Tom Glavine, his former teammate in Atlanta, would pump his hands as a timing mechanism during his delivery. Sanchez talked it over with Righetti and decided to try it. Perhaps not coincidentally, that's when Sanchez's season took off.

Mostly, DeRosa tried to keep younger players like Sandoval as upbeat and confident as possible. He reminded him: if you deliver in the postseason, nobody remembers your batting average. When the opportunity presented itself, the Panda just needed to slow the game down, keep his weight back, react to the pitch, and resist trying to get two hits in one at-bat.

Only the precocious Panda could find a way to do all of the above.

His opportunity came in the sixth inning when right-hander Chad Durbin issued a leadoff walk to Burrell and allowed a double to Ross. Sandoval followed by pulling a pitch down the right-field line, causing the crowd to rise and pray it would hit grass on the fair side of the chalk.

It did, just catching the inner edge of the line. Replays showed it clearly. But right-field umpire Dan Iassogna blew the call, and Sandoval clapped his hands to his helmet in disbelief. After such a long, wasted season, he thought he had come through with the most important hit of his young career.

Now he'd have to do it again.

He did. Sandoval remained composed and lined a two-strike pitch that split the defenders in left-center field, giving the Giants a 5–4 lead. He really did hit two doubles in one at-bat.

Sandoval stutter-stepped into second base, pointed to the sky, maniacally clapped his hands, and looked into the Giants' dugout.

"Everything going crazy," he said of the scene. "I just couldn't believe it. I was so excited. When you're a little kid, you dream of going to the World Series. It's one of the best moments of my life."

Torres couldn't believe it, either. Before the game, Sandoval had called him into the laundry room and told him, "Hey, kid, I'm going to do something special tonight."

There was just one problem: Sandoval gushed like that before every game. No, he wasn't a very good Karnak. It didn't make the laundry-room prediction any less magical in Torres' eyes.

This Game 4 washing machine had more tumbles in it, though.

Lopez, who had been so marvelous since the Giants rescued him from the Pirates, threw a scoreless seventh inning but gave up a double to Howard leading off the eighth. Romo couldn't pick up his bullpen mate, giving up another double to Werth that tied the score.

But Bochy stuck with Romo, just as he had stayed with Casilla. And Romo did not crumble after losing the lead. With the go-ahead runner at second base, he got Rollins to pop up and used his Frisbee slider to strike out Francisco and Ruiz.

The Giants summoned Wilson to pitch a scoreless ninth, setting themselves up for a chance to win it in the bottom of the inning. They already had let a huge opportunity slip in the seventh, when they loaded the bases on Posey's one-out double, a walk, and an error. That chance was wasted when Sandoval failed to come through a second time, grounding into a double play against tough setup man Ryan Madson.

The Phillies wanted to save closer Brad Lidge for a potential save situation, but they didn't want to send out Madson for a third inning. So Oswalt, who had overwhelmed the Giants with simple fastballs in Game 2, campaigned to take the ball in the ninth. The instant Werth's tying double landed in the grass in the eighth, Oswalt had sprinted back into the clubhouse to put on his spikes. He already had thrown his side session earlier in the day, but he told pitching coach Rich Dubee that he was fresh and ready despite just two days of rest.

The Giants did not try to wait out Oswalt's fastballs this time. By now, they were deep enough into this postseason that the jitters had subsided. The Giants pitchers had been great when they needed to be, especially in the Braves series, allowing the club to sneak through the first round. Now players like Huff and Freddy Sanchez had seen enough pitches in huge situations to calm down and trust themselves.

Even against a pitcher who was undefeated in 10 postseason appearances, a pitcher who had just dominated them three days earlier, the Giants did not lack for confidence. Sanchez pounced on a pitch but lined out to right field. Huff followed with a good swing, grounding a single through the right side on a change-up that floated back across the plate. Then came Posey, who already owned three hits in this game.

Posey didn't have much experience playing baseball this deep into a season, and when the Giants sent him to the Arizona Fall League a year earlier, he hit just .225. Scouts noticed he looked tired in Arizona's October sunshine and his bat was slow. Now he was battling heavy legs in the postseason, catching every inning of every game, while also facing the best pitching in the big leagues. His golden bat looked a bit leaden.

But Blanton was the first truly mediocre starter the Giants had seen all postseason—and Posey proved time and again that he was so much better than mediocre competition.

There was nothing mediocre about Oswalt, though, and Posey went up determined to battle. After taking a rip and missing the first pitch, Posey fouled off the next three. Rookies were supposed to be afraid of hitting with two strikes. Posey wasn't your average rookie.

He almost seemed to be calibrating Oswalt's fastball, and whenever the pitcher tried to make him chase, Posey didn't take the bait.

This was a double-play situation, and Oswalt wanted a ground ball. He tried to jam him. Posey, that sum'gun, flared it to right field.

"The guy throws hard. He's got an electric fastball, and good offspeed stuff as well," Posey said. "So the goal was to let the ball travel, try to see it, and I think when I'm going good, that's what I do."

Posey was going good, all right. And so were the Giants. Huff alertly went from first to third on the single, putting runners at the corners with one out.

The next batter: Juan Uribe.

Bochy had double-switched three times in the game and inserted Uribe at third base when he brought in Wilson to pitch the ninth. Now he had the right man up in the perfect spot.

Uribe already had made one contribution, using all his range and arm strength to rob Ross Gload of an infield hit leading off the ninth. It was a play Sandoval probably wouldn't have made.

Uribe had taken batting practice earlier in the day, and while he wasn't able to turn loose his swing because of his swollen wrist, he still had one good arm. For Bochy, that was enough.

In Bochy's Dirty Dozen, Uribe was the original member. He had joined the Giants on a minor league contract in 2009, unable to find a guaranteed deal on the free agent market, even in a backup role. The Giants liked him because he had power and some versatility on the infield. A World Series ring with the 2005 White Sox didn't hurt, either.

When Uribe made the club as a reserve, it was a heartwarming story for Giants fans—a chance to rekindle memories of a former favorite and break out a chant that hadn't been heard since the last days of Candlestick Park.

Jose Uribe had been the Giants' sunny, smooth-fielding shortstop through most of the late 1980s, filling out their iconic infield of Will Clark, Matt Williams, and Robby Thompson. Whenever Uribe would dive up the middle, spring to his feet, and make a throw, the fans would serenade him: "OOOO-ree-bayyy!"

Jose wasn't a marvelous hitter, but his every trip to the plate was a moment for an opportunistic cheerleader in the stands to yell out a guttural "OOOO." The other fans in the section would respond with the rest.

Now the call-and-response cheer was part of the everyday experience at AT&T Park, a thread of continuity from the blustery days of Candlestick. And on April 12, 2009, the Giants started an Uribe at shortstop for the first time in almost 17 years.

Sometimes Juan Uribe described Jose as his uncle. Other accounts listed them as second cousins. But there was no doubt they considered themselves family, and they were very close. Juan didn't go a day without thinking of Jose, who died in a car accident in December 2006 at the age of 47.

During Jose's playing days, he would return to the Dominican Republic after every season and tell Juan about what life was like in the big leagues. He didn't regale his nephew with talk of fast cars, fancy hotels, or personal achievements. His passions ran so much deeper than that.

"He said everybody on your team is your family," Juan said. "You're together every day and you work hard for each other to win. I try to be like him."

Righetti vividly remembered details of Jose Uribe's last game as a Giant. It was October 4, 1992, the season finale, at Cincinnati. The Giants won 6–2 in 13 innings, and Righetti pitched two relief innings to get the victory.

The nimble shortstop started a double play to help him escape the 11th inning.

"[Manager] Roger Craig gave me the game ball," Righetti said. "It was a big deal because we thought it was the last game in San Francisco Giants history. Everyone was thinking we'd be in Tampa the next year."

Righetti remembered Jose Uribe as "a heck of a guy. We all miss him. He was well loved by everyone on the team. Just his demeanor, the way he carried himself…every team needs that infectious kind of personality."

Soon after Juan became a Giant, it was clear the team would have that kind of personality once more.

Most players sprayed themselves with cologne after their postgame shower. Uribe would self-fumigate as his last act before jogging out for the pregame stretch. Then he'd turn into a game-show host during batting practice, pitting groups of fans against each other and throwing baseballs to those who cheered loudest.

Any time players were hitting on the field and you heard a commotion, it was usually Uribe down in the left-field corner, entertaining the fans along with himself.

On most baseball teams, the Latin players formed their own social circle. But Wilson and Lincecum were regulars at Uribe's dominoes table. They played for cash stakes, and anyone with a stack of 20s was welcome. Uribe usually stood up from the table with the fattest bankroll, too. When Wilson and Lincecum received multimillion-dollar raises before the 2010 season, nobody was happier than Uribe. The first thing he did after arriving in the clubhouse that spring was zip open his bag, take out his tin of dominoes, and give it a shake.

Mostly, Uribe's comedy defied explanation. He just knew how to make everyone laugh and feel at ease around him. And he found unending humor in the simplest of things.

He absolutely loved the office supply store commercial in which one of the shoppers exclaims, "Wow! That's a LOW price!" And another shopper replies with, "I KNOW!"

It was an insipid ad. Uribe couldn't get enough if it. He and Sandoval would shout it across the room to each other for most of the season, and somehow, the gag never got old. Probably because they enjoyed it so darn much.

When Uribe played for the White Sox, he'd look forward to the annual trip to Toronto. Not for the cuisine or the nightlife or the novelty of going to Canada. Uribe loved it because he got to hear the Canadian national anthem. And his teammates knew, for at least the next four to six weeks, they'd hear Uribe belting out the opening line every day on his way to batting practice:

"Ohhhh Cann—DAHHHH!"

Uribe simply never had a bad day in the major leagues, although one came close in 2009. He felt awful when his error was the only thing that stood between Jonathan Sanchez and a perfect game. But Sanchez still got his no-hitter that day, and his teammates forgave and forgot. That's what families do.

There was no doubt Uribe had established himself as a starting player again in 2010. But by late June, he had fallen into a terrible slump. He hadn't said anything to trainers, but his middle finger was so swollen that he could barely grip a bat. Finally, he told Bochy, who rested him for two games at Milwaukee. Someone in the clubhouse draped Uribe's

Juan Uribe reacts after hitting a tiebreaking home run during the eighth inning of Game 6 of the NLCS. Uribe also hit the game-winning sacrifice fly in Game 5 that scored Aubrey Huff to beat the Phillies 6–5.

jersey and cap over an overstuffed, leather recliner and tilted it all the way back. They also festooned the scene with Uribe's bat, complete with two Band-Aids in an X-pattern affixed to the barrel.

With Uribe, it was more about show than tell. His English was barely functional, yet he found a way to get the point across with limited vocabulary. In fact, the results often had a poetic beauty.

The same was true for many players and coaches for whom English was a second language. Former manager Felipe Alou would say things that sounded more like proverbs than statements. When the Giants' aging roster began to crumble on Alou's watch, and he had to release popular players like Marquis Grissom and Kirk Rueter, the morose manager said his players were "dying in my hands."

The translation might be inexact, but never inelegant.

Uribe wasn't a team spokesperson, and he wasn't the easiest player for reporters on deadline, since the chances weren't great that they would get something to put quote marks around. Yet the writers made a habit of talking to Uribe after he'd hit a big home run or made a play. They needed to store up goodwill for those times when he might kick a ball in the late innings, or heaven forbid, with a perfect game at stake.

The reporters were often at Uribe's locker in 2010. There were so many victories that he impacted during the regular season. He finished second on the club with 24 home runs, 11 of which either tied the game or gave the Giants the lead—none bigger than that shot in the ninth at Dodger Stadium to complete a four-homer comeback.

He had that six-RBI inning at Wrigley Field after the hitters met underneath the bleachers. He also delivered the walk-off single in August when the Giants beat the Padres for just the second time in 11 games. That time, his teammates nearly rubbed the orange dye right out of his hair.

Whenever he'd barrel up a pitch, Uribe let go of the bat in a distinctive way. He'd flash the palms of his white gloves with all 10 fingers splayed, almost posing like Al Jolson in *The Jazz Singer*.

He insisted it wasn't intentional, not an act of showmanship. He was simply reacting to the pitch. But Uribe's "jazz hands" always meant good things for the Giants. And he had plenty of showstopping moments during the year.

One night in Cincinnati the reporters approached Uribe after he hit a 433-foot home run. And even with his limited English, he found the essence:

"I never think I'm a good player or a bad player," he said. "This is what I'm thinking: I can play. And I want to play. Every day I come to the ballpark, and I only try to do something to help the team. One day, you can win the game with your glove. One day, you can win a game with a hit.

"Win the game, go to the playoffs, go to the World Series. If you go, nobody thinks you hit .100 or .200. If you win the game, you're happy. I want to be happy.

"Me, I'm not thinking maybe. I think this team will go to the playoffs. I believe in this team. I believe in the guys. My teammates are good players and good people, too."

Uribe was right. The Giants not only made it to the playoffs, but they were on the verge of taking command of the NLCS against the mighty Phillies.

Uribe stepped to the plate with one good wrist and runners at the corners, staring at Oswalt. The Phillies knew he was hurting and tried to jam him. One pitch busted him inside and actually glanced off his hand, but Bell, the plate umpire, ruled that it hit off the knob of his bat and called it a foul ball.

Uribe had two strikes on him, but he knew Oswalt would keep pounding him inside. He fouled off a pitch. Then he got an inside change-up and lifted it to left field.

It was deep enough. Ben Francisco caught it, Huff waited an extra millisecond on third base to be sure, and he streaked across the plate as the Giants spilled onto the field in full glory mode.

On Uribe's sacrifice fly, they had beaten the Phillies 6–5. They were one win away from the World Series. And in an exultant moment, Uribe found the essence again.

"I go home now, be with my family," he said, "and be a lot of happy."

He kept repeating that same phrase through waves of interviews: "A lot of happy."

There could be no better four-word sequence to describe the joyous scene at AT&T Park. Giants fans saw Sandoval redeem a wasted summer with the biggest hit of his life. They saw Casilla and Romo give up leads only to keep their composure and get huge outs. They saw Posey, their rookie superstar in the making, collect four hits and make an amazing defensive play.

The Phillies were the beasts of the National League. But the Giants didn't just outpitch them to win Game 4. They outfought them, too.

"We saw something special tonight," Torres said. "We never give up. We always come back.

"This team, we believe."

The Phillies still had faith, too. They would send Halladay, Oswalt, and Hamels to the mound if they could make the series go the distance. The difference now: the Giants had defeated all of those vaunted pitchers once in this series.

"I heard somebody—they were asking me today [whether] we like to play with our backs to the wall," Manuel said. "I think we're going to get a chance."

Chapter 15

All Decks on Hand

The Giants needed one victory. They had three chances.

Does this sound familiar?

Back on the final weekend of the regular season, they needed all three games against the San Diego Padres to win the NL West. So it probably shouldn't have surprised anyone wearing a fake beard or holding a "Torture" sign that the Giants did not clinch a trip to the World Series in front of their home fans in Game 5.

The Phillies extended the series, but it wasn't because Roy Halladay threw a no-hitter or Lincecum failed to measure up or the two-time defending NL champs refused to bow.

No, the Giants simply played a bad baseball game at China Basin. They tried to make plays that weren't there. They rushed in the field. They took defensive swings. For the first time in this series, they displayed a little bit of panic.

And so after a 4–2 loss, they had to lug themselves on a cross-country flight and head back to feisty Citizens Bank Park.

The Phillies had beaten Lincecum, although that was more a matter of semantics. All three of the runs scored off him were in the third inning, after Huff turned a routine ground ball into a two-run error.

Huff already was frustrated over what happened in the first inning, when the Giants created an immediate scoring chance on Halladay. Torres had drawn a rare leadoff walk and went to third base on Freddy Sanchez's beautifully executed hit-and-run single.

Huff followed with a scorching line drive, but first baseman Ryan Howard made a diving play. The Giants managed a run when Torres scored on Posey's ground ball, but Huff was ticked off. They should've put up a crooked number. Never before did scoring a run against Halladay feel like a letdown.

They were about to be let down again. The Phillies created a chance when Ibanez hit a leadoff single in the third and Ruiz made no effort to dodge an inside pitch that hit him.

Then the craziness began. Halladay tried to put down a sacrifice bunt, but it hit the plate and started to spin foul. Posey, aware he might have a force play at third base, alertly pounced on the ball, and plate umpire Jeff Nelson called it fair.

Halladay just stood in the box, not realizing he needed to run. The Giants had an easy double play.

But Sandoval had charged as Halladay squared to bunt, and he was confused initially, too. Sandoval took the throw from Posey while drifting back to third base, but he couldn't locate the bag, and his blind attempt to stab it with his leg missed the mark. Ibanez slid in safely, and it took the home dugout screaming at Sandoval for him to realize that Halladay only now had begun jogging down the line.

The Giants managed to get the force at first base. But they should've gotten much more.

The mistakes didn't end there. Victorino followed with a ground ball to Huff, who knew that Ibanez was not a fast runner at third. He thought he could throw home and prevent the tying run from scoring. But in his haste, Huff forgot to watch the ball into his glove. It took a hard deflection off the leather and bounced into shallow center field, allowing two runs to score easily. Victorino made it to second base without a play, then scored on Polanco's single.

Outside of that one messy inning, Lincecum pitched brilliantly. He retired the side in the first two innings. He didn't allow a base runner in the fourth, fifth, or sixth, either. Yet he blamed himself for not shutting down the rally in the third. He also was upset that he hit Ruiz on an 0–2 pitch.

"Aww, man," Huff said. "He's standing up for his first baseman. He's a great pitcher, a great kid. No, this one's on me. Obviously, I made the big one. It's all on me tonight."

Despite letting Halladay off the hook in the first inning, the Giants had more chances to get him. By the third inning, it was clear that he was lacking something on the mound. His cutter wasn't moving as much and his fastball was short by at least 4 mph.

After the game, Charlie Manuel revealed that Halladay had strained his groin in the second inning. Big Roy was so intent on not letting Ross beat him again that he pushed off a little harder while humping up on a fastball.

"He was determined to stay in there," Manuel said.

Halladay lasted seven innings, mostly on cutters, change-ups, and guile. Ross hit an RBI double off him in the fourth inning, but he also made an ill-advised attempt to tag up on Sandoval's fly out to right field. Jayson Werth threw out Ross easily to end the inning.

"It was a split-second decision," Ross said. "It was the wrong decision. It kind of took the momentum out from under us."

Werth hit a solo homer in the ninth to make it 4–2, and the Giants couldn't touch Phillies closer Brad Lidge.

"We're not machines, man," Huff said. "We made mistakes. I made a mistake tonight. I was trying to make a gamble throwing home. I wish I could rewind but…can't.

"I mean, listen," he continued. "We took one there. We took two of three here against a really tough team. If you told us before the series started that we'd be in this position, I think we'd all take it. We have to go out there and play like we did all year. Today just wasn't my day. Sleep it off, go back to Philly, and go to work."

The Giants still had two chances to win the series. But unlike that final weekend against the Padres, they would have to leave their well-feathered nest. They'd have to clinch on the road.

Either the Giants would return to host Game 1 of the World Series or they had played their last game in 2010 on the shores of McCovey Cove.

"We see ourselves more in the driver's seat than them, a little more in control," Lincecum said. "So it's up to us."

The Giants had time to think on the five-hour flight to Philadelphia, plus a little extra time before the plane took off. There was a ground stop on the tarmac because President Obama was on his way back to Washington after making an appearance to support Democratic candidates in San Francisco. Giants players and staff watched out their windows as Air Force One took off.

Bochy could have used a consultation with Obama's national security advisors in selecting a third baseman. Sandoval's inability to find third base on Halladay's bunt play cost the team, and Fontenot, who let an easy pop-up drop in Game 2, wasn't going to get another shot. It seemed clear that Uribe would move to third, and Renteria would reclaim his role as the starting shortstop.

There were other story lines prior to Game 6. The Giants did not have a robust franchise history when they hit the road with a 3–2 lead in a postseason series. It had happened on two other occasions in the team's 53 seasons in San Francisco. The first time, the upstart 1987 club went to Busch Stadium needing to beat the Cardinals just once to win the NLCS. They didn't score a run in two games, and outfielder Candy

Maldonado's ill-advised sliding attempt made the difference in the first one. Atlee Hammaker got blasted in the deciding Game 7, giving up a three-run home run to Jose Oquendo—who had hit just one homer during the regular season.

The Giants' other failure came on an even grander stage. They had two chances in Anaheim to win the 2002 World Series, and every Giants fan had the numbers painfully etched in their memories.

Five-run lead. Seven outs away.

Russ Ortiz handed over the baseball after allowing consecutive hits in the seventh inning, and the game devolved from there. Scott Spiezio somehow kept his three-run homer fair against Felix Rodriguez, and the Angels stormed back to take the lead against stalwart closer Robb Nen, whose arm throbbed with every pitch.

The Angels' annoying Rally Monkey had done the backflip of his little simian life. The Giants suffered a concussive loss in Game 6, and they couldn't wake themselves from the shock in time for Game 7. Livan Hernandez got hit hard, and the little team from Orange County once owned by Gene Autry rode off into the sunset.

These 2010 Giants did not have Bonds hitting a home run every seventh or eighth at-bat. In fact, they had played three consecutive games against the Phillies at AT&T Park without hitting a homer—the first time that had happened since August 4 through 7. Aside from Ross, who had three homers in the series, no other Giant had gone deep against the Phillies.

It would be Jonathan Sanchez against Roy Oswalt one more time in Game 6, and the Phillies' right-hander insisted he was at full strength, despite throwing 18 pitches while taking the loss in relief in Game 4.

Bochy was sending out more psychological ripples of confidence with his decisions. The Phillies brought Cole Hamels, their Game 7 starter, to the media interview room before Game 6. The Giants had no interest in letting Cain speak to reporters, though. They didn't want to acknowledge the possibility they'd need him to start a deciding game. They sent Torres, instead.

But privately, Bochy fretted over Game 6. He had confidence knowing he could send Cain to pitch the following day, yet he also knew the Phillies would be emboldened if they stormed to tie this series. So would their fans. Even with Cain in reserve, Bochy did not like his chances in a winner-take-all game for the pennant in South Philly. This would be the game he was determined to win, and so he planned to draw a line in the sand. He stood ready to manage like it was an elimination game.

Bochy also worried about his Game 6 starting pitcher. The Phillies had a good approach against Jonathan Sanchez in Game 2. He wasn't throwing quite as hard as he did to finish the season, and aside from his dominant start against the Braves' poor lineup in the NLDS, he'd been walking a lot of batters.

Bochy had Bumgarner ready to back up Sanchez, but the manager also told Lincecum to hold off throwing his side session. He might use his ace for a few batters, maybe more.

It would be, to use Bochy's phrasing from earlier in the postseason, "all decks on hand"—the most hilarious malaprop uttered by a Giant since Barry Bonds once famously said he'd "tackle that bridge when we come to it."

The Phillies all but tackled Sanchez in the first inning. They scored a pair of runs on a walk, a wild pitch, a double by Utley, and Werth's sacrifice fly that nearly left the ballpark. With Guillermo Mota already warming up behind him in the bullpen, Sanchez escaped further damage by getting Ibanez to pop up to strand two runners.

But while Sanchez was wild out of the strike zone, Oswalt was careless within it. And the Phillies' infield defense, which struggled most of the series, did not play clean behind him.

It was Sanchez's surprising leadoff single in the third that touched off the Giants' tying, two-run rally. Torres followed with a deep drive to center field that Victorino appeared to catch, but the ball dislodged as the outfielder's back hit the wall. Sanchez, unsure if the ball had been caught, had to stop at second base. It was a good break and a bad one for the Giants, all at once.

A sacrifice bunt advanced both runners, and Huff came through in another RBI spot, punching a single up the middle. Sanchez scored, and Flannery gambled by sending Torres to the plate. He would've been safe, but Victorino's throw took a lucky bounce off the mound, and Ruiz applied the tag.

For every play the Phillies executed, though, they bungled another. Oswalt should've been out of the inning when he got Posey to ground to Polanco. But the third baseman threw wide to first base, and Huff, who had advanced to second base on Victorino's throw to the plate, made his second smart base running decision of the inning. He saw the ball squirt away from Ryan Howard and instantly reacted to score the tying run.

It was a new ballgame, but Sanchez would last only two more batters. Without his legs under him, he walked Polanco on five pitches to lead off the bottom of the third, then threw a 2–0 fastball that drilled Utley in the back.

Utley immediately turned toward first base, and when the ball bounced right to him, he couldn't resist flipping it dismissively to the mound.

There was history between these two. A year earlier, Utley got buzzed by a Sanchez pitch and took a long look at the mound. Then he purposefully called timeout as Sanchez was about to begin his windup, just to get in the pitcher's head. Utley won that battle, hitting a home run into the right-field arcade. Later in that game, both sides were warned when the Phillies hit then-Giant Ryan Garko with a pitch.

This time, the warnings were about to come out—along with everyone on both teams.

Sanchez could not let Utley's dismissive gesture go without comment.

"That's bullshit," he yelled.

"What's bullshit?" responded Utley, as he stepped off first base and took a step toward the mound.

Huff immediately moved in front of Utley, and so did umpire Derryl Cousins. Both benches emptied, almost playing out a scene from *West Side Story*. Ruiz screamed at Sanchez, and Renteria screamed right back, but it barely qualified as a tussle.

The relievers spilled out of the bullpens in center field, too, even though they were so far away it was almost farcical. By the time they arrived, it was clear the hostilities wouldn't escalate. But the baseball codes say you always join a fight. So that's what they did.

Only one player stayed put. Left-hander Jeremy Affeldt had been getting loose on the bullpen mound, and coach Mark Gardner grabbed his jersey and ordered him to stay where he stood. Even before the benches cleared, Bochy had decided to go no further with Sanchez. He needed Affeldt to be ready and clear-headed.

Affeldt wore abuse from the Phillies' boorish fans, who were perched almost right on top of him. "Chicken" and "coward" were two of the less vulgar terms hurled in his direction. But Affeldt didn't mind. He knew he was serving a higher purpose.

That was how the tall, good-natured left-hander tried to see everything in life. Affeldt was a devout Christian who often leafed through the pages of his Bible in the dugout before a pregame stretch. But he wasn't like many other religious athletes. Affeldt wasn't a judgmental Christian. He was more into forgiveness and understanding. He didn't condemn sinners or object if a teammate played a rap song with strong language.

That's not to suggest he was passive about his faith, though. He cared deeply about social justice and pledged both time and money to Not For Sale, a nonprofit campaign that fights to end human trafficking and slavery around the world. He was interested in things like clean water and hunger campaigns and assisting orphans in developing nations. He empathized with battered women and anyone else who was a victim of abuse. He was the Giants' nominee for the Roberto Clemente Award, which honors the game's most inspirational humanitarian, and he donated $100 for every strikeout to Not For Sale.

He hadn't donated nearly as much money in 2010, though. Affeldt started slow and dealt with injuries all season. A year earlier, he was the best setup man in the league, posting a 1.73 ERA—the lowest among all NL relief pitchers—and earned a contract extension. But he was having an inconsistent follow-up season even before a strained oblique muscle in July knocked him out for a month. When he returned, Lopez had supplanted him as the team's top left-handed specialist.

During batting practice before Game 6, Affeldt stood in the outfield and said a prayer asking for strength and patience. More than anything, he wanted to pitch in a meaningful situation again. He wanted to use his talents to glorify God.

Affeldt's prayer was answered, but not in the way he intended. Sanchez's start was his shortest of the season, and the shortest by a Giant in the NLCS since 1989, when Rick Reuschel didn't make it out of the first inning in Game 2 against the Cubs.

When players finally calmed down and returned to their dugouts, Affeldt received his chance. And he flat-out dominated.

He struck out Howard, retired Werth on a fly ball, and got Victorino to ground out, stranding both of the runners he inherited. Then Affeldt retired all three batters he faced in the fourth inning, too.

Wilson turned to his mates in the bullpen.

"Guys, this is fitting," he said. "We're going to have to nail it down. We'll get a late-inning run, and it's going to take a combined effort, and we'll celebrate afterward."

Affeldt already had run the toughest leg of this relay, the one Bochy wasn't sure how he'd cover. Next the manager used Bumgarner, the 21-year-old rookie, who was working on just two days of rest. And the kid was put to the test in the fifth when Rollins singled and Howard hit a two-out double. It took a tremendous play by Torres, quickly gathering Howard's double off the wall in left-center, to keep Rollins from scoring. After an intentional walk to Werth, Bumgarner got Victorino to tap out to the mound and leave the bases loaded.

Bumgarner faced an even tougher escape in the sixth inning, when Ibanez led off with a double and took third on a sacrifice. Huff walked over from first base to make sure the rookie was good and calm. Instead, Bumgarner ended up easing Huff's nerves.

"I'm gonna strike this guy out, and we're out of this thing," he told Huff.

Sure enough, Bumgarner went fastball–change-up–curveball to strike out pinch-hitter Ben Francisco. Then Rollins flied out to end the inning.

Affeldt and Bumgarner made their best pitches to strand runners. Next it was Lopez's turn to preserve the tie.

Years earlier, Lopez saw his minor league career going nowhere in the Arizona Diamondbacks system. So he valued pragmatism over his pride and asked sidearm reliever Mike Myers to help him drop down. It was a decision that changed his life, and while he wasn't a household name, he was proving to be one of the Giants' most valuable players. Over the years, Lopez had learned to read hitters' swings and vary his looks to the plate, dropping down a little lower when he felt an opponent was beginning to time him.

Lopez didn't need to drag his knuckles against Utley and Howard. He kept them guessing to the end. The sidearm lefty had disarmed two of the best left-handed hitters in the game, retiring them nine out of 10 times in the series. And in Game 6, he made it 11-for-12, getting Utley to hit a harmless tapper in front of the plate and then striking out Howard on a slider to end a perfect seventh inning.

For all the invective directed at Brian Sabean at the trade deadline, the GM ended up acquiring the biggest difference maker of all.

It was getting late now and the game remained tied. The Giants had used their best lefties. They weren't equipped to handle extra innings. They needed one more big hit from the offense.

Uribe provided it.

The jovial soul of the team and original member of Bochy's "Dirty Dozen," Uribe stepped to the plate against Ryan Madson with the bases empty in the eighth. His wrist still wasn't 100 percent, and scouts noticed he hadn't been catching up to quality fastballs for the better part of a month. Madson threw him one that caught more of the plate than he wanted.

Uribe wasn't out in front, but he was strong enough to make solid contact to right field. He hadn't hit a home run down the right field line all season. He busted out of the box, thinking the drive might be off the wall. Werth also sprinted back, ready to play a carom. But the ball did not bounce back. It disappeared into the first row, stunning the crowd.

Uribe was wearing his black batting gloves, so the effect wasn't as dramatic. But he flashed those jazz hands of his, and the Giants had their first lead of the ballgame. They could smell the pennant now.

Bochy had an ace up his sleeve, and he wasn't about to save it for Game 7. He brought in Lincecum, a two-time Cy Young setup man for one night only. Lincecum made his pitches to strike out Werth, the most dangerous right-handed hitter in the Phillies' lineup. But then Victorino and Ibanez hit consecutive singles, and Bochy decided it was time to hand the ball to his closer.

A few years earlier Wilson took a trip to Ireland with his buddy, Oakland A's pitcher Dallas Braden. They stayed in hostels, backpacked through the countryside, and toured castles. They kissed the Blarney Stone, which is supposed to impart the gift of eloquence and persuasiveness.

Wilson must've tongue wrestled with the thing.

Perhaps it imparted some luck, too. Braden threw a perfect game in 2010. And Wilson was about to tap into some seriously good fortune.

He gave up a rocket to Ruiz, but it was right at Huff. This time, the first baseman didn't rush the play. He watched the line drive into his glove, then stepped to double off Ibanez. Wilson's assignment was a five-out save. He'd just lucked into two of them on a ball that Ruiz hit on the screws.

The Giants were three outs away from the World Series, but there remained plenty of mines in the Phillies' lineup for Wilson to sidestep. He walked Rollins with one out. He walked Utley with two outs. And he ran the count full against Howard, who had the potential to end the game with one swing.

"I don't want to leave anything middle, but then again I still have to challenge him," Wilson said. "Because, worst-case scenario, we have a game tomorrow. If the season's going to come down to it, it's going to come down to this. Let's go for it."

Sometimes Wilson referred to his tight little breaking pitch as a slider. Other times it's a cutter. Does it really matter? This is a guy who wouldn't admit he dyes his beard black.

Whatever the pitch was, it took stones to throw it with a full count. It dipped perfectly, brushing the bottom of the strike zone, and umpire Tom Hallion pumped his arm. Howard turned and tilted back his head in defeat. The Giants won 3–2.

Moments after the Giants clinched the NL pennant, Brian Wilson crosses his arms and points to the sky as Buster Posey rushes to congratulate him. Wilson struck out the Phillies' Ryan Howard to seal a victory in Game 6 of the NLCS.

Wilson let out a scream as he crossed his arms, then turned back to find Posey already upon him. Burrell was the first one out of the dugout to reach the mound. Freddy Sanchez jumped into Renteria's arms. The Giants had been winning these torturous games for the better part of two months. They were winning them still.

Now, for the fourth time in 53 seasons in San Francisco, they were National League champions.

Ross was the easy choice as NLCS Most Valuable Player, after hitting .350 with three doubles and three home runs among his seven hits. His .950 slugging percentage was the highest in a six-game series in NLCS history.

Lopez wasn't the series MVP, but it was fitting that he received the victory in Game 6. Howard had led the NL in RBIs in three of the last five years. He'd driven in 130-plus in four of the last five seasons. He didn't knock in a single run in the NLCS, and Lopez was most responsible for that.

Uribe had a lot more happy to celebrate. His two game-winning RBIs in the series would assure a lasting place in Giants history, right there with his beloved uncle.

"POWW!" Uribe said. "It's big like me. It's for the World Series."

Bochy had managed teams with more talent in the lineup, but he said he'd never managed a group of players with more heart. Bochy showed plenty himself, too, while making one genius move after another in the series.

"It's not easy to get here," Bochy said. "You've got to go through two tough teams. We played the best team in the National League, the team with the best record, and we had to play our best ball to beat 'em. And they found a way to do it, with their heart and determination."

The Giants staged their second champagne celebration on the road, and it lasted long into the night. After making a mess of the visiting clubhouse at Citizens Bank Park, they rented out a ballroom at their team hotel and kept right on raging.

Huff was ready for one more party.

"All these years I'm watching the postseason on the couch, wondering how these guys are so up to play these games," he said. "I get it now, man. I get it.

"And it's not over yet. I know America probably wanted to see the Yankees and Phillies, but it's time for some new blood."

Over their history, the Giants won pennants behind Will the Thrill, with Kenny Lofton's little flared single, and, going back to the Polo Grounds, with a Shot Heard Round the World.

This time, they reached out nearly all their best arms to grab it. Bochy fearlessly used three-fourths of his playoff rotation to win a non-elimination game. Wilson had saved so many victories for Sanchez, Bumgarner, and Lincecum. This time, he saved it for all three.

"You knew it wasn't going to come easy," Wilson said. "You knew we're going to have to fly to Philly. It was going to come down to a late-inning run. But we knew when we finally did this, we'd look at each other and say, 'This is well earned. It's exhausting, and it feels good, and it's going to be that much better of a celebration.'"

Wilson was holding the NL trophy as he spoke—a giant hunk of wood and brass. He remarked on how heavy it felt and almost had to laugh at the absurdity of it all. The beards, freaks, rejects, and thong-wearing misfits—and yes, even the mysterious Machine—were going to the Fall Classic. And they were ready to crank it at full volume.

What did Wilson imagine the World Series trophy was like to hold?

"I hope it's a skyscraper," he said.

Chapter 16

High Noon

The Giants held home-field advantage in the World Series, just as Wilson crazily suggested all those months ago when he caught a flight to Anaheim for the All-Star Game.

Except the Giants didn't meet the Yankees or Red Sox or even the Tampa Bay Rays on the shores of McCovey Cove. As Huff proclaimed, it was time for new blood. The American League entrant was the surprising Texas Rangers, and their catcher was none other than Bengie Molina.

Four months earlier Molina stood in the aisle of a bus on a dark night in Denver and told the Giants they were going places. He had no idea that he'd meet them there.

This was not the first time a team had traded a player midseason and faced him in the Fall Classic that year. In 1985 the St. Louis Cardinals dealt Lonnie Smith to the Kansas City Royals. Smith was a catalyst against his former team, hitting .333 and stealing two bases as the Royals won in seven games.

Molina wasn't exactly a threat on the base paths. But for the Giants, facing their former catcher was a much bigger deal. He had been the brains of their on-field operation for the previous three seasons. He knew Lincecum, Cain, and Jonathan Sanchez inside and out while hand-feeding them into the big leagues. And he'd match wits against the extraordinary rookie who made him expendable.

Molina wasn't motivated by revenge, nor did he begrudge anything to Posey. But the veteran catcher still didn't like the way the trade to Texas went down. And now he was especially cross with Sabean after the GM revealed during the NLCS that he had planned to trade Molina from the moment he re-signed the catcher.

"That was rehearsed—set in stone, really—once we decided not to start the year with Buster," Sabean said. "Bengie was going to be a bridge, and once Buster was ready, we were going to bring him into the mix and trade Bengie. That was the plan almost going all the way back to the winter meetings.

"We were fortuitous that Bengie turned down the Mets and signed with us. But [if not], we would've signed another catcher and lined it up the same way, because Buster wasn't ready."

Molina had turned down more money from the Mets. Now he wished he had taken it.

"Hell no, I wouldn't have signed. Big time," Molina said. "Because you don't want to be in a place that doesn't want you. I wish they had been honest with me."

Molina didn't care that Sabean also was complimentary toward him, calling the veteran "way above board" in how he dealt with the Posey situation and assisting in the rookie's development after his promotion in May.

"Well, yeah, that's not going to make anything better," Molina said. "That tells you what kind of person he is. That tells me. He should have kept his mouth shut. He probably shouldn't say it. But that's all right. That's him.

"That is not the way I feel about everybody."

As much as the Giants admired Molina, they weren't lacking for leadership behind the plate. Posey had grown into the role he seemingly was destined to hold. It wasn't much different than back in Tallahassee: he had baseball and school, and what else was there? Now he was studying opposing hitters instead of prepping for finance midterms, and the Giants' talented pitchers were executing his plan. Whether it was Jason Heyward in the division series or Ryan Howard in the NLCS, the Giants had neutralized their opponents' most dangerous hitters. Sabean's two best advance scouts, former big leaguers Joe Lefebvre and Steve Balboni, had provided Posey with many of the answers.

Posey wasn't just studying the scouting reports. He had learned the fine art of reading hitters in the box. He'd steal occasional glances at their stance, their setup, whether their weight was centered or slightly on the balls of their feet. He wasn't just breaking them down on paper. From an arm's length away, he was reading their tells, their moods, how tensely they were gripping the bat.

Posey aced Steve Decker's crash course at Triple A Fresno. Now he was applying those lessons as the baseball world watched. And when his pitchers shook him off, it wasn't always a sign of disagreement. Posey often had Lincecum do it intentionally when he'd want to plant one more distracting thought in the hitter's mind.

Posey's growth wasn't just remarkable, it was close to unprecedented. He would become the first rookie catcher to start a World Series game since Bengie's brother, Yadier, for the 2004 St. Louis Cardinals. No rookie starting catcher had won a World Series since Andy Etchebarren did for the 1966 Baltimore Orioles. But Posey was doing more than that, too. Lest anyone forget, he was batting in the middle of the Giants' lineup, often in the cleanup spot.

The last rookie catcher to hit in the middle of the order in a World Series game? Why, that would be Yogi Berra for the 1947 New York Yankees—when he won the first of his 10 rings.

Posey's confidence was soaring, but he remained humble and economic in his dealings with reporters. After his four-hit performance in Game 4 of the NLCS, he was asked: how do you digest what you did tonight?

"I helped the team win," he said. "I guess that's how I digest it."

But do you understand that it's an epic night in a postseason game?

"Well, thank you."

Molina was not surprised that Posey had won the confidence of the pitching staff and coaches. He had a father's admiration for the kid catcher, and said he looked forward to the moment when he could dig in the box and tap Posey's shin guards with his bat.

"I consider these guys brothers," Molina said. "But in between the lines, I have to defend my colors, and they have to defend theirs."

This would be the second time Molina would defend his colors against the Giants in the World Series. The last time he stepped into the visiting clubhouse at AT&T Park, it was 2002 and his Angels were the upstart team from the AL West with a lineup full of gritty, tough outs, smart base runners, and power threats.

"In 2002 the Giants were very powerful," Molina said. "They had Barry Bonds, Jeff Kent. Now they have young guys who can do the job.... It's hard to say which one is better. But I think these guys are more dangerous because of how they play the game. I know what is inside of them."

These Rangers were not unlike those Angels. They took out the Rays before beating the heavily favored Yankees in six games, and now, even in their first World Series, they found themselves the surprising favorite in the eyes of the oddsmakers.

The Rangers didn't have a Rally Monkey, but they boasted their own zoology, complete with hand gestures. When one of them did damage with the bat, the Rangers' dugout saluted the player with the Claw—sort of a slashing, long-distance high five. And when someone used speed or hustle on the base paths, the Rangers would flash the Antlers—holding their hands above each ear to imitate a swift deer.

The phenomenon leapt the dugout and took to the stands, where tens of thousands of fans in Arlington wore claw and antler T-shirts. And the Rangers didn't let their fans sit on their hands. Their high-scoring lineup could beat you with small ball, speed and hustle on the bases. Or they could knock it out of the park.

The Rangers had perhaps the best player in baseball and the hottest hitter in the postseason, Josh Hamilton, who was almost Bondsian while hitting four home runs and drawing eight walks against the Yankees in the ALCS.

And as scorching as Ross had been for the Giants in the playoffs (.324, four home runs, four doubles, eight RBIs), he was no better than either of the Rangers' two hottest hitters, Hamilton and Nelson Cruz (.375, five home runs, five doubles, eight RBIs).

The Rangers had two guys rodeo-clowning their way through this postseason.

Unlike the Phillies, who seemed to grow old overnight, the Rangers' lineup presented a multidimensional threat. They had 15 stolen bases in 17 attempts over their 11 postseason games. That posed a problem for Lincecum, who wasn't particularly good at holding runners and often got distracted by them. He had allowed 27 steals out of 30 tries during the season—a 90 percent rate that was the worst among all major league pitchers with at least 25 attempts against them.

Even Molina had hit for the cycle shortly after joining the Rangers, if such a feat could be believed.

Lincecum did not look forward to facing his former catcher. Molina had stayed in touch with him during his miserable, winless August, sending him motivational text messages. He was more than just a friend and guide.

"I've said it before and I'm going to say it again, he's been half of the reason why I got here outside of my dad and my family and my other teammates," Lincecum said. "He's meant a lot to me, and he's meant a lot to this team. He's a part of the reason why we're here and obviously part of the reason why they're there, too."

Lincecum had to deal with more than the Rangers' multidimensional offense and the emotion of facing his former catcher. He also would oppose Texas left-hander Cliff Lee, who was building a career résumé as perhaps the most dominant playoff pitcher of all time.

It didn't seem possible that Lincecum's task could get any tougher than to outpitch Roy Halladay, who was coming off a no-hitter when he took the mound for the NLCS opener. But Lee was 7–0 with a 1.26 ERA in eight career playoff starts. He simply did not fall behind hitters or issue walks.

Against the Rays and Yankees, two of the best offensive clubs in the game, Lee was 3–0 with a 0.75 ERA and had struck out 34 against a single base on balls.

Like Molina, Lee didn't begin the season with Texas. He helped pitch the Phillies to the World Series the previous year after coming over in a trade from the Cleveland Indians. Then he found himself on a last-place club in Seattle to begin 2010 after the massive, three-team deal that sent Halladay to the Phillies. The bankrupt Rangers surprised everyone in baseball when they swung a deal for Lee in July, and when he reported to the All-Star Game a few days later, he was disillusioned to be wearing yet another new uniform.

Lee would be a free agent in a few weeks. Even if he felt less than a full kinship with his new Texas teammates, he knew every strike he threw into Molina's glove would earn him tens of thousands more on the open market. And wherever he signed, he'd make sure he received a no-trade clause, too.

Once again, the national media wrote the story before the first pitch was thrown: the Giants and their merry band of misfits weren't supposed to be any match for Lee.

It would be up to Lincecum to pitch with him, and Lee almost delivered a backhanded compliment when asked about the Giants' ace.

"The way he does it…no one else does it that way. I like that," Lee said. "I like when unorthodox works."

Lee was a paragon of orthodoxy. He didn't look to the sky like Fernando Valenzuela or contort his body like Lincecum or seem to touch you as he released the ball like Randy Johnson. He simply used his fastball like a scalpel and churned through lineups with a perfect array of secondary pitches.

"You look in, and he'll go away," Rowand said. "You look away, and he'll bust you in. He throws a two-seamer and a cutter and a back-foot curveball. He's got enough velocity, and he locates. He's got a lot of ways to get you out. He keeps you off balance, and that's what makes him so effective."

Once again, Lincecum entered as the smaller, less-heralded pitcher in the matchup. The only difference: this was Game 1 of the World Series.

"He's not a guy who gets wavered by nerves," Wilson said. "He doesn't pitch on negative emotion. He's a guy who knows what he's capable of doing, he grabs the ball and makes his pitches. He's a big-time pitcher and that's what the postseason is all about.

"It's his time to shine."

The Giants understood and accepted that they were underdogs against the Phillies, who had won consecutive pennants and finished with the best record in the National League. But privately, they were annoyed that the so-called experts stamped the Rangers as the clear favorite. Hadn't the Giants won two more games than them in the regular season? Didn't they have a better pitching staff, top to bottom? Sabean certainly thought so. He didn't think his pitchers got enough credit for shutting down the Phillies, and he liked their chances to subdue Hamilton, Cruz, Elvis Andrus, and the rest of the red-hot Rangers where the Rays and Yankees could not.

"If you ask me straight up, we like our pitching staff better than the Yankees' pitching staff," Sabean said. "Simply put, we don't have the Yankees' pitching staff that gave up all the runs they gave up against Texas.

"We just beat a pretty good team. So I don't think our pitching staff is going to be intimidated by Texas."

The Giants weren't bent on proving the experts wrong, though. Their motivation didn't spring from a negative source. Within their free-spirited and familial clubhouse, winning for each other was enough. They wanted to accomplish something grand for themselves and their city.

The nation had a couple days of buildup to learn about these teams. Ross the Intern from *The Tonight Show* interviewed Ross, the Giants' upstart right fielder. Wilson answered so many questions about his beard that he said it needed its own podium.

But after all the waiting and all the workouts, the flyovers, the anthem by John Legend, and yes, a warm ovation for Molina as he tapped his chest in the introductions, it was time to stage a World Series game in San Francisco.

And Lincecum had the brain fart of his life.

Texas put immediate pressure on him in the first inning, as three of the first four batters reached base. The Rangers scored a run when Vladimir Guerrero's line drive pelted Lincecum's leg for an infield single, and they had runners at the corners with one out.

Lincecum needed to make a pitch, and he did, getting Cruz to hit a tapper in front of the mound. Lincecum bounded to scoop up the ground ball, then turned to catch Michael Young midway down the third-base line. It was a terrific reaction play, and Lincecum had Young in a rundown.

But inexplicably, Lincecum held the ball and jogged toward third, running Young all the way back to the base. Uribe couldn't understand why Lincecum didn't throw it to him. The ballpark buzzed with confusion, and when Lincecum looked back to second base, he frowned. He immediately knew.

He screwed this one up, big time.

"A brain fart," he said, admitting he thought the bases were loaded. "It's a first for a lot of us and [a] different atmosphere…and I got outside of myself there."

Uribe helped him dial it back in. He made a deft pickup of Ian Kinsler's ground ball to start a step-and-throw double play that got the Giants out of the bases-loaded situation.

But the Rangers would flash more claws and antlers in the second inning. Molina, hitting against Lincecum for the first time, started off the rally by punching a single to right field. Then, with one out, Lee showed bunt early.

It was an odd move. Everyone on both teams knew Molina was too slow to advance on a sacrifice. It's the main reason that Bochy never wanted to hit him seventh or eighth in the lineup. But the Rangers were slicker than they let on. Lee pulled back the bat at the last instant and executed the age-old "butcher boy" play, taking a quick hack at a fastball down the middle.

The Giants should've seen the trickery coming. Instead, they fell for it, and their infielders were charging as Lee pulled the string. Their outfielders were playing so shallow that the line drive to left field had no trouble splitting the gap for a double as Molina advanced to third base.

The Rangers kept right on gambling. Andrus lifted a fly ball to center field that might have been deep enough to score most runners from third, but not Molina. Texas sent him anyway.

Even a decent relay would've gotten Molina at the plate. But Torres unleashed all his adrenaline with his heave from center field, and it was so wild that Molina scored easily. Lee broke for third base on the play, and Posey had a terrific shot at gunning him down, but his throw was off line, too. It was a total breakdown.

The Rangers were harassing Lincecum at the plate and on the bases, and he was pitching like a cornered animal. Instead of pounding fastballs from the start, as he often did, Posey had him mixing up mostly offspeed pitches. It was clear by now that his slider, the pitch that resurrected him in September, wasn't anywhere near sharp.

But Lincecum found a way to minimize the damage. And after two innings, for all their sloppy play and brain farts, the Giants only trailed 2–0.

That should have been a mountain range to overcome against Lee. But he was off his game, too. His cutter lacked its usual buzzsaw movement and accuracy. He couldn't throw his curveball for strikes. He still had his smarts and ability to change speeds, but he lacked his put-away stuff.

The Giants ran up Lee's pitch count to 75 through four innings. Uribe fouled off several in a 10-pitch at-bat while striking out in the fourth. Yet the Giants seemed so bewildered to be in 2–0 and 3–1 counts that they helped out Lee by overswinging. They weren't thinking about "keeping the line moving," as Bochy so often preached. They didn't know how many hitting counts they'd get against a pitcher who practically wore a halo in the postseason. So they were swinging big on him.

Freddy Sanchez was the only hitter who stayed within himself at the plate. All of a sudden, he didn't look like the skittish former Pirate who might not have the nerve and toughness to handle the postseason. In Game 1 of the World Series, he shined like a batting champion.

Sanchez hit a broken-bat double in the first inning. He doubled in the Giants' first run in the third. And he hit another double in the fifth that put them ahead. He used every part of the ballpark, from the right-field chalk to the left-field line to the gap in left-center, while becoming the first player in World Series history to double in his first three career at-bats in the Fall Classic.

"At the beginning of the postseason, I was feeling real anxious and not relaxed at the plate, and as the postseason went on, I started to get more comfortable," Sanchez said. "I started to find my swing a little bit."

Being a rookie in the World Series wasn't easy. But perhaps it was even tougher for a player like Sanchez or Aubrey Huff, veterans who were in the playoffs for the first time. They had spent a decade or longer thinking about being in this moment. They fully understood how fleeting and precious it was. It was natural to tighten up, to be ruled by fear, to think that if they blew this chance, they'd forever live with regret.

Sanchez was just 2-for-16 in the Atlanta series, and he was still battling two sore shoulders. But he and Huff and all the other playoff newcomers were allowed to receive more chances because the Giants' dominant pitching staff had picked them up and carried them through to the next round. Now feeling settled in, it was their chance to return the favor.

After Sanchez provided the boom-boom-boom, Uribe brought his unique brand of pow.

Consecutive RBI singles by Ross and Huff made it 5–2 and drove Lee from the game in the fifth, and Uribe greeted right-hander Darren O'Day by crushing a hanging slider deep into the left-field bleachers. This time Uribe didn't need to hustle down the line. He could stand and admire it while flashing his white batting gloves. Jazz hands were better than claws any day.

It was a three-run shot, and it completed a six-run fifth inning that gave the Giants an 8–2 lead. It was the Giants' first six-run inning in the World Series since 1937.

All of a sudden the story wasn't about Cliff Lee, the second coming of Sandy Koufax. It was about the Giants' no-name lineup, which had found a way to beat the league's best pitchers all season.

"You know, we've got some pretty good players, too," Burrell said. "We may not have all the accolades, but some guys know how to hit over here."

Lincecum struggled while giving up two more runs in the sixth and didn't survive the inning. The Giants needed Wilson to stem a three-run rally in the ninth, too. But for once, the Giants had scored enough to cover up a few mistakes. For a team that had six one-run margins in their first seven postseason wins, their 11–7 victory in Game 1 of the World Series was like Christmas morning in October.

"We don't have the most talented lineup," Ross said. "We don't have superstars. But we play with a lot of heart. We like the fact nobody really gives us a chance. We feed off that. We're not scared, that's for sure.

"Everyone in here had confidence that we'd win today."

But win a slugfest?

"Oh, no, no, no," Ross said. "Not like this. I was thinking 2–1, something like that."

Freddy Sanchez thought of a conversation he had with Sabean months earlier. He was in a slump and having a pity party for himself as he watched video.

"Freddy, why are you so upset?" Sabean said. "The season isn't over yet. There's a reason we brought you over here. We know the kind of player you are."

He was the kind of player who had four hits in his first World Series game.

"It's crazy to have my name up there," said Sanchez when told the unprecedented nature of his three doubles. "It's something special for just a little guy like me to be able to do it."

But the Rangers made enough hard contact in the later innings to remind the Giants that they wouldn't be tamed easily in this series. Bochy knew his club needed to play a cleaner Game 2 if they hoped to take control. He adjusted his rotation one more time, moving Cain in front of Jonathan Sanchez to pitch at home.

Someone asked Cain: how do you try to sleep the night before you start a World Series game?

"Close your eyes," he replied.

Yep. The Giants had the right man on the mound.

It was hard to believe Cain had been a Giant longer than anyone on the roster. He was just 26 years old—a few months younger than Lincecum, actually—and he had to shake his head and laugh softly when Duane Kuiper came up with the torture theme that would describe their season.

Cain's whole career had been a dungeon of unspeakable wrongs.

By so many measures, he ranked as one of the best, most consistent pitchers in baseball. Dan Haren, CC Sabathia, and Roy Halladay were the only others in the majors to throw 200 innings and record an ERA below 4.00 in each of the last four seasons. Cain held opponents to a .195 average with runners in scoring position over 2009–2010. Among all full-time major league starters, only Milwaukee's Yovani Gallardo was stingier.

Want more? Cain ranked sixth in the NL with 223⅓ innings in 2010 and had become the first Giant to throw a fourth consecutive 200-inning season since Jim Barr in 1977. The other Giants pitchers on that list were luminaries—Jack Sanford, Juan Marichal, and Gaylord Perry.

Cain threw a quality start (at least six innings, no more than three earned runs) in 25 of his 33 outings, tying him with Chris Carpenter,

Tim Hudson, Adam Wainwright, and Halladay for the most in the NL.

He had an unbelievable five-start run from May 22 to June 13, tossing at least seven innings while allowing no more than one earned run each time out. There had been just two other five-start spans like that in 53 seasons in San Francisco. Vida Blue owned one of them, in 1978. And Cain owned the other, as a 22-year-old in 2006.

This run was even better. It included three complete games in a four-start span, and Cain went eight innings in the other one. One of those complete games came in Cincinnati's lively ballpark against the league's highest scoring team. No pitcher had gone the distance against the Reds in 2010 before Cain did it.

Cain knew if he wanted to pitch deeper into games and maybe give himself a better chance to win, he needed to tame the wildness and deep counts that often disrupted his outings as a younger pitcher. And he succeeded. He walked one batter or fewer in each of his final 10 regular season starts.

He had a highly respectable 3.45 career ERA.

He had taken a no-hitter to the seventh inning or beyond five times.

And one more statistic: his career record.

57–62.

It's almost criminal that a pitcher as good as Cain could have a losing record. True, the Giants weren't a .500 team in any of his first four seasons. But the explanation went beyond that.

Every year, one pitcher on every big league staff seems to draw the short straw and cope with poor run support. Every year, the fates rigged the lottery against Cain. In 2007 he threw 22 quality starts. He had a 6–8 record in them.

It became such a common occurrence that it needed its own term: to pitch a 2–1 game and lose was to get Cained.

Reporters honestly felt bad when they'd have to approach Cain's locker after one of these starts. How could they ask about the lack of run support again? How could they not?

Even in his youth, Cain kept his emotions under wraps. He didn't purse his lips or sigh or flail his arms in frustration. Even when speaking with a friendly reporter off the record, he wouldn't give any indication that he was frustrated with his teammates. There were no trade requests. Not so much as a sniffle of self-pity.

When he was in the minor leagues, his coaches marveled at how mature Cain seemed for his age. He was just 17 when the club took him toward the back of the first round in the 2002 draft, a little higher than most prognosticators expected him to go. Some wondered if this was another of the Giants' cheap, below-slot signings.

It wasn't. The Giants had liked Cain ever since scout Lee Elder, in charge of the southern states at the time, happened to see the right-hander on a trip to Alabama. Elder had driven from his home in Augusta, Georgia, to see Cain's high school teammate, a pitcher named Conor Lalor, but the ace had a sore arm. Elder got a look at Cain instead. He knew the kid was first-round material.

Cain already knew how to pitch. He began taking lessons when he was 11 from Mauro "Goose" Gozzo, a former relief pitcher with the Toronto Blue Jays who lived not far from the Cain house in suburban Memphis. Gozzo owned some horses on his 10-acre spread and employed a farrier who also happened to do some work for Cain's grandfather, Guy Miller. One day Miller brought three of his grandsons to be evaluated. Cain was among them.

"You never tell how a kid that young will develop," Gozzo said. "But I definitely saw a loose arm, and I sensed some serious desire. Those are the two things you look for."

Gozzo quit his job at a waste management company to give lessons full-time, and Cain was one of his prodigies. He pulled Cain out of the local Dixie Youth League to face tougher competition. Gozzo talked about mound presence and confidence, and Cain soaked it up.

"Even from T-ball up, he's been so competitive," said Cain's father, Tom, a custom woodworker. "He just picked up the game really fast. He knew all the rules. He knew where to throw the ball. He had a knack for baseball from day one. We tried to do everything we could to support him and send him to get all the instruction he could get."

Cain never caused any problems as a kid, and his fourth-grade teacher never had to write his name on the blackboard. His mother would know. It was her classroom.

"He's always been a good boy," said Dolores Cain, smiling.

Barely three years after his high school graduation Cain was in the major leagues—the youngest Giant to start a game since Mark Grant in 1984. And five years after that Cain would rank as the longest tenured Giant, their union representative, their steadiest pitcher, and a seawall in any storm. Coaches still had to remind themselves how young he was.

One veteran pitcher who took Cain under his wing was Matt Morris, the fiery former Cardinals ace who had joined the Giants as a free agent in 2006. When Morris arrived in Scottsdale that first spring, he went to a local music shop and bought a honey-colored Martin guitar, but his purchase soon became a problem. The shop owner didn't tell Morris that he needed to keep the guitar in a humidor, and it warped overnight in the dry, Arizona air.

Morris sent it to get repaired and shared his lament with Cain during fielding drills the next day. The kid perked up. He'd been meaning to buy a guitar and offered to pay cash for it. Morris said no, he wouldn't take money from a rookie making the league minimum.

They became friends from that day forward, frequently going to dinner together on the road. Morris even made conditioning work fun by incorporating a soccer ball and Frisbee.

"With Cainer, he's so talented that I just didn't want to mess him up," Morris said with a laugh.

On the last day of the 2006 season, which also happened to be Cain's 22nd birthday, Morris presented him with a gift. It was the Martin guitar, bearing Morris' autograph in silver pen along with a good-luck inscription.

Like Morris, Cain had learned to become a tough competitor. He didn't like making anything easy for an opponent, even if it was something as simple as an opposing pitcher trying to sacrifice. But Cain had a much different way of channeling his aggression. Unlike Morris, who was known for his bursts of body language, Cain was Gary Cooper on the mound.

Bochy often talked of Cain having "that look" when he'd check on him in the late innings. Posey didn't have any idea what his manager meant.

"He's got it all the time," the rookie catcher said. "He does. It's a confident look, and determined. It's a good feeling when the guy out there is pitching without fear."

Cain didn't mind that Lincecum received all the accolades, magazine covers, and video game commercials. In fact, he liked it that way. He could sit in a corner, maybe strum his guitar a little, then tie on his work apron when it was his day to pitch.

To watch Cain pitch to an isolated hitter, or even see him for a full inning, you might not think he was anything special. He didn't get hitters to screw themselves in the ground, as Lincecum did with his change-up or Jonathan Sanchez did with his slider. Cain simply found a way, time after time, to keep hitters the slightest bit off balance and their contact just the slightest bit off center.

Cain learned something from opposing pitchers, too. He went up against Greg Maddux seven times over a two-year span, and the master frustrated him time and again. Cain had several strong outings in those games. The Giants still lost six of seven. Cain couldn't figure out why, but Maddux was able to pitch a little better—and get the better of him—every time.

In Maddux's final major league start, on September 27, 2008, Cain held the Dodgers to two earned runs in seven innings at AT&T Park. Maddux allowed one on two hits through six. The Dodgers Cained Cain 2–1.

When Cain went home after that season, he thought of ways he could improve. He wanted to be more like Maddux—always calculated, always cool, always keeping hitters a fraction of an inch off center. And all through 2010, Cain did exactly that.

Cain didn't have Lincecum's rock-star stuff and style. He might get an unsexy pop-up to second base instead of a fist-pumping strikeout. But he had a compact, clean, and tight delivery, and he was repeating it on every pitch. His fastball had that heavy, late explosion that kept surprising hitters. He was around the plate with his curve and change-up, too, and when he missed, it was more often a competitive ball than a mistake in the strike zone.

He was the young gun with an old soul, and he had reached a unique point in his career. He still had giddy-up on his fastball, yet he was wizened enough to know how to use it. He could add and subtract from his heater, sometimes saving a hump-up pitch for the late innings when he really needed it.

He'd never admit to it, but one thing continued to nag at him. Entering the year, he had faced the Dodgers 13 times. And he'd never defeated them. The streak became 14 when he lost another to the Giants' archrivals in June.

Cain finally broke the streak on August 1, throwing 7⅔ shutout innings to complete a sweep of the Dodgers at AT&T Park. Even then, he refused to exhale or to admit a weight had been lifted or acknowledge all those times he pitched well against the Dodgers and didn't get any runs.

He simply said he was happy the team won, and when asked about how such a peculiar streak could happen, he just shrugged.

"Didn't pitch well enough to win," he said in a way that drew a few chuckles from reporters.

"A lot of times, I didn't," he said, firmly.

It was Renteria who helped Cain finally break through for that victory over the Dodgers. With first base open, L.A. manager Joe Torre had Clayton Kershaw intentionally walk Rowand to pitch to Renteria. The ailing shortstop hit a screaming triple off the right-field arcade. It was the hit Cain had been denied so many times in his young, torture-filled career.

Renteria provided one of the year's best quotes after that game, admitting the intentional walk to Rowand bruised his pride.

"You never wake up the baby," he said.

Now Cain was locked in another tight battle. It was Game 2 of the World Series. And the baby screamed once more.

Renteria, his place in the lineup secure again, connected on a pitch from left-hander C.J. Wilson in the fifth inning. His solo home run over the left-field wall broke a scoreless tie.

Cain watched with approval from the dugout. So many times in his career, the Giants failed to support him with a single run. Now he had a lead in the World Series, and he already had received an even more obvious gift from the baseball gods—one of the zillions owed to him.

In the top half of the fifth, Ian Kinsler hit a deep drive to center field that hit the very top of the padded wall, bounced straight up in the air,

Matt Cain's performance in Game 2 of the 2010 World Series earned him the win and a deafening ovation when he walked off the mound in the eighth.

and fell back into play. Torres snatched it with his bare hand. Kinsler didn't miss a home run by inches. It was more like a millimeter.

"I don't know how that happened," Torres said. "But things happen for a reason."

Kinsler had to settle for a leadoff double, and Cain all but staple-gunned him to second base while retiring the next three hitters, excluding an intentional walk.

"I cashed it in as one run," Cain said. "Then I saw Torres had thrown it in and he was standing on second. From there, I just said, 'We'll just get the next guy and see how it works out.'"

It was working out brilliantly. Cain gave up only three other hits in his 7⅔ innings. But two of them came on consecutive singles with one out in the sixth, and a wild pitch advanced both runners. It was still just a 1–0 game, and the Rangers had Nelson Cruz, their dangerous power-hitting threat, at the plate.

Cain had struck him out twice on a series of diving change-ups and sliders earlier in the game, and although Cruz was a fearsome fastball hitter, those offspeed pitches were stuck in his mind and slowed down his bat. Cain spotted a fastball on the inside edge, Cruz couldn't get out in front, and he popped up to Huff in foul ground. Cain followed the same plan with Kinsler, throwing another no-frills, inside fastball that resulted in a pop out to shallow right field. The crowd roared as Cain resolutely walked off the mound.

The Giants manufactured another run in the seventh inning to take a 2–0 lead, and Cain's pitch count was starting to climb. With two outs and a runner on second base in the eighth, Bochy came out for the ball.

The orange-splashed sellout crowd yelled with all the strength nearly 100,000 lungs could muster, showering their love on Cain, their quiet, humble, and doggedly determined pitcher who was so underappreciated every place except where it most mattered.

The song played upon his exit was by Fatboy Slim:

We've come a long, long way together
through the hard times and the good.
I want to celebrate you baby,
I want to praise you like I should.

Cain deserved to win this game, and he did. Lopez, fresh off neutralizing Chase Utley and Ryan Howard in the NLCS, moved right along to the next dangerous lefty, getting Hamilton to fly out to strand Cain's runner. And the Giants went on to wreck the Rangers' wild bullpen in a seven-run eighth inning—a final outpouring of generosity from the baseball gods to Cain—on their way to a 9–0 victory in Game 2.

Cain hadn't allowed an earned run in three postseason starts, spanning 21⅓ innings. He became the fifth pitcher in major league history to throw at least 20 innings with a spotless ERA in a single postseason. Christy Mathewson and Carl Hubbell, two New York Giants Hall of Famers, were among the others.

In the postseason, hitters were 1-for-15 against Cain with runners in scoring position—and the Rangers were hitless in seven tries in Game 2.

"That's the Cain I saw the last 3½ years, and he was probably even better tonight," Molina said. "He gets that curveball over for strikes all the time now. He's been a good pitcher for a long time, but wow, he seemed to take it to another level."

Said Bochy: "He's the oldest Giant we have here."

Yet when Cain exited to the ovation of his life, he didn't wave or tip his cap. He cast his eyes downward the whole way, walking off like a grim town sheriff.

The streets were safe for another day.

If Cain didn't acknowledge the cheers in a World Series game, leaving a shutout in the eighth inning, when would he?

"Awww, you can't do it with runners on base," he said. "It just didn't seem right. But it is cool—really cool. To walk off the field and hear 43,000 people cheering for you…definitely."

Cain chased off the bad guys. The Giants held a 2–0 lead in the World Series. And now, all of Northern California could envision the end credits.

Chapter 17

I'll Say It Now

This would be the first World Series Gala in North Texas, and the invitation called for "cowboy chic" attire.

Giants owner Bill Neukom, who owned degrees from Dartmouth and Stanford Law, who had just completed a term as president of the American Bar Association, who had more Microsoft bucks than anyone not named Gates or Ballmer, was going to find out how bow ties looked with a pair of shit kickers.

No, his boots probably hadn't seen many cattle drives. But he was getting into the spirit.

His team was a Texas two-step away from winning its first World Series in 56 seasons—four years before packing up at the Polo Grounds and heading west. All of San Francisco braced for a party that nobody in the city would ever forget—unless they were too hung over to remember it.

For many, the party already had begun. Josh Hamilton said he smelled marijuana smoke while playing center field in Game 1 at AT&T Park, and because his recovery from drug addiction was well chronicled, his olfactory experience became a fairly significant story in the Dallas area. One local TV reporter did his live shot from near the Willie McCovey statue on the opposite side of the cove, shouting with incredulity that people were getting high just a few feet away from him. Other Texas-based reporters were astonished that local police didn't seem to care about enforcing laws or issuing citations.

"We are truly in San Francisco," said Newy Scruggs, a reporter for the NBC affiliate in Dallas. "I'm standing here and I'm like...that's not cigarettes. That's weed. *That's weed!*"

History favored the Giants lighting a victory cigar, or whatever else they chose to fire up. Of the 51 teams to take a 2–0 lead in the World Series, 40 of them hoisted the trophy, including 13 of the last 14 clubs.

But history was no consolation for anyone sober enough to remember McCovey's line drive in 1962 or those infernal Rally Monkeys in 2002. And how could it get any worse than a natural disaster—the devastating Loma Prieta earthquake—just minutes before the start of the Bay Bridge World Series in 1989?

The Giants didn't hold a 2–0 lead in any of those World Series, though. They were up two games to none for the first time since 1954, and you didn't need to be Vic Wertz's grand-nephew to know what happened in that Fall Classic. Willie Mays made "the Catch" and the Giants went to Cleveland, completing a stunning sweep over the 111-win Indians.

Giants fans had waited ever since. Only the Indians (1948) and Chicago Cubs (1908) had longer World Series droughts among active franchises.

This series was not secure yet, though. Texas is a state that issues plenty of conceal-and-carry permits, and the Rangers had all the requisite offensive firepower to make a statement at home. This was the first World Series in the Metroplex, and for the first time anyone could remember, baseball was a bigger local story than the Dallas Cowboys on a weekend in late October. Even with their team trailing in the series, the antler- and claw-clad faithful were ready to make noise.

The Rangers played with more confidence in their lively home park, where they had a 51–30 record during the regular season. And Hamilton knew how to take advantage of the jet stream to right field.

Hamilton was 1-for-8 in two games at San Francisco, but he was a .390 hitter with a staggering .750 slugging percentage at home in 2010. He'd hit 22 of his 32 home runs there, too.

The Rangers also would have Vladimir Guerrero back in the lineup at designated hitter; his attempt to play right field was a disaster in Game 1, and Texas manager Ron Washington had little choice but to bench him the following night.

Plus the Giants were more worried than ever about Game 3 starter Jonathan Sanchez, whose fastball barely hit 90 mph as he failed to get out of the third inning in the final game of the NLCS. This time, Bochy wouldn't have two more starting pitchers ready to back up Sanchez in the bullpen.

Bochy's fears were well founded. Sanchez battled as well as could be expected while pitching in the upper 80s, but Rangers first baseman Mitch Moreland popped a three-run home run in the second inning, and Texas took a 4–2 victory.

Moreland, a former college pitcher who made his major league debut in July, had just 28 big-league at-bats against left-handers, without a home run. But he fouled off four consecutive pitches with two strikes— all curveballs and change-ups—before Posey called for an inside fastball. In a rare instance in the postseason, the Giants' brilliant rookie catcher second-guessed himself for a pitch selection.

"I'll take as much blame for it," Posey said. "I thought it was a good pitch, and the guy just put a good swing on it."

There was plenty of blame to go around after the Giants failed to put consistent pressure on right-hander Colby Lewis and two relievers. Ross and Torres hit solo home runs, but Sandoval flopped in the designated hitter spot, grounding into a double play and striking out.

Burrell had become a major concern, too, after striking out in all four of his at-bats—something no Giant had done in a World Series game since Josh Devore in 1911. After Game 3, he was 0-for-9 with eight strikeouts in the series and had 19 strikeouts in 38 postseason at-bats.

"I picked a bad time to struggle," Burrell said. "There's no way around it. I'm getting pitches to hit and just not doing anything with them. I'm chasing some balls off the plate.

"I'm supposed to…be a presence at the plate. That's what I'm here for, and I just didn't do that. You've got to be accountable for what you do, and certainly I didn't get the job done tonight, not even close."

Bochy said he'd sleep on the Game 4 lineup. He also sidestepped questions about Sanchez, who loomed as a major concern because he'd be lined up to pitch a deciding Game 7. Righetti answered honestly, though, when asked if the coaches would discuss alternatives to the tiring left-hander.

"Darn right, absolutely," Righetti said.

It was more important than ever that the Giants win at least one of the remaining two games in Texas, giving Cain a chance to crimp the seal in Game 6 at home. The Giants couldn't let this series go to a seventh game.

They had to reverse the momentum, which Hamilton now claimed for the Rangers.

"Obviously we're still down one game, but it's shifted," said Hamilton, who clocked a homer off Sanchez in a fifth inning the left-hander didn't escape. "I mean, we're at home, we've got the fans behind us. We're right where we want to be."

But one of the Giants had come home, too.

Aubrey Huff already was caught up in a whirlwind, advancing all the way to the World Series in his first postseason. It was too much to absorb. Not only was he playing in the biggest games of his life, but now he was competing against the team he grew up watching.

His earliest memories of baseball were listening to Rangers games on the radio or watching them on TV with his grandparents, who would babysit him when his mother was working late or attending night school. Huff's grandparents remained devoted Rangers fans through all the lean years, and Aubrey had vivid memories of the games he attended at old Arlington Stadium. It was a sweltering, sun-bleached, obviously converted minor league park with aluminum bleachers that could give you third-degree burns on a hot afternoon.

"I thought that was the most beautiful park I had ever seen in my life," Huff said.

He'd stomp on the metal bleachers with hundreds of other kids, delighted by the sensation that they were creating their own earthquake. He stuffed his face in the upper deck on Dollar Hot Dog Night. He was 16 years old when he attended the final game in the stadium's history, and watched the ceremony when they moved home plate from the old ballpark to the new one.

Fonda Huff had made so many things possible for her son despite being a widow on a Winn-Dixie salary. Aubrey only begrudged her one thing: the day he had tickets to see Nolan Ryan pitch against the Toronto Blue Jays in May 1991 but didn't go.

"My mom was too tired from work that day to take us," he said. "And he threw a no-hitter that night, and we missed it. I was so upset. I'd been a Rangers fan my whole life, and obviously he was the face of the franchise."

Now Ryan was the president and co-owner of the franchise, and he threw out the ceremonial first pitch before Game 3.

"For me just to see what he's done with that organization already since he's been there, it's been amazing," Huff said. "It's pretty cool being able to play in the World Series against a team I grew up rooting for."

A part of Huff never left Texas. Sure, he had an iPod full of cheesy '80s hits that he'd blast in the clubhouse before batting practice. He chose the campy disco beat of "Stayin' Alive" as his walk-up music. But his soul was pure country, and he had enough gravel and twang in his voice—and personal heartbreak—to handle the lyrics.

Huff gave his full Johnny Cash rendition in spring training, taking the stage with beer in hand for a benefit concert that Zito helped to organize. And a few years before that, Huff recorded a track on a CD that featured cover songs sung by Major League Baseball players.

Huff sang a deeply mournful version of "Letters From Home," a John Michael Montgomery ballad about a wartime soldier who isn't ashamed to show his personal correspondence to his combat buddies. It was hard to miss the personal meaning of one lyric:

> *Dear Son, I know I ain't written,*
> *But sittin' here tonight, alone in the kitchen, it occurs to me,*
> *I might not have said, so I'll say it now*
> *Son, you make me proud.*

Huff had become a father for the second time during the season, when his wife gave birth to a son they named Jagger. And Huff still wore his orange wristband, too, the one he'd slipped on for every game during the season. He hadn't forgotten seven-year-old Joe Turner, the little man he inspired to keep on battling.

Now the Giants had a battle on their hands with Tommy Hunter, the pudgy right-hander who, like Bumgarner, didn't begin the season in the big leagues yet found himself starting Game 4 of the World Series.

Hunter did not have good stuff. He labored to throw strikes and only escaped the second inning when Hamilton made a tremendous catch to rob Nate Schierholtz of a two-run double. It was buzzard's luck, to borrow one of Bochy's favorite phrases, and if the Giants kept letting Hunter squirm out of jams, they'd surely regret it later.

Huff was making his first start of the year at designated hitter, and he stepped to the plate in the third inning of a scoreless game. Torres had good wheels as he led off second base, and Huff had 12 singles among his 14 postseason hits. Just one more grounder through the middle would get the Giants on the board.

But Huff was thinking bigger this time. It was the same thought he had when he took a rip on his first pitch of spring training.

Screw it.

He took a home run cut on a first-pitch fastball, and the result was obvious from the moment it struck his bat. Huff posed with his bat still in his hands and watched the ball soar down the right-field line, landing 30 rows deep.

Huff led the Giants with 26 home runs in the regular season. But this was his first in the playoffs. He hadn't gone deep since September 25, and he enjoyed the hell out of his trot around the bases.

"It's in the back of your mind you'd like to hit a big homer to put you ahead," he said. "It's pretty surreal right now."

Hunter threw 72 pitches in his first three innings and didn't generate a single swing and miss. But other than Huff's two-run shot, the Giants weren't able to score off him.

The Giants knew it wouldn't be easy to hold down the Rangers' lineup on this Halloween night. They had inexperience on the mound, too, and behind the plate. Bumgarner and Posey were the first all-rookie battery to start a World Series game since Spec Shea and Yogi Berra teamed for the New York Yankees in Game 1 of the 1947 World Series. Bumgarner was the youngest pitcher to start in the World Series since Fernando Valenzuela looked to the sky for the Dodgers in 1981.

Just eight months earlier, Bumgarner wasn't physically or mentally equipped to face hitters in a Cactus League game. Now he had to subdue a Rangers lineup that was dangerous and confident, knowing that if he failed, Texas would turn this series into a best-of-three free-for-all.

Bumgarner had joked earlier in the playoffs that he hadn't felt this much pressure since the North Carolina high school championship game. His comment didn't come out the way he meant it, and it drew chuckles. Observers wondered: did the 21-year-old even have the perspective to grasp the enormity of his current situation? Maybe not. And maybe that was for the best.

However Bumgarner perceived his environment, he took the mound in Texas showing no nerves and no fear. He yanked a few fastballs in the first inning while walking leadoff hitter Elvis Andrus. But then he fell into a rhythm with Posey, and the Giants' infield was nothing short of phenomenal behind him.

They flashed more leather than the Machine.

At second base, Freddy Sanchez's strained rotator cuff appeared to be a non-issue, and he covered the infield like a caffeinated acrobat. He started a double play on Hamilton's hard grounder to get Bumgarner out of the first inning. When Jeff Francoeur smoked a line drive in the second inning, Sanchez climbed an invisible stepladder, leaping to make a snow-cone grab. Not since Omar Vizquel graced the Giants with his presence had one of their middle infielders made a catch like that.

And Sanchez wasn't done. In the fourth he made an incredible reaction play when Josh Hamilton's line drive went off Bumgarner's glove. Sanchez, who had been moving to his right, abruptly changed direction and charged to scoop up the carom. He picked it up cleanly and reached across his body to tag Michael Young, who was running from first base. Sanchez managed to transfer and get off a strong throw, too, and nearly completed a double play.

The Giants created highlights in the outfield, as well. Bochy had made the decision to sit strikeout-prone Pat Burrell, who certainly wouldn't have been able to catch Ian Kinsler's deep drive in the fifth inning. Ross, who had shifted over to left field, ran a marathoner's distance to flag it down near the wall.

Bumgarner wasn't just getting by on guts and glovework, though. His fastball hit 94 mph, and the Rangers couldn't see the ball out of his syrupy, sidearm motion. He struck out Guerrero three times—looking in the first at-bat, then twice more when the long-armed DH couldn't check his swing.

Something like this simply didn't happen to Guerrero. He destroyed lefties. Only once had he struck out three times against a southpaw in his career, and that came more than a decade earlier—in June 1998 against Al Leiter of the New York Mets.

But Posey kept calling the right pitches, and Bumgarner kept hitting the catcher's glove—establishing his fastball inside, sweeping his breaking ball down in the zone, and baffling the Rangers with his change-up.

Only once did Posey feel compelled to go to the mound, after Uribe made an error with one out in the seventh inning. Nelson Cruz followed with a two-out single, and for the first time all game, the Rangers had a runner in scoring position.

"I went out there more or less because, well, you're kind of supposed to, I think," Posey said. "But I don't think I really needed to. I mean, you can tell by just looking at the guy's face sometimes.

"I didn't stay out there too long. He had that look like nothing was going to faze him."

Bumgarner broke Kinsler's bat on a line out to end the inning.

"There are some 21-year-olds right now in a costume trick-or-treating," Duane Kuiper said on the Giants' radio broadcast.

"Bumgarner is pitching in the World Series, and he's shutting out the Texas Rangers."

Posey could've worn a superhero's cape and cowl, too. He made the right calls. He threw out a runner at second base. And in the eighth inning he connected on a pitch from Darren O'Day that kept carrying and carrying until it landed on the grassy berm beyond the center-field fence.

It was a glorious moment for Posey, and not just because it was his first career postseason home run. In a way, the at-bat summarized everything about his tremendous season.

The previous night in the Game 3 loss, Posey had represented the tying run in the eighth inning when he faced O'Day. The at-bat went to a seventh pitch, and Molina wanted a slider away. O'Day kept shaking off. He wanted to throw an inside slider. Molina jogged out to the mound and explained to O'Day that the outside pitch was the place where Posey was least liable to hurt them. And sure enough, Molina had the right idea. Posey made weak contact while grounding out, and Molina got the better of the rookie who had made him expendable.

But in Game 4, O'Day came on to face Posey again. And the rookie had cataloged every pitch in his mind from the previous night. It was another seven-pitch battle. Posey fouled off a fastball. Molina called for another slider away. This time, Posey made the adjustment. And he hurt them.

"I threw him a slider away once too often, and he got it up in the air," O'Day said.

Posey, 23, became the youngest catcher to hit a home run in the World Series since Johnny Bench was a 22-year-old in 1970. Posey had met the Reds' Hall of Fame legend as a junior at Florida State, when he won the Johnny Bench Award as the best collegiate catcher in the nation.

Posey studied old tapes of Bench, naturally. And he said one thing stood out: "massive backspin." That's what creates the near-magical force

Madison Bumgarner strikes out the Texas Rangers' Vladimir Guerrero for a third time during the seventh inning of Game 4 of the World Series in Texas.

that allows a fly ball to carry as if being pushed by a friendly breeze. Bench had it. And so did Buster.

His home run gave the Giants a 4–0 lead, and Bumgarner held the Rangers scoreless through eight innings. Bochy only needed to call on

Wilson for the final three outs, and he retired the side, striking out Hamilton to end it.

The Giants had thrown their fourth shutout in this postseason—tying the 1998 Yankees and the 1905 New York Giants for the most in major league history. And they did it behind their No. 4 starter, who became the youngest pitcher to throw eight shutout innings in a World Series game since Jim Palmer in 1966.

"He made every young kid in the country look up to him today," gushed Affeldt. "He's honestly pitching like he's pitched his whole life. This might hit him in the off-season. We'll go hunting, and I'll remind him about what he's done. But hopefully right now he stays unconscious."

Bumgarner's tenacity, his location, his moving cutter, and even his pickoff move reminded some of another decorated playoff lefty—the Yankees' Andy Pettitte.

"He didn't make many mistakes [over] the plate," Posey said. "He was able to throw that cutter back door, throw the cutter in, down, throw his heater in when he needed to keep them honest. He pretty much did that with everybody all night."

More than anything, he pitched with Pettitte's confidence and guile—even though he had none of the experience.

"I didn't expect this in my wildest dreams, but I'm definitely glad to be here and have this opportunity," Bumgarner said. "This might be the only opportunity I get. Hopefully there's a lot more, but you never know. It's definitely going to feel good to finish the year with a win, if this is the last game I throw."

Just a few months earlier Posey and Bumgarner were down Highway 99 in Fresno, representing the far-off future of the Giants organization. But after they led the Giants to a Game 4 victory on Halloween night, the future was now. Boy, was it ever.

The Giants were nine good innings from winning the first World Series in San Francisco history.

You couldn't count on rookies like Posey and Bumgarner to understand this context. They hadn't lived and died with this organization through the decades. They'd never played amid the blowing hot dog wrappers at chilly Candlestick Park. They had no idea how many times Giants fans had had their hearts broken.

After the Game 4 victory, it would be up to others to provide some perspective—someone like Sabean, the baseball lifer and longtime general manager.

But he couldn't find the words.

"I have a lump in my throat," Sabean said. "I can't even talk, that was so amazing."

Chapter 18

Fully Healed

Felipe Alou was a proud man and a baseball pioneer.

When the Giants called him up as a 23-year-old outfielder in 1958, only one of his countrymen from the Dominican Republic was on a major league roster. And Ozzie Virgil had moved to New York City when he was 14 years old. Truly, Alou was the first man to venture from the Caribbean nation straight into a major league organization.

He did not break the color barrier—Jackie Robinson had done that 11 years earlier—but in some ways, Alou's obstacles were almost as difficult to overcome. Robinson knew he would encounter hatred, anger, no shortage of racist epithets, and even acts of violence, both on the field and off it. At least he had the chance to steel himself for what he was about to endure.

Alou was not prepared for any of it. He had a college education at the University of Santo Domingo. He starred in the javelin at the Pan Am Games. He had plans of becoming a doctor before a Giants scout offered him $200 to play baseball—and his family had a grocery debt to pay. Upon arriving in the U.S., Alou was received an entirely different education. And when he endured angry shouts from white fans in the segregated minor leagues of the Jim Crow South, he did not understand what they were saying. In moments like these, he was glad he did not speak English.

Alou's arrival in 1956 was delayed because of a paperwork problem with his visa, so the Giants sent him to Lake Charles, Louisiana, in the Class C Evangeline League. That year, the Louisiana state assembly passed a bill that outlawed integrated sporting events, and one club, the Baton Rouge Rebels, ferociously enforced it. Alou was told to take off his uniform and sit in the left-field bleachers—the only place blacks were allowed to watch the game. Until then, Alou hadn't realized he was considered one of them.

He sat with Ralph Crosby, a shortstop from New York, and Chuck Weatherspoon, an outfielder from Pineland, Texas. He would never forget their names.

Within another day or two, the few black players in the league were transferred out, and Alou was put on a bus to Cocoa, Florida, where the Giants had a Class D team. Things would be better for him there, someone told him. But Cocoa was segregated, too. He couldn't enter restaurants with his teammates, who often brought him hamburgers to eat on the bus. In one or two cities, restaurant owners wouldn't even let the bus park in their lot. The driver would drop off the white players and park across the street, leaving Alou in the dark with only his thoughts to nourish him. It was a miserable, lonely time.

Alou played even harder in response. He hit .380 for Cocoa that season. He was in the major leagues two years later. He became the first Dominican All-Star during a 17-year playing career. And much later, he became baseball's first Dominican manager.

Much later. He was 57 years old when the Montreal Expos appointed him to the job. He had spent a dozen years in their minor league system, including six consecutive seasons without a promotion at Class A West Palm Beach.

In 1994 Alou managed an Expos roster that was as talented as any baseball team in decades. Pedro Martinez. Larry Walker. John Wetteland. Ken Hill. Marquis Grissom. Mike Lansing. Cliff Floyd. Mel Rojas. His son, Moises. They were 74–40 and had the best record in baseball when the strike hit in August. It was the only season in the last 105 years that a World Series wasn't played.

Alou had so many reasons to be hateful and angry, feel cheated and wronged. But he also knew the ways he had been blessed beyond belief. He did not allow injustice to harden his heart. It simply made him stand up a little straighter, a little taller, and a little prouder. He was a man of dignity and poetry, and four years after his last season as the Giants' manager, he still carried himself with a regal presence.

But there was one regret he held in his chest.

It was Game 7 of the 1962 World Series. The Giants trailed the Yankees 1–0, and his brother, Matty, bunted for a leadoff single off Ralph Terry. Now it was Felipe's duty to advance his brother to second base with another bunt.

"I can replay it to this day," he said. "It was fair for a while, and the wind blew it. Moose Skowron, the first baseman, let it go foul. The next pitch was a hit-and-run, and I fouled it into the catcher's mitt. The next one was a swing and miss.

"It was my last World Series swing."

Willie Mays hit a two-out double to right field. Roger Maris collected it so quickly, it would've been folly to send Matty home. He had to stop at third base.

"If I had gotten the bunt down," Felipe thought, "Matty would've scored the tying run."

Then came Willie McCovey's line drive—the one that ended the game, the series, and the season. The one Charles Schulz could not purge without shouting his frustrations through Charlie Brown.

"With myself, McCovey, and [Orlando] Cepeda coming up, we had some kind of team," Alou said. "There were some serious people there, Hall of Fame people, and we didn't win.

"I struck out. I thought there would be another opportunity, but it didn't work."

Now a special assistant to Sabean, a gray-haired Alou watched the Giants take batting practice before Game 5, shielding his eyes in the dugout from the clear Texas sun.

The entire Giants front office was here in Arlington, and not just Sabean's circle of scouts and assistants. Marketing people, group sales associates, accountants—anyone who wanted to make the trip was there, along with a guest. Neukom had instructed the team's charter jet to turn around and fly back to San Francisco to make a second pickup.

"We want to reward all their good, smart, and hard work," Neukom said. "And we hope to give them the memory of a lifetime."

For Alou, a World Series title for San Francisco would be more than a lifetime memory. It would be absolution. After 48 years, he could take the deepest, most fundamental sin he made as a player, hold it in his hands like a dove, and set it free.

"Of course, yeah," he said. "I want to pick up a newspaper in San Francisco that says, 'We won it.' For this group of players to be the group to win it, it would really be something.

"You have to be ready to bunt in a World Series. I was not ready. I drove in 98 runs. I hit 25 home runs in Candlestick, and Candlestick was big. I saw the bunt sign, and I had my doubts.

"But this is what this team is all about. Bochy has these guys ready, and they have responded to it."

In the hours before Game 5, Bochy was nervous inside but outwardly loose. In the interview room a reporter asked about the little boy who dressed as Ron Washington for Halloween, complete with the crown of his head shaved to duplicate the Texas manager's bald spot. Could there be a little Bochy somewhere out there, too?

"Well, he'd have to blow his head up somehow," said Bochy, to a laughing audience. "I don't know how he would do it. Put a lot of air in it, and he would get close."

Later, someone asked Bochy if he liked "swagger" in a team and if he had any himself.

"Do I have it? Yeah, in the respect that I believe in these guys, that when they hit the field, we expect to win," Bochy said. "And if that's swagger, then I guess I have it a little bit."

Bochy drew more uproarious laughs when he stood up from the dais and strutted like a peacock on his way out of the room.

The pregame question on everyone's mind: would Cliff Lee have his swagger back? The Texas ace didn't shed much light on his struggles from Game 1, saying he just left too many pitches over the plate. He also sought to backtrack a bit from his earlier comments, when he responded to a question about the Giants' lineup by instead praising their pitchers. It wasn't too hard to interpret it as a slight against the hitters he'd be facing.

"They've got guys that [put up] quality at-bats and make you throw a lot of pitches," Lee said. "They've got a good lineup, no doubt about it. They proved it in San Francisco. They know what they're doing with the bat. The more pitches they see, the better they get.

"They're pitchable, but if you make mistakes over the plate, 2–0 and 3–1 [counts], that's what happens."

Lincecum, despite getting the win, also had an erratic start against the Rangers in Game 1, struggling at times to control his focus and adrenaline. But the Giants had a good feeling with him on the mound. Ever since his rookie year, folks in the front office greeted each other with a "Happy Lincecum Day" whenever it was the pliant little right-hander's turn to pitch.

This had the potential to be the happiest Lincecum Day of all.

Righetti felt reassured the moment Lincecum walked up to him in the dugout after that uneven performance in Game 1.

"I'll be good next time," he told his pitching coach. "I'll be good."

"He was trying to be too calm out there," Righetti said. "I said, 'Let it take you. Posey will rein you in if he has to. Use the adrenaline, because you'll need it. It's November.'"

The Giants hadn't ever played a game in November before. And as much as they wanted to celebrate a World Series in front of their home fans, they were eager to nail this down right here in Texas behind their ace.

In Game 5 Lincecum and Lee gave the nation the unblinking duel that everyone expected in the World Series opener. Neither pitcher allowed a runner into scoring position until the seventh inning.

Lee had his curveball working again, established the inside half with his cutter and threw four of his pitches to all four quadrants of the strike zone. Lincecum was just as resolute, twisting his body over his front leg as he put extra fade on his change-up and snap on his breaking pitches. His slider was back, too, and the Rangers simply couldn't cope with so many weapons at once.

Lee gave up a two-out single to Torres in the third, but the pitcher reached up to snare Freddy Sanchez's line drive to end the inning. Huff reached on an error in the fifth, but Lee threw a biting pitch and Renteria grounded into a double play. Posey made the purest contact in the sixth, but Nelson Cruz made a leaping, wall-bumping catch to take away a potential RBI double.

Lincecum had allowed only a walk and two singles through his first six innings. Josh Hamilton, who would win American League MVP honors and who destroyed the Yankees in the ALCS, couldn't manage to hit a ball out of the infield.

Lee finally allowed a runner into scoring position in the seventh, when Ross led off the inning with a ground-ball single up the middle. It came on a 1–2 pitch, and Uribe followed with another good piece of two-strike hitting—a single up the middle on an 0–2 fastball that he was strong enough to keep from jamming him.

The Giants had their first decent scoring opportunity of the night. And Huff, who hit a moon shot a day earlier, walked to the plate.

Huff led the Giants with 26 home runs and 86 RBIs during the regular season. He had been their most consistent run producer all year. He looked to third-base coach Tim Flannery for the sign.

Bunt.

"Don't care," Huff thought. "I was gonna do it anyway."

Huff had played in 1,479 games over 11 major league seasons. He had 6,112 plate appearances. Unbelievably, he did not have a sacrifice hit in his career. Not even one.

In fact, there were only three active big leaguers who had amassed more plate appearances without a sacrifice, and two of them—Burrell and Vladimir Guerrero—were in the ballpark.

Huff only practiced bunting on the first two pitches he saw in batting practice every day, and as any ballplayer could tell you, that was just eyewash. Going through the motions, nothing more.

"But you know what?" he thought. "When I do my B.S. bunts in BP, the only one I do well is the one I push. If I go down the third-base side, I might pop it up. I know what I've got to do."

It wasn't just a good bunt. It was nearly an infield hit. The Rangers were surprised when Huff squared at the last instant and dropped his bunt to the first base side of the mound. It took some thick grass, an athletic play by Lee, and a strong throw to retire Huff by a fraction of a second.

"You know what?" a grinning Huff said. "That might've been the best pitch I saw all night."

Huff's college buddy, Burrell, was up next. The Giants had one out and two runners in scoring position. And just like his last at-bat in a Phillies uniform in 2008, it was time for Burrell to join the show.

Burrell was 0-for-13 in that '08 World Series before his double led to the clinching run. Now he was 0-for-11 with nine strikeouts in this World Series, and he only returned to the Game 5 lineup in the DH spot by virtue of Bochy's faith in him.

Burrell had drawn a key walk against Lee in Game 1, and he was determined to see more pitches this time. He worked the count full, and in the on-deck circle, Renteria noted that all three of Lee's curveballs were wide of the zone. Burrell didn't chase any of them.

But Lee still had that cutter, and he back-doored one that snapped to the outside corner as Burrell swung through it. He closed his eyes in resignation, then turned his head and asked plate umpire Jeff Kellogg if the pitch would've been a strike. Yes, he was told.

"Damn," Burrell said, defeated.

But as he passed Renteria, he shouted a message: "C'mon, Papi!"

So much time had passed since Renteria was that 21-year-old kid, waving his arms in elation as he ran down the first-base line, knowing he had just delivered the hit that won the 1997 World Series for the Florida Marlins. That clip from the 11th inning of Game 7 against the Cleveland Indians had been replayed so many times, and with every viewing, it was striking to see so much pure joy on his face.

Renteria had not experienced much joy as a Giant, though. His two-year, $18.5 million contract was panned long before he played his first game with the club. Renteria had looked like a player in decline with the Detroit Tigers in 2008, and the critics were proven right when his two seasons as a Giant were marred by injuries. In 2009 he played most of the season with three bone fragments in his elbow. In retrospect, trainer Dave Groeschner had no idea how Renteria was able to swing a bat for all that time. The chunks of bone removed after the season were so impressively big, Groeschner kept them in a jar in the trainer's room as a souvenir.

When Renteria arrived in the spring of 2010, he insisted that he felt great and he would rebound to become the player the Giants envisioned. He had a scorching opening week in April, too, collecting 11 hits in his first 15 at-bats. Included in that run was the tying, two-run home run in the ninth off Billy Wagner—the one that forced extra innings in what turned into a dramatic Giants victory in the home opener.

But then the 35-year-old shortstop began to fall apart. He went on the disabled list three times during the season, each time with a different injury. He had a strained groin that forced him out in May. When he returned to the lineup, he played just three games before going back to the DL with a bad hamstring.

"Unbelievable," he said.

He moved his locker across the clubhouse, hoping to change his mojo. It didn't work. When he returned in June, he was a nonfactor over a 12-game span, scoring one run with one RBI and four double-play grounders. The Giants were 2–9 in his starts over that miserable stretch.

Renteria was moving glacially at shortstop and was in an 0-for-15 spell in July when a reporter approached him in Milwaukee with a blunt but honest question.

Did he have anything left?

Renteria was stunned by the question. He had wondered privately if his body would make it through the season. But was this really how everyone perceived him? Did they think he was done? Did he have something to prove?

"Myself, I am too proud," Renteria answered. "I always say if I can't play this game, I'd be home. But I can help this team win."

During that critical road series in Milwaukee, the one that changed the course of the Giants' season, Renteria delivered the same message to Bochy in a private meeting. He needed his manager to believe in him, too.

"He hit a skid, and when that happens with an older player, the question will come up," Bochy said at the time. "He's had setbacks, but he's shown he still has game left. More important is his attitude—what he thinks."

But the disabled list would swallow up Renteria one more time. He pinch-hit against Wagner on August 5 in Atlanta and tried to repeat his heroic swing from the home opener, gearing up and letting loose on a 97 mph fastball. This time, he lined out to Wagner. And he felt a searing pain in his left arm. He had partially torn his biceps tendon.

The inflammation didn't subside the next day, and Renteria couldn't swing a bat. At one point, Bochy sent Renteria to the on-deck circle as a bluff. Atlanta Manager Bobby Cox wasn't fooled.

"C'mon!" shouted Renteria, as he descended the dugout steps. "I don't scare nobody anymore?"

Renteria tried to play through the inflammation, but it was obvious to trainers and coaches that he was too compromised. To his great protestations, he went back on the disabled list. He refused to go on a minor league rehab assignment.

Renteria begged to come off the DL as soon as he was eligible, but by now Uribe had taken the everyday shortstop job, and the Giants faced a roster squeeze following the additions of Ross and Guillen. Renteria had become such a marginal player that he had to wait for rosters to expand September 1 before the Giants would activate him.

At that point, Renteria was on the team for no better reason than he was under contract. He was just an occasional starter in September, mostly getting time against left-handers when Uribe would move to third base in place of Sandoval.

Renteria's elbow flared up again in September, and he started just one of the Giants' final 14 games. When the regular season ended, he had set career lows with 72 games, 67 hits, and 22 RBIs. It was the first time in his 15-year career that he failed to appear in 100 games.

But he started the first game of that final weekend series against the Padres, partially so Bochy could find out if Renteria was healthy enough to be an option for the postseason roster. If not for Renteria's recent history against Wagner, he probably would've been left off the club.

Bochy found his spot to use Renteria in Game 2 of the NLDS against the Braves, sending him up to pinch hit against Wagner in the 10th inning of a tie game. And in another fateful moment between the two players, Renteria felt a sudden pain while swinging through a first-pitch fastball. This time, it was excruciating.

Remember Renteria's brilliant bunt single? Remember how he nearly set up the winning rally with it?

"Here's the part that nobody knew," Groeschner said. "He had to bunt. He couldn't swing the bat."

Back in August, Renteria had torn his biceps tendon against Wagner. Now, facing the same pitcher two months later, he tore it the rest of the way. What were the odds?

That wasn't all. After Renteria's surprising bunt, Wagner's major league career would last just one more hitter. He sustained his own injury, straining his oblique muscle while trying to field Torres' bunt. It was playing out like the final scene from a Western, when most of the main characters bite the dust.

After the Giants' Game 2 loss to the Braves, Renteria sat in an MRI chamber at 1:30 AM, assuming his season—and possibly his career—was over, too. His tendon had torn completely. Bochy and Sabean huddled with Groeschner, strategizing on who should replace Renteria on the roster.

But the following morning, Renteria arrived for the Giants' flight to Atlanta. He stretched his left arm in disbelief.

"You know," he said to Groeschner, "I don't feel anything. I'm good to go."

Groescher didn't know what to make of it. Was it divine intervention? Magic? A medical miracle?

"Madness," Groeschner said. "Just…madness."

Renteria's tendon had rolled down his forearm. His left biceps bulged out a little, but it was just a curiosity. The tendon offered no resistance, and he felt no pain.

It didn't change the fact that Renteria was still a bench player. It took Sandoval's defensive struggles, and then another bad game in the field by Fontenot in the NLCS, for Bochy to make a gutsy call. He moved Uribe to third base and reinstalled Renteria at shortstop.

"It's a twist of fate," Sabean said. "He became the shortstop somewhat by default with Pablo's failings."

Bochy simply wanted a leader on the field.

"You know, he's a guy all the players look up to," Bochy said. "Once we got to that point, I knew I wanted to turn it over to him and put Juan at third base. That was our best club. I couldn't have two better guys on the left side of the infield, the way they play, their experience, their composure. It's all about winning with them."

Renteria had sent that message to his teammates September 23 at Wrigley Field, when they stood a half-game back in the NL West and felt their season slipping away while scoring one run over a two-game span.

Eventually, the secret was revealed: it was Renteria who took the floor in that meeting underneath the bleachers. He told his teammates that he didn't care if he had a marginal role on the club. He would make any sacrifice to win another World Series, and he stood behind every person wearing a Giants uniform.

And he wept.

"He broke down, and we all broke down with him," Huff said. "Since then, I've wanted this more for him than anybody. What a leader he is."

This had become the overriding dynamic in the Giants' clubhouse. This was the missing element that nobody could identify, the hidden power that Mat Latos couldn't see, the cement that bonded this group of bearded, thong-wearing rejects, misfits, and castoffs.

They wanted to win for selfish reasons, sure. But more than anything, they looked around the room with admiration. They wanted to win for each other.

"It is a long time ago. Thirteen years ago, you know?" Renteria said of his moment of elation in 1997. "But I feel great. I was always ready for a moment like now. I'm trying to trust in whatever I've got."

Before Game 5 of the World Series, Renteria told Torres that he would do something special. He would hit a home run. This was not the exuberant boast of a young kid like Sandoval. Renteria had a glint in his eye when he said it.

Now he stepped to the plate against Lee, who had just struck out Burrell and was on the verge of spoiling the Giants' only scoring opportunity of the night. Renteria took a cutter and a change-up, both just missing the zone. He knew that Lee, behind in the count, wouldn't throw him a curve. He tapped his front foot, stood in his familiar, closed stance, and waited for another cutter.

"The ball," he said, "it no cut."

Lee made a mistake over the plate, and Renteria lashed it to left-center field. His eyes opened wide with hope as left fielder David Murphy went back to the track and looked up.

Renteria was a 21-year-old baby again. And the Texas Rangers just woke him up.

Edgar Renteria blasts a three-run homer during the seventh inning of Game 5 of the 2010 World Series on November 1, 2010. Renteria, the series MVP, followed through on his promise to Andres Torres that he would do something special in the game.

In the on-deck circle, Rowand watched the ball disappear over the wall and held up a tentative fist in disbelief. Ross stepped on home plate with a twisting, skipping, joyful dance move.

Up in the broadcast booth, radio announcer Dave Flemming had been fighting a respiratory ailment all night and was trying his hardest to keep it smooth. When Renteria's ball landed over the fence, Flemming's excited voice broke as if he were graduating from the Vienna Boys Choir.

"It is…GO-AAAA-OHHHHN!"

It wasn't the call Flemming anticipated or wanted, but the effect was perfect. Back in San Francisco, every voice was cracking and every heart was skipping a beat.

Renteria, other than his wide eyes, did not react. He simply ran the bases at a standard pace. The Giants' dugout met him with potent high fives.

Renteria did not have a single three-RBI game during the regular season. This was his second in this World Series. And his home run was just the second Lee had allowed in 76 postseason innings.

In the home stadium of George W. Bush, the Giants led 3–0. They were nine outs away from accomplishing their mission.

Lincecum knew this was no time to be passive. He gave up a home run to Cruz in the bottom of the seventh, but struck out three. He kept throwing more of those unhittable change-ups. And the Rangers kept swinging over the top of them.

Lincecum was taking Righetti's advice. He was letting the adrenaline carry him.

"I'm just thinking I don't want to be complacent," he said. "More than anything, it's going back to this organization and its philosophy, how it's so important to pound the strike zone.

"Watching Bumgarner yesterday gave me motivation. I mean, obviously, I didn't need too much motivation, considering it was the World Series clincher. But you know what I mean."

Yes, Timmy, everyone did.

Lincecum had gone through so many trials in 2010, but he was on the verge of achieving infinitely more than both his Cy Young Award seasons smashed together. It was a running gag that he had left the two trophies on the back seat of his car for a few weeks. It's safe to say a World Series ring wouldn't leave his sight.

He was about to become the 15th player in history to win four games in one postseason, outpitching Halladay once and Lee twice. The Giants needed a legitimate ace to match up against those elite arms, and for a long time, Lincecum wasn't even close to being that pitcher. Now he was committed to being nothing less.

Proving the doubters wrong? That didn't matter. He only wanted to win for his comrades in arms and for the city that accepted him for who he was.

He made quick work of the Rangers in the eighth, recording three outs on nine pitches. No claws, no antlers. Just deer in the headlights.

The final act belonged to the most dramatic performance artist in the house. It would be Wilson and his black beard, looking like he dropped straight out of the World Wrestling Federation. He called himself a ninja and a mental assassin. He said he envisioned nailing down the final out of a World Series when he was five years old.

After 53 years of heartache and lament, of old wounds and fresh ones, too, Wilson did the prudent thing. He prolonged the torture no longer than necessary.

Hamilton struck out when he watched a fastball blow past him below the letters. Guerrero grounded out to Renteria. And when Cruz swung through a 3–2 cutter, clinching the Giants' 3–1 victory, the ground almost opened up with a release of elation, relief, and pure joy.

Charlie Brown could kick the football. Felipe Alou could let go. All of Northern California could party like never before.

The Giants were World Series champions.

Wilson tapped his chest and crossed his arms, remembering his late father. Then he turned and let out a primal scream as Posey tackled him. Burrell was the first one out of the dugout, of course, converging on Wilson along with Huff. Freddy Sanchez leapt into Renteria's arms.

The Giants had clinched on the road for the third consecutive time in this dogged playoff run of theirs. And for all the torture they inflicted on their fans, they didn't play an elimination game all season.

Who would have believed it? The Giants' first title since 1954 was improbably accomplished by a team of grinders and goofballs who stood in fourth place at the All-Star break. And their deliverance came on a swing from a broken-down shortstop who insisted he still had something to offer.

"This was our season," Wilson said. "Since spring training, this was storybook. It's been written. It's been destiny.

"As torturous as it seemed all year, we knew what we had. And we prevailed."

Anything else?

"I'm feeling…I'm feeling like I want to rage," Wilson said. "*Right now.*"

Chapter 19

Nailed It

The celebration began. The Commissioner's Trophy arrived in white-gloved hands, and Bud Selig presented it to Neukom, Sabean, Bochy, and club president Larry Baer. Congratulations were accepted and heartfelt speeches made for the television audience.

When the camera lights clicked off, Neukom took the gleaming trophy, with its iconic circle of flags, and he knew who should present it to the team. He found Mike Murphy off to the side and charged the beloved clubhouse man with the most important task in his five-plus decades with the team.

"Take it, Murph," Neukom said. "Take it to the players."

Nobody had waited longer for this day than Mike Murphy. He was the only Giants employee who had been with the club from its first day in San Francisco, when he showed up at 6:00 AM to see if the newly arrived equipment manager had a job for him.

Murphy had been a batboy for the San Francisco Seals since he was 12, and his first emotion was sadness when he heard that Major League Baseball was coming to town. It meant all his favorite Seals players would go somewhere else.

He grew up in the Excelsior District, played baseball at City College and USF, and loved everything about Seals Stadium, where the Giants played during their first two seasons while Candlestick Park was under construction. There was the heavenly scent from the Langendorf bread bakery mixed with the wafting odor from the Hamm's beer factory. There was the iconic neon sign that showed the Hamm's glass filling up. There was the neighborhood feel to the ballpark at 16th Street and Potrero Avenue, now the site of a Safeway grocery store.

Murph ran the visiting clubhouse from 1962 to 1979 and moved to the home side in 1980, eventually saying good-bye to clammy Candlestick Park and relocating with the Giants to their beautiful new home on the waterfront at China Basin.

No matter when they came or went, everyone who had worn a Giants uniform knew Murph—hundreds upon hundreds of players and coaches. And they knew they could trust him. When they would come back to visit, he was the first person they asked to see. He was the common thread that spanned decades.

Murph was a creature of habit. In spring training, he ate at Don & Charlie's every single night. He called everyone "kiddo." He answered the phone the same way every time, with a hearty, "HAYYY-lo." And whenever anyone would ask him a controversial question, or try to get him on their side of an argument, he'd shrug, walk away, and say, "Ahhh, I don' bother nobody."

On the afternoon of Game 5 in Texas, Murph left his glasses somewhere in the clubhouse, and they fell on the floor. One of the clubhouse kids accidentally stepped on them. Wouldn't you know it? The Giants won the World Series that night, a sight that Murph waited and hoped for 53 years to see. It was fuzzy to his tearful eyes, but no less rapturous.

After bringing the trophy to the wildly appreciative team, Murph quickly got out of the way and found a quiet place. Then he called Willie

Mays, the greatest Giant and his very good friend. For the first time since "the Catch," the Giants were the kings of baseball. Neither of them could believe it.

Murph agreed to a few interviews but was bashful about it.

"The boys did it," he said softly. "Go talk to them. The boys did it."

The boys were living it up , spraying champagne and dousing each other with crumpled cans of beer for the fourth time in a month. Neukom got hit with a point-blank blast from Uribe, interrupting an interview. Then the corporate lawyer began jumping up and down in joyously bizarre fashion, yelling, "Juan Juan Juan Juan Juan OOOOO-Reeeeebayyyyy!"

Special assistant Shawon Dunston watched quietly from one corner of the clubhouse, stunned speechless for the first time anyone could remember. His final big-league at-bat came in Game 6 of the 2002 World Series. He hit the home run that put the Giants ahead that night, only to see the Angels steal away their championship. Dunston spent years with the Chicago Cubs. He understood baseball's cruelty.

Now Dunston was stunned to witness the party scene in front of him, and so was former teammate J.T. Snow.

"Erased a lot of ghosts, right?" Snow said. "I'm happy for the people of San Francisco. They can call themselves winners now."

Huff grabbed a reporter's arm and used his sleeve to wipe the stinging alcohol from his eyes.

"This team is legendary in San Fran, man! That's all I know," he shouted. "We better not pay for a meal the rest of the year."

Sabean, his usually stoic face flush with emotion, thought of Ted Uhlaender and Pat Dobson and all the others who couldn't be there to experience this. He credited his advance scouts, a group headed by Joe Lefebvre, his boyhood friend, and assisted by Steve Balboni—trusted connections from his Yankees years.

Champagne flows as the 2010 World Series champs hoist the Commissioner's Trophy high overhead. The city embraced this band of misfits, and they, in turn, gave San Francisco a championship the city had waited more than a half-century to celebrate.

The Giants shut down their opponent's best hitters all postseason. Atlanta's Jason Heyward was 2-for-16 without a run or RBI. The Phillies' Ryan Howard and Chase Utley combined to drive in one run. And now they had neutralized a Rangers lineup that entered the World Series with bats that seemed to have heat-seeking technology.

Josh Hamilton was 2-for-20. Vladimir Guerrero was 1-for-14.

"I can't speak enough to our advanced scouting and how the pitchers executed the plan," Sabean said. "And the catcher we have, Posey, is really off the charts in terms of his intellect and ability to stay calm in the moment and call the games that he did. This kid's a genius in his own right."

The Giants became the first team to throw two shutouts in a World Series since 1966, when the Baltimore Orioles blanked the Dodgers in three of four. And looking ahead, each of the Giants' starting five, plus most of their bullpen and Posey, would remain under club control for the foreseeable future.

"I expected our pitchers to pitch good," said Tidrow, covered in champagne instead of dirt. "They pitched a little better than good."

Even Zito, the $126 million left-hander who didn't make the playoff roster, had kept throwing in the bullpen until the very end, doing his tedious arm exercises and pitching live batting practice when he could. He stayed ready, and Sabean was proud of him, too.

"The group we have going wild in this room has a lot of determination and a lot of will," said Sabean, "and they wouldn't be denied."

The party moved out of the clubhouse and back onto the field a half-hour later, where a small but vocal contingent of Giants fans stayed to cheer them on. They chanted "Rookie of the Year" for Posey and "MVP" for Renteria and "Thank you, Giants" for everyone else.

Maybe the Giants didn't have the most talent on their roster. Maybe their lineup was jerry-rigged in midsummer. But that was the beauty of this game. The best teams usually lost at least 60 games, and the worst teams usually won at least 60. There's an element of unpredictability in a nine-inning baseball game that no computer program or statistical method can simulate.

You could only hope to sneak into the postseason, when it starts anew. Then it's a bunch of nervous guys, many of them in the playoffs for the first time, a few of them wearing lucky underwear.

It happens every year: someone makes a devastating mistake. Someone rushes a routine play. Someone emerges as a hero. He's probably an unlikely one.

In 2010 the Giants were the team with magic in the ether. They were hardened by a 162-game battle to clinch the NL West. They showed confidence in the hitter behind them or the next pitcher in the bullpen, allowing them to stay within themselves in outsized moments. And they had one heck of a rotation.

They competed as well as anyone, and whether you called it mental toughness or certifiable lunacy, they didn't need a standing-eight count to regain their bearings after the worst of losses.

Perhaps they weren't the best team when they arrived in the spring or in April or August. But when it most mattered, they nailed it.

Or, as Sabean put it, "You don't always pick the time. The time picks you."

Twice in 13 years, the time picked Renteria. He became the fourth player to own game-winning RBIs in two World Series clinching victories, joining an extremely distinguished list. The others: Lou Gehrig, Joe DiMaggio, and Yogi Berra.

So many Giants players and coaches said they were happiest for Renteria, who might have been the most unlikely World Series MVP in history. He had assumed he would retire after the season. Now he was reconsidering. (And he eventually would sign a one-year contract with Cincinnati after the Giants declined his $10.5 million option.) The desire to play again was strong after he hit .412 with two home runs and six RBIs in five World Series games.

Renteria held together his emotions when he accepted the MVP trophy on national television. But later, during an interview on the field with ESPN Deportes, he suddenly bent over at the waist and covered his face. He was unable to hold back from sobbing.

All through the night, Renteria kept coming back to the same word to describe this night, this season, this career.

"Unbelievable," he said over and over, clutching the MVP trophy. "Unbelievable."

Here's something else that was hard to believe: Lincecum didn't drop any F-bombs on live television. Not intentionally, anyway. He kept his interview with Flemming as clean as a cotillion luncheon. But as the interview ended and Flemming prudently yanked the microphone away, Lincecum got a gleam in his eye and a huge smile on his face. And for the benefit of a few people around him, he mouthed the words that so many Giants fans were shouting:

"F— yeah!"

Asked in another TV interview what he hoped the scene was like in San Francisco, Lincecum said, "Just a lot of craziness, a lot of beer flowing. Smoke in the air, I'm hoping…"

The Giants would find out soon enough. They landed at SFO at 3:00 AM and were shocked to find that hundreds of fans were camped outside AT&T Park when their bus rolled up, for no other reason than to express their gratitude.

It was just a taste of what was coming next.

The players and coaches already knew this season was magical. They were about to realize it also had been so integral—and it would hit them with the full, high-decibel fury of nearly 1 million fans.

The BART trains were packed, and the streets were full hours before the victory parade was scheduled to begin. The celebration drew hundreds of thousands, with some estimates at 1 million. Aides to Mayor Gavin Newsom called it the largest civic event turnout in San Francisco history.

It was the first time the Giants cruised down Market Street since 1958, when Mays waved to fans from the back of a convertible and the city heaped ticker tape on their brand new baseball club. More than a half-century later, Mays led the procession again. And the city, after such an interminable wait, could festoon their lovable lads once more.

The Giants rode on motorized cable cars for the two-hour procession through the streets, and none of them were prepared for the overwhelming sights and sounds—and yes, smells—when they turned from Montgomery onto Market.

Wilson left his cable car several times during the parade to slap hands with fans, once nearly causing a chain-link barricade to collapse. Prop 19, which would have legalized recreational marijuana use in California, had failed at the ballot box a day earlier. But that didn't seem to deter thousands of revelers.

"I'm kind of having a mini heart attack," Wilson said. "I'm not sure what it's from. Maybe the electricity of the crowd. Maybe the smell of Prop 19. I don't know."

After waving to the endless sea of fans, the team arrived at City Hall where California Governor Arnold Schwarzenegger congratulated the Giants while making a special reference to Wilson's mysterious friend.

"I thought I was the only machine, the Terminator," Schwarzenegger said. "But I hear there is a machine on this team. Congratulations to the Machine, also."

Governor Schwarzenegger and President Obama probably wouldn't agree on much, but it turns out they shared a mutual fascination with Wilson's beard. When Obama placed his congratulatory phone call to Sabean and Bochy, he asked if Wilson's beard had magical powers.

On the streets of San Francisco, there was magic inside, outside, and everywhere in between. The players and coaches took turns speaking to the biggest mass of humanity they'd ever seen.

"My knees are weak, my heart is racing, and I've got a lump in my throat," Sabean said. "We deserved this. San Francisco deserved this. Northern California deserved this. It's the most interesting life experience anyone could ever have. I can only think of one word, and that's *closure*.

"These guys were junkyard dogs on a bone. They wouldn't let go."

Sabean introduced Bochy with a joke about his head expanding, but the manager had his own dry witticisms ready to go, including a jab at Wilson's unnaturally dark beard.

"Now, we apologize a bit for the torture, for the gray hairs," Bochy said. "I can bring in my closer. I think he can help you with that."

When the Giants clinched the NL West title on October 3, the last day of the regular season, Bochy asked players to take a lap of gratitude around AT&T Park. The Giants weren't able to thank their fans again, having clinched all three of their playoff series on the road.

But Bochy made sure they knew.

"We felt your presence against San Diego. We felt your presence in Atlanta. We felt it in Philly, and we certainly felt it in Texas," Bochy said. "You guys were out in full force, and you made it an incredible ride. Believe me, this trophy belongs to you, San Francisco, as much as it belongs to any of us."

Duane Kuiper, who created one of the most identifiable mottoes for the season, used his turn at the microphone to make a slight alteration to the slogan: "Thanks to these gentlemen here, the torture is over!"

The players spoke in groups of three, each delivering a different message. With Posey, of course, it was about looking ahead. The confident catcher made it clear he wasn't satisfied with just one ring. Yogi Berra won 10, didn't he?

"Let's enjoy this today, tomorrow, maybe a week or a month," Posey said. "Then let's get back to work and make another run at it."

Posey slapped the podium as he abruptly walked away. The crowd went wild. They were going to love watching this kid for a long, long time. A few weeks later, Posey was announced as the NL Rookie of the Year, receiving more than twice as many first-place votes as Heyward, his high school rival. Posey became the first Giant to receive the award since John "the Count" Montefusco in 1975.

Artifacts from this Giants season were going to tell the team's story in the Hall of Fame. Museum officials asked for Renteria's bat and Lincecum's jersey from the World Series clincher.

They must've forgotten to request the Rally Thong.

During the ride through the streets, Huff held the most famous underwear in America over his head like a title belt. And when it was his turn to speak in front of City Hall, he had something special planned.

"Nine years of my life, fourth place or dead last…," he said. "This organization had the heart to bring me here, and here I am in front of all you beautiful people. And I've got a little present for you."

Huff reenacted a scene from *Zoolander*. He stuck his hand down his jeans, theatrically twisted and contorted, produced the Rally Thong, and held it on high.

"Rally Thong is going to the Hall of Fame," he yelled. "Or maybe we'll just wear it next spring training.

"WHOOO! Nailed it!"

From Huff's irreverence to Wilson's oddball antics to Lincecum's long-haired laissez faire, the Giants were a cast of characters, all right. They had Ross the Boss, the Town Sheriff, a Kung Fu Panda, two southern-born gentlemen rookies, Pat the Bat, OOOO-Ree-bay, the amazing Andres "Yungo" Torres, a pair of Sanchezes, and the most unlikely World Series MVP of all. No matter where their careers and lives would go, they would remain forever legends in the City by the Bay.

There was just one problem. They still had to believe it all really happened.

"It hasn't really settled in," said Lincecum after returning from the parade to pack up his locker. "On the field, you're waving your hands in the air, saying, 'Can you believe it?' That's what you're asking everybody. That's what you're asking yourself.

"I'm still waiting for those tears. We'll see when it happens."

These Giants were a band of misfits, but they couldn't have meshed together any better. And San Francisco accepted them just as they were.

They turned a glorious day in November into a full-on summer of love.

"Pass this story on. Keep the love alive," broadcaster Mike Krukow said. "And when you tell the story, simply say, 'We're the Giants! We're San Francisco! And we are world champions!'"